# MACHINE INTERPRETATION OF LINE DRAWINGS

**The MIT Press Series in Artificial Intelligence**
Edited by Patrick Henry Winston and Michael Brady

*Artificial Intelligence: An MIT Perspective, Volume I: Expert Problem Solving, Natural Language Understanding, Intelligent Computer Coaches, Representation and Learning* edited by Patrick Henry Winston and Richard Henry Brown, 1979

*Artificial Intelligence: An MIT Perspective, Volume II: Understanding Vision, Manipulation, Computer Design, Symbol Manipulation* edited by Patrick Henry Winston and Richard Henry Brown, 1979

*NETL: A System for Representing and Using Real-World Knowledge* by Scott Fahlman, 1979

*The Interpretation of Visual Motion* by Shimon Ullman, 1979

*A Theory of Syntactic Recognition for Natural Language* by Mitchell P. Marcus, 1980

*Turtle Geometry: The Computer as a Medium for Exploring Mathematics* by Harold Abelson and Andrea diSessa, 1981

*From Images to Surfaces: A Computational Study of the Human Early Visual System* by William Eric Leifur Grimson, 1981

*Robot Manipulators: Mathematics, Programming and Control* by Richard P. Paul, 1981

*Computational Models of Discourse* edited by Michael Brady and Robert C. Berwick, 1982

*Robot Motion: Planning and Control* by Michael Brady, John M. Hollerbach, Timothy Johnson, Tomas Lozano-Pèrez, and Matthew Mason, 1982

*In-Depth Understanding: A Computer Model of Integrated Processing for Narrative Comprehension* by Michael G. Dyer, 1983

*Robotics Research: The First International Symposium* edited by Michael Brady and Richard Paul, 1984

*Robotics Research: The Second International Symposium* edited by Hideo Hanafusa and Hirochika Inoue, 1985

*Robot Hands and the Mechanics of Manipulation* by Matthew T. Mason and J. Kenneth Salisbury, Jr., 1985

*Legged Robots That Balance* by Marc Raibert, 1985

*The Acquisition of Syntactic Knowledge* by Robert C. Berwick, 1985

*The Connection Machine* by W. Daniel Hillis, 1985

*Object Oriented Concurrent Programming* by Akinori Yonezawa and Mario Tokoro, 1986

*Machine Interpretation of Line Drawings* by Kokichi Sugihara, 1986

Peter Denning, consulting editor, computer science books

# MACHINE INTERPRETATION OF LINE DRAWINGS

Kokichi Sugihara

The MIT Press
Cambridge, Massachusetts
London, England

© 1986 by The Massachusetts Institute of Technology

This book was printed and bound in the United States of America.

Library of Congress Cataloging-in-Publication Data

Sugihara, Kōkichi, 1948–
  Machine interpretation of line drawings.
  (The MIT Press series in artificial intelligence)

  Bibliography: p.
  Includes index.
  1. Computer vision. I. Title. II. Series.
TA1632.S86 1986        006.3'7        86-2982
ISBN 0-262-19254-3

# CONTENTS

# SERIES FOREWORD

Artificial intelligence is the study of intelligence using the ideas and methods of computation. Unfortunately, a definition of intelligence seems impossible at the moment because intelligence appears to be an amalgam of so many information-processing and information-representation abilities.

Of course psychology, philosophy, linguistics, and related disciplines offer various perspectives and methodologies for studying intelligence. For the most part, however, the theories proposed in these fields are too incomplete and too vaguely stated to be realized in computational terms. Something more is needed, even though valuable ideas, relationships, and constraints can be gleaned from traditional studies of what are, after all, impressive existence proofs that intelligence is in fact possible.

Artificial intelligence offers a new perspective and a new methodology. Its central goal is to make computers intelligent, both to make them more useful and to understand the principles that make intelligence possible. That intelligent computers will be extremely useful is obvious. The more profound point is that artificial intelligence aims to understand intelligence using the ideas and methods of computation, thus offering a radically new and different basis for theory formation. Most of the people doing artificial intelligence believe that these theories will apply to any intelligent information processor, whether biological or solid state.

There are side effects that deserve attention, too. Any program that will successfully model even a small part of intelligence will be inherently massive and complex. Consequently, artificial intelligence continually confronts the limits of computer science technology. The problems encountered have been hard enough and interesting enough to seduce artificial intelligence people into working on them with enthusiasm. It is natural, then, that there has been a steady flow of ideas from artificial intelligence to computer science, and the flow shows no sign of abating.

The purpose of this MIT Press Series in Artificial Intelligence is to provide people in many areas, both professionals and students, with timely, detailed information about what is happening on the frontiers in research centers all over the world.

Patrick Henry Winston
Mike Brady

# PREFACE

This book presents a computational mechanism for the interpretation of line drawings by means of which a machine can extract three-dimensional object structures from their pictures drawn on a two-dimensional plane. It is easy for a human being to understand what is represented by line drawings, so that they are frequently used in many stages of human communication, such as illustrations in books and engineering drawings in factories. For a machine, on the other hand, line drawings are simple collections of two-dimensional line segments; some intelligent mechanism is required to extract three-dimensional information from them. How the machine can possess such intelligence is the main problem attacked throughout this book.

From a theoretical point of view this book provides a typical example of making humanlike intelligence by a simple computational mechanism. We are apt to think that the human ability to interpret line drawings is based on various kinds of human experiences, and hence a mechanism that mimics this ability should be supported by extensive and complicated knowledge about the outside world. However, it turns out that this ability can be realized by a simple mathematical procedure at least when the objects are restricted to planar faced solids. The computational mechanism presented here is not accompanied by a large database, but is composed of several simple procedures based on linear algebra and combinatorial theory; it can still mimic human flexible intelligence in picture perception.

From a practical point of view the results in this book can be applied to man-machine communication and robot vision. One of the main problems in a computer-aided system for geometric design is how to input data about object structures that are born in a designer's mind. The computational mechanism in this book makes the communication flexible in the sense that the system can extract object structures automatically from pictures drawn by the designer. In a robot vision system for recognizing the outside world, the present results can be used as an intermediate stage, which receives line drawings from an image processing stage and offers the descriptions of three-dimensional object structures to an object recognition stage.

This book is mainly based on the author's work during the past ten years, the first half of which was spent at the Electrotechnical Laboratory and the other half at Nagoya University, on understanding line drawings. Among many others the author would like to express his thanks to Prof. Noboru Sugie of Nagoya University and Dr. Yoshiaki Shirai of the Electrotechnical Laboratory for guiding him to this interesting field of research; Prof. Masao Iri of Tokyo University for suggesting the importance of the combinatorial aspect of line drawings; Prof.

Jun-ichiro Toriwaki of Nagoya University, Dr. Hiroshi Imai of Tokyo University, Prof. Henry Crapo of INRIA, Prof. Walter Whiteley of McGill University, Dr. Masaki Oshima of the Electrotechnical Laboratory, and Prof. Ken-ichi Kanatani of Gumma University for valuable communications; and Mr. Hiroki Iguchi of NEC Co. Ltd. for help in writing computer programs when he was a student at Nagoya University. Many of these people, in particular Profs. Iri, Sugie, and Kanatani, gave the author valuable comments on earlier versions of the manuscript. The author also wants to thank his wife Keiko Sugihara for helping him not only mentally but also physically by keeping their daughters from his room and thus giving him time for writing this book. The text was generated by ATF (Advanced Text Formatter for science) at the Nagoya University Computation Center.

K. Sugihara
March 1986

# MACHINE INTERPRETATION OF LINE DRAWINGS

# 1. INTRODUCTION

## 1.1. Aim of the Book

Human beings invented a noble class of pictures called "line drawings" as a means of representing three-dimensional shape of objects. The line drawings, though they consist of only line segments on a plane, convey much information about three-dimensional object structures; when we see them, we can easily understand what is represented there. The line drawings are widely used in various fields of human communication, from engineering drawings of mechanical parts to illustrative figures in popular books.

For computers, on the other hand, line drawings are simple collections of line segments on a two-dimensional plane. In order to extract three-dimensional information from them, some intelligent mechanism is necessary. However, we cannot mimic the human visual process, because we know for the present almost nothing about how human beings understand line drawings.

The aim of this book is to present a computational mechanism for extracting three-dimensional structures of objects from two-dimensional line drawings. The objects considered here are polyhedrons, that is, solid objects bounded by planar faces, and the line drawings are single-view pictures of these objects. Probably this mechanism is quite different from what is employed in human perception. It can nevertheless make a computer intelligent in the sense that, given line drawings, the computer generates three-dimensional descriptions of objects automatically.

One of potential applications of this mechanism is flexible man-machine communication. Computer aided systems are widely used for the design of geometric objects, such as mechanical parts and buildings. These systems provide many facilities by which designers can analyze, deform, and monitor various kinds of characteristics of shape of objects interactively. However, these systems are not completely comfortable for users. One of the problems is how to generate numerical data about shapes born in a designer's mind. It is tedious work for designers to convert their thoughts into numerical forms, such as three-dimensional coordinates of vertices and incidence relations among vertices, edges, and faces. The present mechanism can undertake this work automatically; all that the designers have to do is to draw pictures of what are in their minds, and, if necessary, to give a small number of additional data, such as lengths of edges and angles between faces. Thus, the mechanism can lessen human labor.

Another application of the mechanism is computer vision systems for recognizing the outside world. Using optical sensors such as a television camera, these systems obtain visual images from the outside, and analyze them by these three stages: first, some features, such as edges, regions, and textures, are extracted from the images; next, these two-dimensional features are interpreted as three-dimensional structures; and finally, objects in the scenes are recognized. The present mechanism can be used as a component for the intermediate stage, the feature interpretation stage, which receives line drawings from the image processing stage and offers descriptions of three-dimensional structures to the object recognition stage.

In order to meet these fields of application, line drawings treated in this book are assumed to be either those drawn by human hands or those extracted by computer processing of digital images. Consequently, they are not necessarily perfect; some lines may be missing, some lines may be superfluous, and/or vertices may be in a wrong position. Given a line drawing of this kind, the mechanism carries out the following tasks. First, the mechanism judges whether it represents a polyhedral scene correctly or not, and, if not, tries to correct it. Next, the mechanism specifies the set of all scenes that the correct (or corrected) line drawing can represent. Finally, it selects a unique scene that is most consistent with other information, such as edge lengths given by a designer or surface texture given in the image.

## 1.2. Philosophy

When compared with languages, another means of human communication, line drawings are easier to understand; they can be read without much training by anyone in any country. This is probably because line drawings are analogical in nature, whereas languages are symbolic. Line drawings are based on physical results of the imaging process, that is, projections of three-dimensional scenes onto two-dimensional planes, and hence they reflect configurations of three-dimensional structures directly.

However, line drawings also have a symbolic aspect. First, they are not direct representations of the distribution of light intensity on the retina. For example, texture details on a surface are usually omitted, whereas invisible edges are sometimes represented by broken lines. These conventions are artificial rules, not direct consequences of the imaging

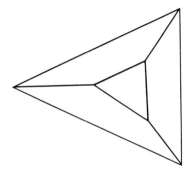

**Fig. 1.1.** Example of a line drawing.

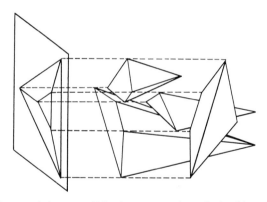

**Fig. 1.2.** Unnatural but possible interpretation of the line drawing shown in Fig. 1.1.

process. Second, from a mathematical point of view a line drawing in general can admit many possible interpretations, but it seems that most of them are never evoked in human perception. The line drawing shown in Fig. 1.1, for example, is usually interpreted as a picture of a truncated pyramid seen from above. It is possible at least mathematically to regard it as the projection of four objects floating in a space and aligning accidentally on the picture plane, as is shown in Fig. 1.2, but this kind of an interpretation is rarely adopted. This implies that in human communication line drawings involve some implicit assumptions so that

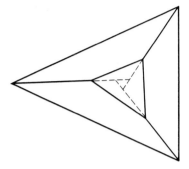

**Fig. 1.3.** Inconsistency in the interpretation of the line drawing in Fig. 1.1 as a truncated pyramid.

"unusual" interpretations are excluded. Third, we can extract three-dimensional information from line drawings even if they are mathematically incorrect. Consider the line drawing in Fig. 1.1 again. We extract from it a structure of a truncated pyramid, but it is incorrect from a mathematical point of view. Indeed, if it were a truncated pyramid, the three quadrilateral side planes should share a common point in a space when extended, and hence the three side edges should meet at a common point on the picture plane, but they do not, as is shown in Fig. 1.3. The line drawing can never be a projection of any truncated pyramid. It is nevertheless used in human communication as a description of a truncated pyramid.

Thus, line drawings are not purely geometrical consequences but mixtures of geometry and human conventions; they have both an analogical aspect and a symbolic aspect.

Basically, the interpretation of line drawings is an inverse problem of the image forming process, where the analogical aspect plays the main role. However, the symbolic aspect of line drawings is equally important in that if a computer deals with only the analogical aspect, man-machine communication is almost impossible. Suppose that we draw a line drawing like Fig. 1.1 and show it to a computer. If the computer ignores its symbolic aspect, the computer will reject it simply because it is mathematically incorrect. Even if we notice that the three side edges must be concurrent, it does not make sense to try to draw a precise picture because digitization errors are inevitable. Thus, we must not be satisfied with a mechanism that works correctly merely in a mathematical sense. A computer should have some flexible mechanism that can extract three-dimensional structures even if line drawings are not strictly correct.

It seems interesting to note that this point is important also in a computer vision system. The input to the computer vision system is an image obtained by means of a visual sensor, and hence it is not contaminated with human conventions. Nevertheless, the three-dimensional structure cannot be reconstructed at all if the data are treated in a purely mathematical manner, because inevitable errors would make the line drawing incorrect. The data must be treated as if they had the symbolic aspect.

In this book we study line drawings from both an analogical point of view and a symbolic point of view, and construct a mechanism that can extract three-dimensional information from both the aspects in a balanced manner just as human beings do.

It should be said here that this book places emphasis on engineering rather than human science. Our aim is to construct a computational mechanism by which a computer can practically process line drawing data. Hence, our mechanism can be independent of the human visual mechanism on one hand, but it must be correct, robust, and efficient on the other hand.

What we search for is a mechanism that is suitable for a computer; its internal structure need not be the same as that in the human brain. Of course, we must know what kind of spatial information the human visual system can extract, because a machine should possess the same, or at least similar, abilities for flexible man-machine communication. For this purpose we consider the human visual system. For the design of internal structures of our mechanism, however, the human visual system seems of little help, because we know for the present almost nothing about the human visual process at such a high level as the interpretation of line drawings. Therefore, we learn what to do from the human visual system, whereas we decide how to do it from an engineering point of view.

Needless to say, a mechanism cannot be applied to engineering use unless it works always correctly, and a mechanism that works always correctly cannot be searched for unless the tasks of the mechanism is well defined. This point is important when we try to replace human intelligence with a machine, because human intelligence is not a well defined concept. "To make a machine that extracts three-dimensional information as human beings do" is not a good specification for the design of an intelligent machine. Different persons may extract different information from the same line drawing, and even the same person may extract different information in different situations. In order to define the problem well, we have to specify in mathematical terms what aspects of human intelligence we want to realize. This is why we restrict our objects to polyhedrons.

In polyhedrons, faces are all planar and hence can be recovered easily from their boundaries. Thus, most of the important information about polyhedrons are contained in ˜skeletal structures˜ consisting of edges and vertices. Line drawings, which are projections of the skeletal structures, consequently contain much information about the objects. In contrast, curved surface objects cannot be reconstructed uniquely even if their skeletal structures are given. Hence, line drawings do not convey enough information. Interpretation of line drawings of curved surface objects seems to depend on each particular situation in human communication, and in general it is very difficult to specify what shape should be extracted from what line drawings. In the polyhedral object world, on the other hand, we can specify clearly the input-output relation the intelligent machine should achieve. Thus we can define the problem in a mathematical manner, and consequently can search for a mechanism that works correctly in a mathematical sense.

Mathematically correct mechanisms are sometimes too weak for practical purposes. As we have seen in Fig. 1.3, only slight errors in positions of vertices on the picture plane often make line drawings incorrect. If line drawings are treated simply in a mathematical manner, a large part of line drawings are judged incorrect though they are usually treated as correct in human communication. Therefore, a desired mechanism must be robust (or, in other words, be flexible) in the sense that it can extract what are intended in line drawings even if they are not strictly correct. How to attain this robustness is the most important and interesting point of our study.

In addition to being correct and robust, a desired mechanism must of course be efficient. Therefore, we search for efficient algorithms for all the components of our mechanism. For this purpose we employ whatever results in other fields, such as linear programming theory, network flow theory, and matroid theory. In case that we cannot find a polynomial order algorithm for a strict solution to a subproblem, we do not hesitate to introduce heuristics in order to avoid the combinatorial explosions.

## 1.3. Short History

Line drawings of three-dimensional objects have long been studied in descriptive geometry and projective geometry, but the main problem there is how to "describe" given objects on two-dimensional planes (for example, Gurevich, 1960; Hohenberg, 1966). The converse problem, the problem of how to "reconstruct" three-dimensional structures from line drawings, started to draw attention only in later 1960s, when digital computers were developed so that they could process image data.

Probably the earliest attempt at machine interpretation of line drawings can be found in Roberts' system for object recognition (Roberts, 1965). Given an image of an object taken from a certain fixed set of a finite number of prototypes, his system identifies the object by first extracting a line drawing from the image and next searching for a prototype whose projection coincides with the line drawing. Though his system requires the strong assumption that objects are isolated in the images and that line drawings can be extracted completely, his method forms a sound starting point for "prototype-based" interpretation of line drawings, where objects are taken from a finite number of prespecified prototypes. The prototype-based interpretation was further developed by Falk (1972) and Grape (1973) so that imperfect line drawings and/or partially occluded objects can also be dealt with.

In the case where the object world is not restricted to a finite set of prototypes, interpretation of line drawings contains problems that are quite different from those in the prototype-based interpretation. One class of problems arises in the interpretation of multi-view drawings (Shapira, 1974). This class includes an important subclass, that is, the interpretation of three-view drawings, such as engineering drawings composed of top, front, and side views (Idesawa et al., 1975; Wesley and Markowsky, 1981; Preiss, 1981; Haralick and Queeney, 1982; Aldefeld, 1983). Here, the main problems are twofold; one is to establish the correspondence between different views, and the other is to find a consistent way of packing material to exactly one side of each face (Markowsky and Wesley, 1980). Another class of problems arises in interactive systems for extracting three-dimensional structures from single-view drawings, where the main problem is how to realize smooth and flexible interaction between users and machines (Lafue, 1978; Liardet et al., 1978; Fukui et al., 1983).

If only a single-view line drawing is given and no interaction between man and machine is allowed, the problem of interpretation becomes more difficult. This challenging problem, "prototype-free" interpretation of single-view line drawings, was first attacked by Guzman (1968a, 1968b), who tried to find a systematic way of decomposing a line drawing of a pile of objects into regions so that each region may correspond to one object. In his method, configurations of lines at junctions are used as keys for the region decomposition. Though his method was based on only a collection of *ad hoc* rules, it worked well for many complicated line drawings. However, his rules were not based on any logical foundation and hence did not always work correctly; indeed we can easily generate line drawings that cheat his method (for example, see Ballard and Brown, 1982). His method is nevertheless a milestone in the sense that it showed that prototype-free interpretation, though it seemed impossible without some knowledge about human everyday experiences, can be achieved fairly well by a relatively simple mechanism based on configurations of lines at junctions.

The configurations of lines at junctions were exploited in a more theoretical manner by Huffman (1971) and Clowes (1971). Huffman introduced labels in order to classify lines in pictures into three categories, that is, lines representing convex edges whose both side faces face toward a viewer, those representing convex edges one of whose side faces face opposite to the viewer, and those representing concave edges. A crucial point he found is that possible configurations of labeled lines at junctions (that is, configurations that can appear in line drawings of polyhedrons) form a very small subset of all the combinations of assignments of labels to lines around junctions. Therefore, once all possible configurations at junctions are enumerated and registered in a computer, the problem of interpreting line drawings can be reduced to a problem of assigning labels to lines consistently in the sense that the resultant configurations at junctions are all in the list of possible configurations. Huffman (1971) demonstrated the validity of this scheme in a so-called "trihedral object world," where every vertex of objects is shared by exactly three faces. Clowes (1971) also proposed an equivalent method with slightly different notations, and hence this scheme is usually called the *Huffman-Clowes labeling scheme* (see also Mackworth, 1977b; Winston, 1977; Nevatia, 1982; Cohen and Feigenbaum, 1982).

The validity of this scheme has been verified in various kinds of line drawings, such as pictures with shadows and cracks (Waltz, 1972, 1975), pictures in which hidden edges are represented by broken lines (Sankar, 1977; Sugihara 1978), pictures of curved objects bounded by quadric surfaces (Turner, 1974; Chien and Chang, 1974; Lee et al., 1985), pictures

of paper-made objects (Kanade 1980, 1981), and pictures of  dynamic  scenes
(Asada et al., 1984).  There are also some attempts to refine the scheme in
a restricted object world, the world  consisting  of  right-angled  objects
(Nakatani and Kitahashi, 1984; Kanatani, 1986).

It should be noted that the Huffman-Clowes labeling scheme is based on
a necessary, but not sufficient, condition for a line drawing to  represent
a polyhedral  scene.   A correct  line drawing always admits a consistent
assignment of labels, but the existence of  consistent  labeling  does  not
imply  that  the line drawing is correct.  Some incorrect line drawings can
also be labeled consistently.  Thus, a consistent assignment of labels to a
line  drawing  gives  a  mere candidate for a spatial interpretation of the
line drawing.  We have to examine this candidate further in  order  to  see
whether it is a correct interpretation or not.

In  order  to  back  up  the labeling scheme, many new ideas have been
proposed.  Various types of conditions that the correct line drawing should
satisfy  are  found  and  used to check the correctness of the labeled line
drawings.  One of the most appealing ideas is the use of reciprocal figures
in  a  gradient  space (Huffman, 1971, 1976, 1977a, 1977b, 1978; Mackworth,
1973).  For every line drawing representing a polyhedron, we can  define  a
reciprocal  figure  which  is a dual in the sense that vertices, edges, and
faces in the reciprocal figure correspond to faces,  edges,  and  vertices,
respectively,  of  the  original line drawing.  The reciprocal figure has a
remarkable  property:  all  of  its  edges  are  perpendicular  to  the
corresponding  edges  of the original line drawing when the two figures are
superposed upon each other in an appropriate  manner.   This  property  was
found  more  than a century ago, and has been used for graphical calculus in
mechanics (Maxwell, 1864, 1870; Cremona 1890).  It was recently rediscovered
by  Huffman  (1971) and Mackworth (1973), and used for the analysis of line
drawings in such a way that a labeled line drawing can be judged  incorrect
if  it  cannot  admit  a reciprocal figure (see also Whiteley, 1979, 1982).
Other types of conditions were  also  formulated  in  terms  of  such  new
concepts as "spanning angles" (Kanade, 1980), "sidedness reasoning" (Draper
1981),  "cyclic  order  property"  of  edges  and  vertices around  faces
(Sugihara,  1978;  Shapira  and  Freeman,  1979;  Fukui  et al., 1983), and
"maximal sets of relative place" (Shapira, 1984), and used for the check of
labeled  line drawings.  The theory of braids was also applied to the check
of inconsistency of line drawings of torus-type polyhedrons (Cowan,  1974,
1977;  Térouanne,  1980).   Whiteley  (1979)  and  Shapira  (1985)  took  a
figure-construction approach to the  check  of  the  inconsistency.   Those

methods could indeed strengthen the labeled scheme in that a larger class of incorrect interpretations can be recognized. However, all of the conditions employed in those methods are necessary, but still not sufficient, conditions for correct line drawings, and hence they cannot discriminate between correct and incorrect interpretations perfectly.

There is another, and more naive, approach to the analysis of line drawings, that is, an approach using linear algebra. It was known from relatively early days that a polyhedral object represented by a line drawing must satisfy certain linear equations; this fact was pointed out, for example, by Falk (1972) and Duda and Hart (1973). Though this approach seems natural, it has not been taken so widely as the reciprocal-figure approach.

Quite recently, however, Sugihara (1984b) succeeded in representing in terms of linear algebra a necessary and sufficient condition for a line drawing to represent a polyhedral scene. This result reduces the problem of judging the correctness of a line drawing to a problem of checking the existence of a solution to a certain system of linear equations and linear inequalities. Thus, the problem of discriminating between correct and incorrect line drawings was solved "theoretically."

However, this method alone cannot serve practical purposes. Indeed, the condition represented by the system of equations and inequalities is mathematically strict, so that many pictures are judged incorrect only because the vertices are slightly deviated from the correct positions. This difficulty, the superstrictness of the system of equations and inequalities, stems from the fact that the system contains redundant equations. The difficulty was solved by a counting theorem (Sugihara, 1979c, 1982b, 1984c; Whiteley, 1984a), which tells us what equations are redundant, and hence enables us to extract a subset of equations that is no longer superstrict. Thus, the problem of discrimination between correct and incorrect line drawings was solved not only in a theoretical sense but also in a practical sense. Using these results we can construct a machine that, like human beings, extracts the structures of objects from line drawings even if they are mathematically incorrect due to digitization and/or free-hand drawing.

## 1.4. Overview of the Book

The computational mechanism for extracting structures of objects from line drawings presented in this book is composed of four fundamental modules.

The first module is for extracting from a line drawing a set of probable candidates for spatial interpretations. The purpose of this module is to lessen the number of candidates for interpretations, which will be examined more carefully in the subsequent part of the mechanism. Therefore, it may extract some incorrect interpretations, but it must not fail to extract any correct interpretations. This task seems to be achieved most successfully by the Huffman-Clowes labeling scheme. So we shall review this scheme briefly in Chapter 2.

The second module is for discriminating between correct and incorrect interpretations strictly. This module will be presented for two classes of line drawings: for natural pictures in Chapter 3 and for hidden-part-drawn pictures in Chapter 4. In both the cases a necessary and sufficient condition for a correct interpretation is formulated in terms of linear algebra, and thus the problem of discrimination is reduced to the problem of checking the existence of feasible solutions to a linear programming problem.

The algebraic approach taken in Chapters 3 and 4 tells us much about mathematical structures of line drawings. Chapter 5 will summarize them. In particular, the distributions of degrees of freedom in recovering objects from a line drawing will be studied in detail. The results in this chapter will provide mathematical foundations on which the subsequent two modules are established.

Chapters 6, 7, and 8 will present the third module, whose purpose is to provide humanlike flexibility for the mechanism. Employing the first two modules, the mechanism can discriminate between correct and incorrect line drawings strictly. The mathematical strictness, however, causes the mechanism to behave very differently from human visual perception. Human beings can extract object structures even if the line drawings are not strictly correct, whereas the mechanism composed of the first two modules simply judges them incorrect; it does not extract any three-dimensional information. First, in Chapter 6, we shall present a theorem that enables us to tell which equations are redundant in the system of equations associated with a line drawing. On the basis of this theorem, we shall next establish, in Chapter 7, the third module, which can remove the redundant equations and thus circumvent the superstrictness. Moreover, this module enables the mechanism to make necessary corrections to incorrect line drawings automatically if the incorrectness is due to errors in vertex positions. In Chapter 8, the module will be improved from a time complexity point of view. Thus, instead of discriminating between correct and

incorrect line drawings, the mechanism can discriminate between
"correctable" and "uncorrectable" line drawings (where the correctable line
drawings include correct ones), and can extract three-dimensional
structures from the correctable line drawings. This is the way how our
mechanism achieves humanlike flexibility. From a practical point of view,
this module is most important because if this module were not available,
the mechanism would be so sensitive to digitization noises that it could
not be applied to real data.

The last module is for determining the object structure uniquely.
Using the first three modules, the mechanism can specify explicitly the set
of all objects that a correct, or a corrected, line drawing can represent.
This set usually contains an infinite number of elements, because the line
drawing does not convey enough information about the third dimension. The
task of the last module is to choose from this set a unique object that is
most consistent with additional information. Chapters 9 and 10 will provide
two options for this module. The first option, which will be presented in
Chapter 9, uses ranges of some points of objects from the observer or
lengths and angles given by a designer. The second option, presented in
Chapter 10, uses surface cues such as texture and shading. Thus, the
description of the whole mechanism will be completed.

It has long been known that line drawings of polyhedrons have close
relationships with mechanical structures composed of rigid rods and
rotatable joints. In Chapter 11, these relationships will be studied from
our combinatorial point of view, and classical results will be generalized.
This chapter is rather a digression from the main story of the book, but
seems important for future researches on line drawings.

## 2.  CANDIDATES FOR SPATIAL INTERPRETATIONS


Given a line drawing, the mechanism should first collect probable candidates for spatial interpretations. These candidates will be examined in detail in the subsequent stages of the analysis. Hence, the set of the candidates collected here must include all of the correct interpretations. For efficiency's sake, on the other hand, the number of the candidates should be as small as possible. This chapter presents a module that executes the above task by assigning labels that represent at least locally consistent interpretations.

### 2.1.  Polyhedrons and Line Drawings

Objects we consider are *polyhedrons*, that is, three-dimensional solid bodies bounded by a finite number of planar *faces*. Line segments shared by two faces are called *edges*, and terminal points of edges *vertices*. Since faces are planar, edges are straight. However, the objects may have hollows so that faces are not necessarily simple polygons, but may have polygonal holes.

   In order to avoid unnecessary confusion caused by "pathological" objects, we put forth the following assumptions.

**Assumption 2.1.** For every face, one side is occupied with material and the other side is an empty space.

   Hence, we need not consider extremely thin objects such as a sheet of paper.

**Assumption 2.2.** Every edge is shared by exactly two faces.

   Hence, we need not consider unnatural objects such as the one shown in Fig. 2.1, where the edge e is shared by the four faces, two visible faces and two invisible faces. At every edge, therefore, the two side faces form either a ridge or a valley.

   A *scene* is a collection of a finite number of objects. In order to exclude "pathological" scenes, we assume that Assumption 2.2 is still satisfied when the whole scene is considered as one (possibly disconnected) object. In other words, edges of different objects do not come together

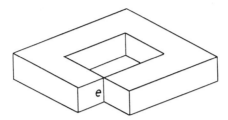

**Fig. 2.1.** Pathological object; four faces meet at the edge $e$.

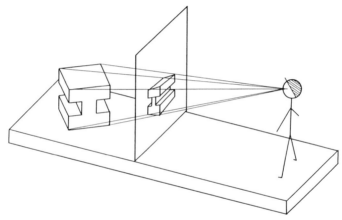

**Fig. 2.2.** Scene and its projection.

accidentally in the scene.

A *line drawing*, also called a *picture*, is a two-dimensional diagram composed of a finite number of straight line segments. The line segments are simply called "lines," and terminal points of the lines are called "junctions." To be more strict, by *junctions* we refer to points where two or more noncollinear lines meet, and by *lines* to the smallest fragments of straight line segments divided by junctions. Thus, a line connects one junction with another but does not have any other junctions between them.

If a scene, an observer, and a picture plane between them are fixed, then a line drawing of the scene is obtained as a perspective projection of the configurations of the edges onto the picture plane with respect to the observer as the center of projection, as shown in Fig. 2.2. If the observer goes infinitely far from the scene in the direction perpendicular to the picture plane, the resultant picture is an orthographic projection. Once the scene, the observer, and the picture plane are fixed, the line drawing is unique up to the choice of whether hidden edges are drawn or not.

On the other hand, even if an observer, a line drawing, and a picture plane are fixed, the associated scene cannot be determined uniquely. There may be no scene or there may be an infinite number of possible scenes. How to specify the set of all possible scenes is the problem we attack in this book.

In order to make the problem clearer we shall put forth three more assumptions.

**Assumption 2.3.** When a scene is projected onto the picture plane, the edges only are drawn.

Hence, even if the object surface is covered with texture or scribbles, they are not drawn. Thus, each line in a line drawing is to correspond to some edge of an object.

**Assumption 2.4.** The observer (i.e., the center of the projection) is not coplanar with any face.

If the observer is coplanar with some face, the face looks like a straight line segment. Assumption 2.4 is to exclude such a degenerate case. Hence, every face corresponds to some nonempty region on the picture plane.

**Assumption 2.5.** The observer is not coplanar with any pair of noncollinear edges.

Hence, no spatially distinct edges accidentally align on the picture plane. The unnatural interpretation shown in Fig. 1.2 can be thus forbidden. As a consequence, every line in the picture corresponds to exactly one edge in the scene. Assumptions 2.4 and 2.5 are sometimes called "nonaccidentalness assumptions" (Marr, 1982).

We consider two ways of generating line drawings. One is to project only visible portions of the edges onto the picture plane. Line drawings generated in this way are called *natural line drawings* or *hidden-part-eliminated line drawings*. The other is to project all the edges of the objects, whether they are visible or not. This kind of line drawing

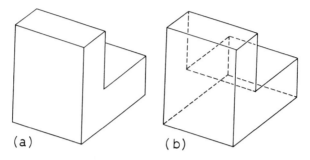

**Fig. 2.3.** Two types of line drawings: (a) is a natural line drawing, and
(b) is a hidden-part-drawn line drawing.

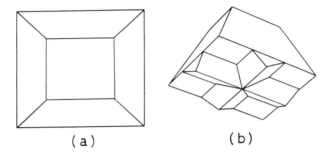

**Fig. 2.4.** Picture that can be regarded both as a hidden-part-eliminated
line drawing and as a hidden-part-drawn line drawing: (a) is a line
drawing, and (b) is an interpretation in which the rear side has a
complicated structure. This interpretation is possible only when the
picture (a) is regarded as a hidden-part-eliminated line drawing.

is called a *hidden-part-drawn line drawing*. In them hidden lines, i.e.,
invisible portions of edges, are usually represented by broken lines.

Examples of line drawings are shown in Fig. 2.3. The picture in (a) is
a natural line drawing, and the picture in (b) is a hidden-part-drawn one.

It should be noted that some pictures can be regarded both as natural
line drawings and as hidden-part-drawn line drawings. An example is shown
in Fig. 2.4(a). When considered as a natural line drawing, this is a
picture of the visible surface of an object consisting of five visible

faces; the picture gives no information about the rear side of the object, so that we cannot tell whether the rear side has only one face or has some complicated structure as shown in (b). When considered as a hidden-part-drawn line drawing, on the other hand, the picture gives information about both the front side and the rear side; hence the interpretation in (b) is not allowed. Unless otherwise mentioned, we will treat such ambiguous pictures as natural line drawings.

**Remark 2.1.** In this book two different types of figures are used. One is a usual type of illustration, whose aim is to give the readers a vivid impression about shapes and relations of geometrical objects. This type of figure should be regarded with common sense. Figs. 2.1 and 2.2 are examples of this type. The picture in Fig. 2.1 represents an edge that has four incident faces. In a mathematically strict sense, however, this figure does not give any information about the invisible part of the object, and hence the edge *e* does not necessarily have four faces. An edge shared by four faces can be seen in this figure only when the invisible part of the object is extrapolated with the aid of the reader's common sense. The second type of figure used in this book is a line drawing as the input data to the machine, that is, material that is to be analyzed by our computational mechanism. This type of figure should be treated as is; we need not use any common sense, heuristics, or knowledge when we see such a figure. The pictures in Fig. 2.3 belong to this type. In Fig. 2.4, the picture in (a) belongs to the latter type, whereas the picture in (b) to the former type. In what follows we shall not state the type of each figure explicitly because we can tell from the context which type is meant by the figure.

## 2.2. Classification of Lines

Let us first consider hidden-part-drawn line drawings; hidden-part-eliminated line drawings (i.e., natural line drawings) will be treated as a special case. Lines in line drawings can be classified into eight categories in the following way.

When two planes meet at a line, they divide the surrounding space into four regions. We call these regions *quadrants*, and number them from I to IV consecutively, as shown in Fig. 2.5. The line of intersection of the two planes forms an edge when some of the quadrants are filled with material. However, we need not consider the case where exactly two quadrants are filled with material. Indeed, if two consecutive quadrants are filled with

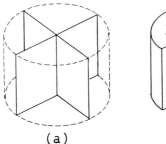
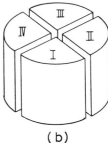

**Fig. 2.5.** Four quadrants generated by two mutually intersecting planes: (a) shows two planes intersecting at a line, and (b) shows the four quadrants generated by the two planes.


material, the line of intersection disappears, and if two mutually opposite quadrants are filled with material, the line of intersection forms an edge having four side faces, which has been excluded by Assumption 2.2. Thus, the line of intersection forms an edge if and only if exactly one or three quadrants are filled with material.

Without loss of generality we assume that the observer is in quadrant I. Then, on the basis of relative configurations of an edge, the side faces, and the observer, lines in a line drawing can be classified into eight categories, as shown in Fig. 2.6. In (a) only quadrant III is filled with material, so that the edge forms a visible ridge and both of the side faces are also visible. In (b) or (c), either quadrant II or IV is filled, and consequently one of the side faces is visible while the other is hidden. In (d) the three quadrants II, III, IV are filled, and hence the edge forms a visible valley. The configurations (e), (f), (g), (h) are obtained from (a), (b), (c), (d), respectively, by interchanging the filled quadrants and the empty quadrants.

Fig. 2.6 exhausts the cases. Indeed, because of Assumptions 2.1 and 2.2 we can restrict our consideration to the cases where either one or three quadrants are filled with material, and because of Assumption 2.4 we need not consider the case where the observer is on a boundary of two quadrants.

In order to represent these categories of lines we introduce the following convention. First, the edge is represented by a solid line if quadrant I is empty as in the cases (a), (b), (c), (d), whereas it is

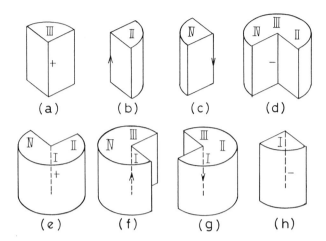

**Fig. 2.6.** Eight categories of lines.

represented by a broken line if quadrant I is occupied by material as in the cases (e), (f), (g), (h). This way of using the solid and broken lines is similar to that in conventional line drawings, but is not the same. In conventional line drawings, hidden lines are always represented by broken lines, but we use solid lines for the edges in (a), (b), (c), (d) even if the edges are hidden by other objects that are between the edge and the observer. Thus, our way of using solid and hidden lines rests only on whether quadrant I is filled with material or not when we see the neighborhood (in a three-dimensional sense) of the edge locally.

Second, on the basis of which portions of the planes form the side faces of the edges, we assign to the lines four kinds of additional labels: the plus label +, the minus label −, and the arrow in each of the two possible directions. If the boundary of quadrant III forms the side faces as in (a) and (e), the plus label is assigned to the line, and if the boundary of quadrant I forms the side faces as in (d) and (h), the minus label is assigned. If either the boundary of quadrant II or that of quadrant IV forms the side faces as in (b), (c), (f), and (g), the arrow is assigned to the line in such a way that the side faces are to the right of the arrow.

Combining the solid and broken lines with the four additional labels, we define the eight labels as is shown in Fig. 2.6. With this convention,

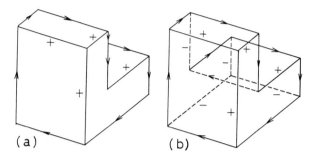

**Fig. 2.7.** Labeled line drawings.

we can represent the categories of lines explicitly in the line drawing. A line drawing is said to be *labeled* if every edge is represented by one of the eight possible labels.

If a line drawing represents only visible edges, the first four labels, (a), (b), (c), and (d), suffice for the categorization of the lines.

Examples of the use of our labeling convention are shown in Fig. 2.7. The set of labels assigned to the picture in (a) corresponds to one of the most natural spatial structures the picture in Fig. 2.3(a) evokes in our mind. Similarly, (b) represents one of the most natural interpretations of the picture in Fig. 2.3(b). Note that the distinction between solid and broken lines in Fig. 2.7(b) is not the same as that in Fig. 2.3(b); some edges represented by broken lines in Fig. 2.3(b) are represented by solid lines in Fig. 2.7(b). This is because in Fig. 2.7(b) broken lines are used when quadrant I is filled with material in the neighborhoods of the edges, whereas in Fig. 2.3(b) broken lines are used when the edges are hidden by other portions which are not necessarily in the neighborhood of the edges.

## 2.3. Junction Dictionary and Consistent Labeling

To put one of the eight labels to a line means to choose one of the eight possible ways of filling the surrounding space with material, and hence to assign labels to the whole lines in a picture means to choose one candidate for a spatial structure the picture may represent. Thus, the problem of the interpretation of line drawings can be reduced to the problem of finding combinations of the labels that correspond to the spatial structures of the objects.

If we ignore physical realizability of an object, a line drawing having $l$ lines can admit as many as $8^l$ different ways of labeling. These labeled pictures can be thought of as the initial set of candidates for the structures of the objects represented by the picture. Most of them are of course nonsense; only a few correspond to realizable objects. Our present goal is to divide the set of all the $8^l$ labeled pictures into correct ones and incorrect ones, where "correct" means that there is at least one object whose projection onto the picture plane coincides with the picture and whose spatial structure is the same as that indicated by the labels. As the first step to this goal, we consider how to delete obviously nonsense labelings. In other words, we try to lessen the number of candidates for spatial structures from $8^l$ to a much smaller number so that we can examine the remaining candidates in detail in reasonable time.

In order to remove nonsense labelings, we construct a set of "rules" labeled pictures must obey. The followings are obvious.

**Rule 2.1.** Each line has exactly one of the eight labels given in Fig. 2.6.

This is because a type of a line does not change as we go along the associated edge unless we pass through a vertex.

**Rule 2.2.** Solid lines should be categorized as the type (a), (b), (c), or (d) in Fig. 2.6.

This is because in hidden-part-drawn line drawings, solid lines mean that quadrant I is empty.

**Rule 2.3.** If the whole part of an object is drawn inside the picture region, the outermost lines should be labeled as solid lines with arrows in the clockwise direction.

This is because the outermost lines correspond to the boundary between the object and the background unless the object is scissored off along the border of the picture region.

Another important rule can be found at *X-type junctions*, that is, junctions where two pairs of collinear lines meet. Because of Assumption 2.5, two distinct edges do not become collinear on the picture plane. Hence the X-type junctions do not correspond to three-dimensional vertices; they

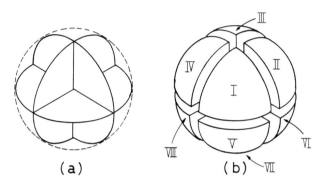

(a)                              (b)

**Fig. 2.8.** Eight octants generated by three mutually intersecting planes:
(a) shows three planes meeting at a point, and (b) shows the eight octants
generated by the three planes.

occur only when two spatially apart edges cross on the picture plane. Thus
we get the next rule.

**Rule 2.4.** At an X-type junction, mutually collinear lines should have the
same label.

The above rules alone are not so powerful as to remove nonsense
labelings. One powerful rule is obtained by constructing a complete list of
possible views of certain types of vertices.

Let us consider, for example, vertices at which exactly three faces
meet. Vertices of this kind are called *trihedral* vertices. All the
junctions that can represent the trihedral vertices can be generated in the
following way.

Three planes meeting at a point divide the surrounding space into
eight portions, which we shall call *octants* and number from I to VIII, as
is shown in Fig. 2.8. Just as we have derived the eight categories of
lines, we put the observer in octant I and consider all the combinations of
packing material to some octants. Then we can generate the list of possible
configurations at junctions corresponding to trihedral vertices. Note,
however, that every way of packing material to some octants does not
necessarily correspond to some junction. Sometimes the point of
intersection of the three planes does not form a vertex (as is the case
where octants VI and VII are occupied by material), and sometimes the

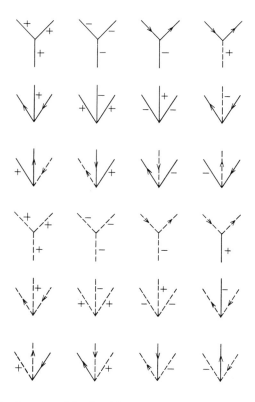

**Fig. 2.9.** Twenty-four possible junctions.

resultant vertex has more than three faces (as is the case where octants VI and VIII are occupied). Moreover, one case can be obtained by rotation of another; for example, the junction generated by packing material to octant IV can be obtained by rotation on the picture plane of the junction generated by packing material to octant II. Checking all the cases similarly, we obtain 24 different types of configurations of labeled lines at junctions, as is shown in Fig. 2.9. The first twelve junctions correspond to the cases in which octant I is empty; the situation for them is illustrated in Fig. 2.10. The latter twelve junctions in Fig. 2.9 are obtained from the first twelve ones, respectively, by interchanging the occupied octants with the empty octants.

The list of possible junctions given in Fig. 2.9 is complete in the

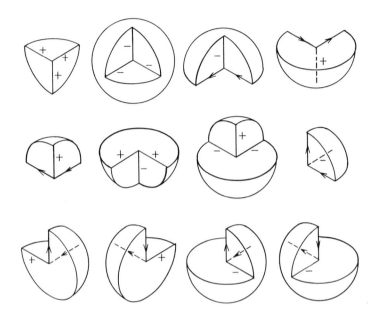

Fig. 2.10. Configurations of occupied octants corresponding to the first twelve junctions in Fig. 2.9.

following sense. We put the observer in octant I, but we are not interested in where in octant I the observer is. Hence two junctions are considered as being of the same type if one is obtained from the other when the observer moves inside octant I. Moreover we are not interested in the exact angles at which the three planes meet, so that two junctions are considered as being of the same type if one is obtained from the other by changing the mutual angles of the planes provided that the observer remains in octant I. Thus, we are not concerned with the exact angles at which lines meet at junctions. We pay our attention only to whether the mutual angles are less than $\pi$ or greater than $\pi$, because the mutual angles change from less than $\pi$ to greater than $\pi$ or vice versa only when the observer goes out of octant I. Consequently, if we ignore labels, junctions representing trihedral vertices consists of only the two types: Y-type junctions where the three mutual angles are all less than $\pi$, and W-type junctions where one of the three mutual angles is greater than $\pi$. What Fig. 2.9 means is that there are only 8 ways of labeling for Y-type junctions and 16 ways of labeling for W-type junctions.

The important point is that the number of possible junction types is very small. If we ignore the physical realizability, the number of different combinations of labels is tremendously large. Since one of the eight different labels can be put to each line, the W-type junction admits $8^3$ = 512 different ways of labeling. Fig. 2.9 tells us that only 3.1% (= (16/512) × 100) of them can appear in line drawings of polyhedral scenes. Similarly, the Y-type junction admits 176 different ways of labeling (note that a Y-type junction has rotational symmetry, and hence there are (8×7×6) /3 = 112 different ways of labeling if the three lines have mutually distinct labels, 8×7 = 56 different ways if exactly two lines have the same label, and 8 different ways if all the three lines have the same label), but only 4.5% (= (8/176) × 100) of them can appear in correct line drawings.

Thus we get the next rule.

**Rule 2.5.** If a junction has exactly three lines, the lines should be labeled so that the resulting configuration at the junction belongs to the list shown in Fig. 2.9.

**Example 2.1.** Let us consider the hidden-part-drawn line drawing in Fig. 2.3(b), and see how the rules work for this picture. First note that because of Rule 2.4 we need not divide the lines at X-type junctions. Assume that the object is trihedral and the whole part is drawn in the picture. Then, it follows from Rule 2.3 that the outermost lines (i.e., the lines 1-2, 2-3, 3-4, 5-6, 6-7, 7-8, 8-9, 9-1 in Fig. 2.11(a), where $i$-$j$ denotes the line connecting junction $i$ with junction $j$) should be labeled uniquely as solid lines with arrows in the clockwise direction. Since four other lines, the lines 1-10, 3-10, 8-10, 4-6, are represented by solid lines, they represent visible edges and consequently should be categorized as type (a), (b), (c), or (d) in Fig. 2.6 (see Rule 2.2). The remaining six lines, broken lines in Fig. 2.3(b), should be categorized as one of the eight types. Thus, if we employ Rules 2.1, 2.2, 2.3, and 2.4 only, there are $4^4 \times 8^6$ different combinations of labeling, which amount to more than 67 million.

Rule 2.5 can drastically lessen the number of possible labelings. Junction 1 is a W-type junction whose two side lines are already labeled with an in-arrow and an out-arrow, respectively. Comparing this configuration with the list in Fig. 2.9, we can see that the middle line,

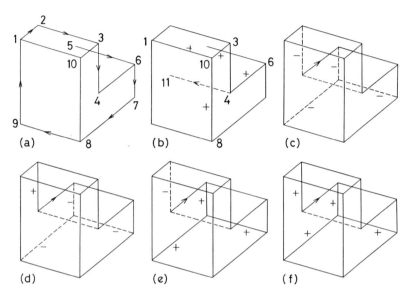

**Fig. 2.11.** Use of the labeling rules. If Rules 2.1, ..., 2.4 only are applied to the picture in Fig. 2.3(b), the eight lines are labeled uniquely as shown in (a), and hence there still remain more than 67 million different ways of labeling the other lines. If Rule 2.5 is also used, five more lines are labeled uniquely as in (b), and the other five lines admit only four ways of labeling, shown in (c), (d), (e), and (f).


the line 1-10 in Fig. 2.11(b), should have a plus label; the line is thus labeled uniquely. Because of the same reason, the three other solid lines, the lines 3-10, 4-6, 8-10, are also labeled with + uniquely. Next, the list in Fig. 2.9 tells us that the remaining line at junction 4 (i.e., the line 4-11) should be labeled with a broken line having the arrow from junction 4 to junction 11. Thus, the five more lines have been categorized uniquely as shown in Fig. 2.11(b). Consulting the list in Fig. 2.9 in a similar manner, we can eventually find that the other five lines can admit only four ways of labeling that satisfy all the five rules, as are shown in (c), (d), (e), and (f) in Fig. 2.11. Of course, even if a picture admits a set of labels that satisfies all the five rules, it does not necessarily correspond to a correct interpretation. In fact among the four possible labelings in Fig. 2.11, only (c) corresponds to a correct interpretation, but (d), (e), and (f) do not. However, we can spend a relatively long time for the check

**Fig. 2.12.** Possible labeling for the T-type junction.

of the correctness of the labelings, because we need to check only the four cases. Thus, the labeling scheme is a powerful method as the first step in the interpretation of line drawings.

## 2.4. Hidden-Part-Eliminated Pictures

The rules we have obtained for the labeling of hidden-part-drawn line drawings can be easily modified for natural pictures, that is, hidden-part-eliminated line drawings. Since every line should correspond to a visible edge, Rules 2.1 and 2.2 can be merged into the following.

**Rule 2.1'.** Every line in natural pictures should have exactly one of the four labels (a), (b), (c), (d) in Fig. 2.6.

Rule 2.3 need not be changed; it remains valid for the present class of pictures.

Unlike hidden-part-drawn pictures, hidden-part-eliminated pictures contain *T-type* junctions, junctions having three lines, two of which are collinear. Junctions of this type are generated from some of X-type junctions when hidden lines are removed. They also convey important information about the structures of the objects. As we have seen, if an object is trihedral, every vertex results in either an L-type, a Y-type, or a W-type junction. Thus, a T-type junction does not correspond to a three-dimensional vertex; it occurs only when an edge occludes another partially. The two collinear lines correspond to the occluding edge, and the other to the occluded one. Hence, a T-type junction should be labeled as is shown in Fig. 2.12, where the asterisk * means that the line can admit any label. Thus, Rule 2.4 is replaced by the next rule.

**Rule 2.4'.** If the object is trihedral, a T-type junction should be labeled as is shown in Fig. 2.12.

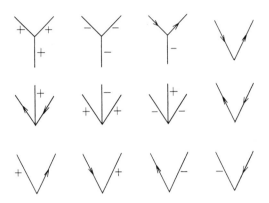

**Fig. 2.13.** Complete list of possible junctions for trihedral vertices (for hidden-part-eliminated line drawings).


Rule 2.5 is changed in the following way. Note that a trihedral vertex can appear in a picture only when octant I in Fig. 2.8 is empty. Hence the list of possible configurations for trihedral vertices can be obtained first by picking up the first twelve configurations in Fig. 2.9, which correspond to the case where octant I is empty, and next by deleting broken lines from these configurations. The resultant list is shown in Fig. 2.13, which was first found by Huffman (1971). Besides Y-type and W-type junctions, the list contains also *L-type* junctions, that is, junctions composed of two noncollinear lines. This is because we have deleted hidden lines from configurations in Fig. 2.9.

The number of junctions listed in Fig. 2.13 is small. If we ignore the physical realizability, every line can have one of the four labels, and consequently L-type junctions can be labeled in $4^2 = 16$ different ways, W-type junctions in $4^3 = 64$ different ways, and Y-type junctions in $4 \times 3 \times 2/3 + 4 \times 3 + 4 = 24$ different ways (note that a Y-type junction admits rotational symmetry, and therefore it can be labeled in $4 \times 3 \times 2/3$ ways if the three lines have distinct labels, in $4 \times 3$ ways if exactly two lines have the same labels, and in 4 ways if all the three lines have the same label). Thus, there are in all $16 + 64 + 24 = 104$ different ways of labeling, and only 11.5% ($= (12/104) \times 100$) of them can represent trihedral vertices correctly.

Thus we get the following rule.

**Rule 2.5'.** If a junction corresponds to a trihedral vertex, the lines should be labeled so that the resulting configuration at the junction belongs to the list shown in Fig. 2.13.

It should be noted that Rule 2.5' is less powerful than Rule 2.5, because in order to apply Rule 2.5' we must know whether a junction corresponds to a trihedral vertex or not. When a picture represents both visible and invisible edges, the picture itself tells us how many edges a junction has. When hidden lines are eliminated from the picture, on the other hand, there is no direct information about invisible edges, so that we cannot tell how many invisible edges there are unless we have some *a priori* knowledge about the object.

Thus, natural line drawings should be labeled subject to Rules 2.1', 2.3, 2.4', and 2.5'.

**Example 2.2.** Fig. 2.14 shows an example of how the labeling rules work for the natural picture given in Fig. 1.1. The picture in Fig. 1.1 has nine lines and each line should have one of the four possible labels, so that there are $4^9$ = 262144 different ways of assigning labels to this picture if we consider Rule 2.1' only. Now assume that this picture represents a trihedral object. If the whole part of the object is drawn in the picture, then from Rule 2.3 the outermost lines are labeled with arrows in the clockwise direction, and next from Rule 2.5' the other lines are uniquely labeled as is shown in Fig. 2.14(a), where an example of a possible section of the object along the indicated line is also illustrated. This labeling corresponds to the structure of a truncated pyramid seen from above. If, on the other hand, the object may be extended outside the picture, the picture can admit also three other ways of labeling, which are shown in (b), (c), and (d). The labeled picture (b) corresponds to a truncated pyramid on a floor, (c) corresponds to a plane with a truncated-pyramid-shape hollow, and (d) corresponds to a board penetrated by a truncated-pyramid-shape hole. Thus, the trihedral object assumption allows only four ways of labeling for this picture.

**Example 2.3.** Some other natural pictures are shown in Fig. 2.15. The picture (a) admits unique labeling if we assume that the object is trihedral and the whole part is drawn in the picture; the result of labeling is shown in (b). Note that the lines in this picture form two connected components, and the component inside the other is not influenced

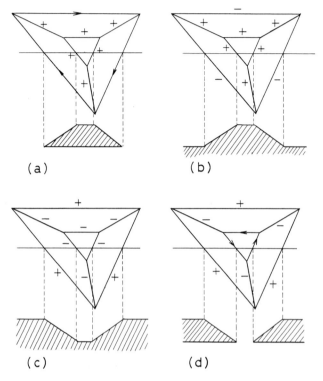

**Fig. 2.14.** Interpretation of a natural picture: if the object is restricted to a trihedral one, the picture in Fig. 1.1 admits these four labelings.

by Rule 2.3. It can nevertheless be labeled uniquely. The uniqueness stems from the T-type junction 2. When Rule 2.4' is applied to this junction, the lines 1-2 and 2-3 are labeled with the arrows in such a way that the third line, the line 2-4, is to the left of the arrows. Next comparing the L-type junction 1 with the list of possible junctions in Fig. 2.13, we can say that the line 1-4 is labeled with either a plus symbol or an arrow directing from junction 4 to junction 1. However, the latter case is rejected at the W-type junction 4, and consequently the line 1-4 is uniquely labeled with a plus symbol. The labeling process proceeds similarly, and we eventually obtain the unique labeling (b). The uniqueness of labeling of this configuration will be discussed in more detail in Section 2.6 (see Fig. 2.18).

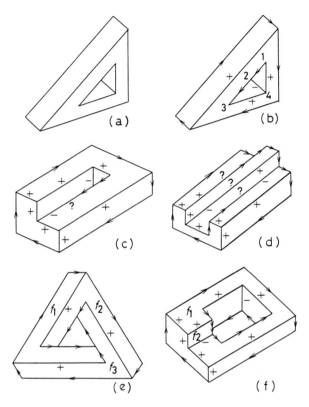

**Fig. 2.15.** Some other examples of interpretation of natural pictures as trihedral objects: the picture(a) admits the unique labeling (b), the pictures (c) and (d) have no consistent labeling and hence can be judged incorrect, and the pictures (e) and (f) admit consistent labelings though they are incorrect (the picture (e) is adapted from Penrose and Penrose (1958)).

The pictures (c) and (d) do not represent trihedral objects. The labeling rules can detect the incorrectness, because there is no consistent way of assigning labels to the pictures. If, beginning with the outermost lines, we try to label lines one by one, we eventually find that the line labels contradict at the lines with question marks; a label determined at one terminal junction is different from that determined at the other terminal junction.

On the other hand, the pictures (e) and (f) can admit consistent
assignments of labels although they do not represent any trihedral object.
The picture (e) is incorrect for the following reason. Note that if it were
to represent a polyhedron, the three faces $f_1$, $f_2$, and $f_3$ should have a
common point of intersection in a space (when they were extended) and
consequently the three pairwise intersection of the faces (i.e., the three
lines labeled with +) should be concurrent on the picture plane. However,
they are not; thus (e) does not represent a polyhedron. The incorrectness
of (f) can be understood if we note that the top face $f_1$ shares two
noncollinear lines with the face $f_2$, which is impossible unless the top
face is curved.

Thus, labeled pictures do not always correspond to correct structures
of objects; they merely represent candidates for spatial structures. The
labeling scheme is, however, powerful in that it can make the set of
candidates extremely small.

## 2.5. Some Extensions and Remarks

### 2.5.1. Non-Trihedral Objects

We have concentrated our attention upon the trihedral object world. Indeed
the complete lists of junctions in Figs. 2.9 and 2.13 together with the
trihedral object assumption have played the main role in the labeling
process. However, the labeling scheme itself can be applied likewise to
non-trihedral objects.

All we have to do is to provide the list of junctions for
non-trihedral vertices. It is of course impossible to enumerate all
possible junctions, because at least theoretically any number of faces can
meet at a vertex, so that the number of possible junctions is not finite.
In practical situations, however, we often have some *a priori* knowledge
about the object world, and hence can construct the complete list of
possible junctions for that object world.

If a three-dimensional vertex is given, the method for enumeration of
possible junctions used in Section 2.3 can be employed straightforwardly.
That is, we extend all the incident faces, dividing the surrounding empty
space into a finite number of convex cones whose apexes are at the vertex,
and see how the vertex appears to the observer who stands in each empty
cone (Sugihara, 1979b). Hence, if, for example, the object world consists

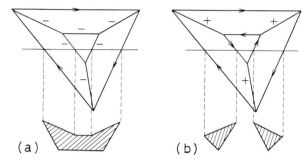

**Fig. 2.16.** Interpretation of the picture in Fig. 1.1 as nontrihedral objects.

of a finite number of prototypes, as is the case of machine manipulation of mechanical parts for assembly, the list of all the possible junctions for this world can be generated automatically.

If, on the other hand, only the number of faces meeting at a vertex is given, it is not so easy to enumerate the possible junctions because unlike the trihedral case it is difficult to list up all possible vertices having the given number of faces. Thus, the method in Section 2.3 cannot be applied directly. However, we shall present in the next chapter a method for judging whether a labeled picture represents a polyhedral scene correctly. This includes a method for judging whether a labeled configuration at a junction represents a three-dimensional vertex correctly. Therefore, given an unlabeled junction drawn on the picture plane, we can generate all ways of consistent labeling for the junction systematically, and use them to search for consistent ways of labeling for the whole picture.

As the underlying object world becomes larger, the number of possible interpretations increases. If we allow any number of faces meeting at a vertex, the line drawing in Fig. 1.1 admits many more interpretations than those listed in Fig. 2.14. Fig. 2.16 shows two examples of interpretations as nontrihedral objects together with possible sections of the objects along the indicated lines. In (a), the outermost three W-type vertices do not belong to the list in Fig. 2.13; each of the three vertices has at least two invisible faces in the rear side. The object represented in (b) can be obtained by connecting three triangular prisms in a cyclic manner, so that every vertex is nontrihedral.

2.5.2.  Other Variations

Other types of variations of the labeling scheme also arise when  the  line
categories and/or the class of objects are changed.

     Waltz  (1972,  1975)  studied  the  labeling  method for pictures with
shadows and cracks.   In addition to the first four categories of  lines  in
Fig. 2.6,  he  introduced  new  labels  for  "cracks"  and  "boundaries  of
shadows,"  and  furthermore  three  new  labels  for  regions:   regions
illuminated, those shadowed, and those facing opposite to the light source.
As a result of augmenting labels, his list of possible  junctions  includes
several   thousand   different   types.   However,   he  observed  that  the
introduction of new labels does not cause more ambiguity in interpretation,
but  can  lessen the number of possible interpretations.   This point may be
understood intuitively if we consider Fig. 2.14 again.   The labeled picture
(a)  represents  a  truncated  pyramid  isolated  in  a  space, whereas (b)
represents the same object on the floor.   If the object  casts  its  shadow
onto  the  floor  and  the shadow boundaries are also drawn in the picture,
then the ambiguity between (a) and (b) would be cleared up.   Thus,  shadows
convey important information about the structures of the scenes.

     Another  new  category of lines was introduced by Sugihara (1979a) for
the analysis of range data obtained by triangulation.   In triangulation,  a
range  to  a  target  point on the surface of the object can be obtained by
determining a triangle composed of  the  target  point  and  the  two  base
points,  so that the range is measured only when the target is visible from
both of the base points.   In the corresponding  picture,  therefore,  there
often remains some regions whose ranges are not observed.   The new category
of lines is  used  to  represent  the  boundaries  of  these  regions.   An
interesting  point  is  that in the case of range data analysis the list of
possible junctions can be used  for  the  "prediction"  of  missing  edges,
because  the  range data enable us to assign labels to lines correctly even
if a line drawing is given partially. See Sugihara (1979a) for the details.

     A typical example of nonpolyhedral object worlds is  Kanade's  Origami
world (Kanade, 1980), where objects are composed of  planar  panels which are
so thin that the thickness is negligible. He constructed a list of  possible
junctions  for  vertices  having three or less panels, and demonstrated the
validity of the labeling scheme to this object  world.   He  observed  that
there  are  some interpretations that are possible in the Origami world but
impossible in the trihedral object world.   The pictures in Fig. 2.16 can be
considered  as  examples  of  such  interpretations,  where we have to read a

line with an arrow as an occluding edge whose right side corresponds to a panel and whose left side corresponds to a background or something farther from the observer. As will be shown in the next chapter, if the number of faces or panels meeting at a junction is not restricted, the difference between polyhedral objects and planar-panel objects disappears. That is, we can show that a labeled picture represents a polyhedral object if and only if it represents a planar-panel object.

### 2.5.3. Other Rules

We have considered only a simple set of rules, Rules 2.1, ..., 2.5 for hidden-part-drawn line drawings and Rules 2.1', 2.3, 2.4', and 2.5' for natural line drawings. These rule are powerful, but not complete; labeled pictures obeying the rules do not necessarily represent correct structures of objects. In order to check the inconsistency that cannot be found by the above rules, many additional rules have been proposed. They include reciprocal figures in a gradient space (Huffman, 1971; Mackworth, 1973; Whiteley, 1979; Kanade, 1980, 1981), theory of braids (Cowan, 1974, 1977; Térouanne, 1980), dual representations (Huffman, 1977a), $\varphi$ and $\varphi'$ points (Huffman 1977b), cyclic order properties of vertices and edges around faces (Sugihara, 1978; Shapira and Freeman, 1979), thickness of objects (Sugihara, 1978), spanning angles (Kanade, 1980), and sidedness reasoning (Draper, 1981).

However, we do not employ any of them here, because they are rather complicated for their effects. Recall that the aim of the first module is to produce a relatively small set of candidates for possible interpretations. It is not expected to produce the precise set of correct interpretations, because the correctness of these candidates will be judged strictly by the second module. In this sense, the present set of rules is powerful enough to reduce the candidate set to a tractable size.

### 2.6. Constraint Propagation

We have seen that although a picture having $l$ lines can admit as many as $8^l$ different ways of labeling, or $4^l$ ways if hidden lines are not drawn, the labeling scheme can successfully extract from them a very small set of candidates for correct interpretations. Now, how much time does it take to select the candidates? If we simply pick up $8^l$ labeled pictures one by one and check whether they obey the rules, it is impossible to finish the task

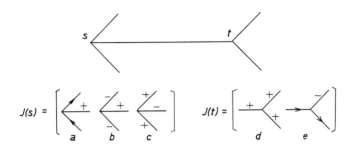

**Fig. 2.17.** Local consistency of labeling.

in a reasonable time unless $l$ is very small. For example, if a picture is composed  of 15 lines, the number of labeled pictures amounts to $8^{15} = 2^{45}$ , and even if each labeling can be checked in 1 microsecond, it would take more than a year to check all the cases.

Fortunately,   however,   each  rule  can  be  checked  "locally"  and consequently we need not examine every labeled picture independently.   For example,  if  a  local assignment of labels to lines incident to a junction turns out to be incorrect, then it implies that all labeled pictures having this  local  assignment  of labels are incorrect.   Thus, we can delete many labeled pictures by only one local  check.   This  idea  leads  us  to  the following  systematic   method;   it  is  sometimes  called  a  constraint propagation method or a relaxation method (Montanari,  1974;  Waltz,  1975; Rosenfeld  et  al.,  1976;  Mackworth,  1977a; McGregor, 1979; Haralick and Shapiro, 1980; Nudel, 1983).

For  each  junction $s$  in  the  picture  we  associate  a  set $J(s)$  of candidates for  labeled  configurations the junction may admit.  Initially $J(s)$ contains all locally possible configurations,  and  if  some  elements turn  out  to  be  inconsistent  with  the  candidates  at  the neighboring junctions, they are removed from $J(s)$.  The inconsistency check is based on Rule 2.1 or 2.1'. The rule says that each line should have exactly one type of a label in a labeled picture, and hence we get the following  definition of local consistency.

Let $s$ and $t$ be two junctions sharing a common line. A configuration in $J(s)$ is said to be *locally consistent* with $J(t)$ if $J(t)$ contains an element having  the  same  label  for  the  common  line  as the configuration has. Consider, for example, two junctions $s$ and $t$ in Fig. 2.17. Assume that they have  the  configuration sets $J(s)$ and $J(t)$ as is shown in the figure.  $J(s)$

contains the three elements $a$, $b$, $c$, and $J(t)$ contains the two elements $d$, $e$. Though a Y-type junction has rotational symmetry, we do not allow here the rotation of elements in $J(t)$. Hence, the line connecting $s$ and $t$ corresponds to the left side horizontal line of each configuration in $J(t)$. The elements $a$ and $b$ are locally consistent with $J(t)$, because the label assigned to the common line (i.e., the + label) appears in the element $d$, whereas $c$ is not locally consistent with $J(t)$ because $J(t)$ has no element having the − label for the common line. Similarly, $d$ is locally consistent with $J(s)$, but $e$ is not.

Given an initial set $J(s)$ for each junction $s$, the next procedure can delete locally inconsistent candidates from $J(s)$. The procedure is written in Pidgin ALGOL used by Aho et al. (1974).

Initially put all lines in stack $E$;
**while** $E$ is not empty **do**
  **begin**
    select and delete an element $e$ from $E$ (let the two terminal junctions of $e$ be $s$ and $t$);
    **if** $J(s)$ has elements that are not locally consistent with $J(t)$ **then**
      **begin**
        delete all such elements from $J(s)$;
        add to $E$ all the lines other than $e$ that emanate from $s$ if they are not in $E$
      **end**;
    **if** $J(t)$ has elements that are not locally consistent with $J(s)$ **then**
      **begin**
        delete all such elements from $J(t)$;
        add to $E$ all the lines other than $e$ that emanate from $t$ if they are not in $E$
      **end**
  **end**

In this procedure, $E$ is used as the stack containing lines along which the local consistency should be checked; hence initially all the lines are put in it. For each line in $E$ we check if the terminal junctions contain locally inconsistent elements with respect to the other. If so, we delete them from the candidate sets, and at the same time add to $E$ the other lines incident to the terminal junctions (if they are not in $E$) for the later check, because the present change of the candidate sets may cause some

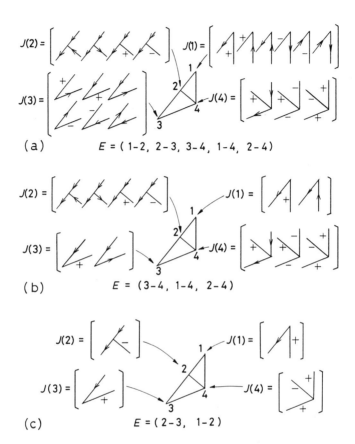

**Fig. 2.18.** Constraint propagation.

change at other junctions. The procedure repeats similar processing until
the candidate sets cannot be changed any more.

**Example 2.4.** An example of the behavior of the procedure is shown in
Fig. 2.18. Let us assume again that the picture is part of a trihedral
object. Fig. 2.18(a) represents the initial state, where the candidate sets
$J(1)$, ..., $J(4)$ contain all possible configurations given in Figs. 2.12 and
2.13, and $E$ contains all the lines. First, the line 1–2 is chosen from $E$
and the local consistency check is carried out at the line. Since the line
1–2 is labeled with an arrow from 1 to 2 in all candidates in $J(2)$, only

two elements in $J(1)$ (i.e., the first and the third ones) are locally consistent with $J(2)$ and the other four elements are deleted from $J(1)$. Next, the line 2-3 is chosen, and four elements are likewise deleted from $J(3)$. The result is shown in (b).

Next the line 3-4 is chosen, and the local consistency check results in two singletons $J(3)$ and $J(4)$ as shown in (c), because the only common label for the line 3-4 is a plus symbol. Since $J(3)$ is changed, the line 2-3 is added to $E$ again. When the lines 1-4 and 2-4 are checked, $J(1)$ and $J(2)$ are respectively reduced to singletons, and the line 1-2 is added to $E$. This situation is represented in (c). Now all the candidate sets have become singletons, and no more change occurs; $E$ eventually becomes empty. Thus the procedure terminates, leaving only one element in each candidate set, and consequently we have a unique labeling that is the same as the result we have obtained in Fig. 2.15(b).

In the above example we happen to have a unique labeling. In general, however, a candidate set may contain two or more elements at the end of the constraint propagation. Therefore, in order to obtain the set of all consistently labeled pictures we have to make a search: for example, a depth-first search. This is not so difficult because the constraint propagation can usually make the set of possible configurations at each junctions very small.

## 3. DISCRIMINATION BETWEEN CORRECT AND INCORRECT PICTURES

The first module, the picture labeling module, has generated a small set of candidates for spatial interpretations, which are represented in the form of labeled pictures. The next task of our mechanism is to divide these candidates into correct interpretations and incorrect ones. The present chapter presents a module that performs this task by reducing the problem to a problem of judging satisfiability of a certain set of linear constraints.

### 3.1. Basic Idea

In this chapter we shall solve the problem of judging whether a labeled picture represents a polyhedral scene. We shall first restrict our consideration to the orthographic projection, but later show that the results are valid also for the perspective projection. The basic idea is the following.

Suppose that an object is fixed to an $(x, y, z)$ Cartesian coordinate system, and the picture is obtained as the orthographic projection of the object onto the $x$-$y$ plane, as shown in Fig. 3.1. Let $(x_\alpha, y_\alpha, z_\alpha)$ denote the position of the $\alpha$th vertex of the object and $a_j x + b_j y + z + c_j = 0$ denote the surface on which the $j$th face lies.

When the picture is given, $x_\alpha$ and $y_\alpha$ are known constants whereas $z_\alpha$, $a_j$, $b_j$, $c_j$ are unknowns. Labels assigned to the picture tell us which vertex should be on which face. If the $\alpha$th vertex should be on the $j$th face, we get the equation

$$a_j x_\alpha + b_j y_\alpha + z_\alpha + c_j = 0 \, ,$$

which is linear in the unknowns $z_\alpha$, $a_j$, $b_j$, $c_j$. The labeled picture also contains information about relative distance; it tells us which part of the object should be nearer to the observer than other part. For example, if the $\beta$th vertex should be nearer than the $k$th face, we get

$$a_k x_\beta + b_k y_\beta + z_\beta + c_k > 0 \, ,$$

which is also linear in the unknowns $z_\beta$, $a_k$, $b_k$, $c_k$.

We shall see that if such linear constraints are gathered in some

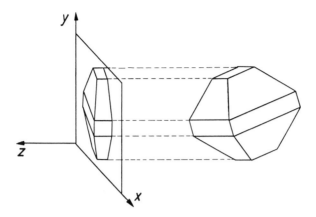

**Fig. 3.1.** Object and its orthographic projection.

systematic manner, the resulting system of equations and inequalities allows us to express a necessary and sufficient condition for the picture to represent a polyhedral scene; that is, the picture represents a polyhedral scene if and only if the system has a solution. Now the most important point is how to extract from the picture relevant equations and inequalities systematically. In order to describe this process clearly we shall introduce a concept called a 'spatial structure,' which is defined for each labeled picture.

Here we restrict our consideration to hidden-part-eliminated pictures; hidden-part-drawn pictures will be treated in the next chapter. Though our objects are polyhedrons, we begin by considering the world consisting of thin objects called planar panels; we shall present a necessary and sufficient condition for a labeled picture to represent a planar-panel scene, and then show that a labeled picture represents a polyhedral scene if and only if it represents a planar-panel scene.

## 3.2. Planar-Panel Scenes

A *planar-panel scene* is a collection of a finite number of planar *panels* fixed to a three-dimensional space. Panels are thin enough (but not transparent), and bounded by a finite number of straight line segments called *edges*. Hence, panels can be regarded as two-dimensional polygonal areas with possible polygonal holes. Panels in a scene may touch each other

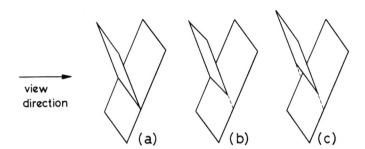

**Fig. 3.2.** Distinction between the concave lines and the occluding lines: scene (a) generates a concave line, whereas scenes (b) and (c) generate occluding lines.

but should not penetrate one another.

In order to exclude "pathological" panels, we assume that panels are homogeneously two-dimensional and hence contain no hanging or isolated structures of different dimension such as solids, lines, or points. Formally, it is assumed that a panel coincides with the closure of its interior in a two-dimensional set theoretical sense.

A scene fixed to an $(x,y,z)$ Cartesian coordinate system is assumed to be seen from the observer that is infinitely distant in the positive direction of the $z$ axis, as shown in Fig. 3.1. Hence, a *picture* of the scene is to be an orthographic projection onto the $x$-$y$ plane of visible part of edges of the panels (note that this is a restatement of Assumption 2.3).

In order to categorize lines in pictures of planar-panel scenes we use the same labels as in pictures of polyhedral scenes. The label + is assigned to a *convex line* along which two visible panels form a ridge with respect to the viewer, the label − to a *concave line* along which two panels form a valley with respect to the viewer, and the arrow to an *occluding line* one side of which corresponds to the panel whose boundary edge yields the line and the other side corresponds to the background or another panel behind (the direction of the arrow is chosen in a way that the right side of the arrow corresponds to the panel and the left side to the background or the other panel behind). It may occur that a panel occludes another along its boundary line segment and at the same time they touch each other along this line segment, as shown in Fig. 3.2(a). We categorize this type of a line as a concave line. Hence, an occluding line implies that the two associated panels must have a gap in their $z$ coordinates, as are shown in (b) and (c); they can touch only at one point.

If two panels in a scene touch along a common boundary line at angle $\pi$, then we remove the common boundary line and merge them together into a single panel. Moreover, we assume that neither any panels are parallel to the $z$ axis (note that this is a restatement of Assumption 2.4), nor any two spatially distinct boundary lines align on the picture plane (this is a restatement of Assumption 2.5). Hence, all lines in the picture corresponding to the scene can be classified into the above three categories without any ambiguity.

A labeled picture is formally represented as a quadruple $D = (J,E,u,h)$ in the following way.

(1) $J$ is a finite set whose elements are called *junctions*.

(2) $u$ is a map from $J$ to $R^2$ (where $R^d$ denotes a $d$-dimensional Euclidean space) such that $u(s)$ represents the position of junction $s$ ($\in J$).

(3) $E$ is a set of ordered pairs of $J$. Element $(s,t)$ of $E$ is called a *line* from *initial junction* $s$ to *terminal junction* $t$.

(4) $h$ is a map from $E$ to the set of line categories {CONVEX, CONCAVE, P-ARROW, N-ARROW}. For any line $(s,t)$,

$h(s,t)$ = CONVEX if the line has the label +,
$h(s,t)$ = CONCAVE if it has the label −,
$h(s,t)$ = P-ARROW if it has the arrow from $s$ to $t$,
$h(s,t)$ = N-ARROW if it has the arrow from $t$ to $s$.

Without loss of generality we furthermore assume the following:

(a) $(s,s) \notin E$ ($s \in J$).

(b) $(s,t) \in E$ implies $(t,s) \notin E$ ($s,\ t \in J$).

(c) Lines in $E$ do not meet each other except at their end points.

(d) Each junction has two or more lines incident to it.

Conditions (a) and (b) are obvious. Condition (c) means that lines in a picture are divided into as small fragments as possible. Hence, the straight line segment connecting junctions 1 and 3 in Fig. 3.3(a) is divided to (1,2) and (2,3); we should not represent it by (1,3) because another line, (2,8), meets it midway. Condition (d) does not place any restriction. Indeed, a junction with a single line never occurs in a

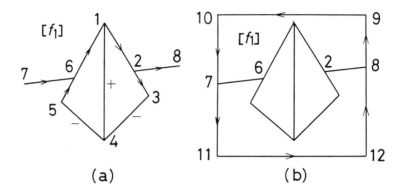

**Fig. 3.3.** Junctions with single lines. Picture (a) contains junctions with single lines, but they are converted to normal junctions by the introduction of a large window, as shown in (b).

perfect picture, because a planar panel can neither intersect itself nor occlude itself.

However, if some panels are too large to be entirely in view, a picture may contain junctions with single lines, just as junctions 7 and 8 in Fig. 3.3(a). For this kind of a picture we introduce, without loss of generality, a new large panel with a rectangular hole through which the scene is viewed, as is shown in Fig. 3.3(b), and thus can make all junctions have two or more lines.

There remains some arbitrariness in the representation of $D$; that is, a line connecting junctions $s$ and $t$ can be represented either by $(s,t)$ or by $(t,s)$. Unless otherwise mentioned, we assume that occluding lines are represented in a way that the direction from the initial junction toward the terminal one coincides with that indicated by the arrow. For convex and concave lines, we use any one of the two alternative representations. However, once we fix the representation, those lines also have their directions. Therefore, we treat them as directed lines, and use expressions such as "the initial junction of a convex line," and "the right side of a concave line."

Now, our problem is to judge whether or not a labeled picture $D = (J,E,u,h)$ represents a planar-panel scene.

### 3.3. Extraction of the Spatial Structure

Given a labeled picture $D = (J,E,u,h)$, we first extract a possible spatial structure from $D$. A *spatial structure* of $D$ is a quadruple $S = (V,F,R,T)$. Elements of $V$ are three-dimensional points $v_\alpha = (x_\alpha,y_\alpha,z_\alpha)$ called *vertices*, where $x_\alpha$'s and $y_\alpha$'s are given constants whereas $z_\alpha$'s are considered as unknown variables. $F$ is a set of visible panels corresponding to two-dimensional regions on the picture plane. We denote by $[f_j]$ a connected region on the picture plane, and by $f_j$ itself the associated panel in the space. $R$ and $T$ are used to represent relative depths among vertices and panels. $R$ is a set of vertex-panel pairs such that the former lies on the latter. $T$ is a set of ordered triple of the form $(\alpha,\beta,\delta)$ such that $\alpha$ and $\beta$ are taken from $V$ and $V \cup F$, respectively, and $\delta$ is taken from the set {BEHIND, FRONT, PROPERLY-BEHIND, PROPERLY-FRONT}. A triple $(\alpha, \beta, $ BEHIND$)$ (resp. $(\alpha, \beta, $ FRONT$))$ means that $\alpha$ has the same depth as $\beta$ or it is behind (resp. in front of) $\beta$, and $(\alpha, \beta, $ PROPERLY-BEHIND$)$ (resp. $(\alpha, \beta, $ PROPERLY-FRONT$))$ means that $\alpha$ is properly behind (resp. properly in front of) $\beta$.

The spatial structure $S = (V,F,R,T)$ associated with $D$ is defined in the following constructive way.

The lines of the picture $D$ partition the picture plane into a finite number, say $m$, of connected regions. We shall denote them by $[f_1]$, $[f_2]$, ..., $[f_m]$, respectively, and put $F = \{f_1, f_2, ..., f_m\}$. This definition is based on the implicit convention that any point on the picture plane corresponds to some panel. Hence, the region $[f_1]$ in Fig. 3.3, which is usually interpreted as an empty space, is also thought of as a certain panel that is sufficiently large and far away. This convention does not restrict our problem domain, whereas it makes the subsequent discussion much simpler.

In the initial state, let $V$, $R$, and $T$ be empty; they are augmented in the following way. Suppose that junction $s$ has $p$ lines ($p \geq 2$). Let $[f_1]$, $[f_2]$, ..., $[f_p]$ be the $p$ regions touching the junction and surrounding the junction counterclockwise in this order, as shown in Fig. 3.4(a). Note that $f_1$, ..., $f_p$ are not necessarily distinct; some of them may be identical because a region may touch the junction twice or more (see Fig. 3.4(b)). Suppose that $q$ out of the $p$ lines are occluding lines and the other $p-q$ lines are convex or concave ones ($q \geq 1$). Let the $q$ occluding lines be $l_1$, $l_2$, ..., $l_q$, which are arranged counterclockwise in this order. Moreover, without loss of generality, we assume that $f_1$ immediately follows

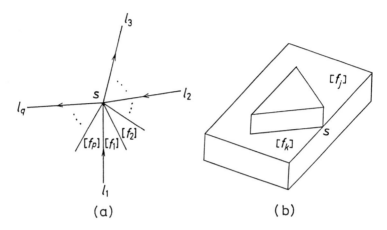

**Fig. 3.4.** Regions surrounding a junction.

$l_1$ in the counterclockwise order, as shown in Fig. 3.4(a). If we see the junction locally, the $q$ occluding lines partition the surrounding plane into $q$ fan-shaped areas and, consequently, partition the set $\{f_1, \ldots, f_p\}$ into $q$ subsets, say $F_1, F_2, \ldots, F_q$. Recall that panels have gaps in depth only at occluding lines. Hence, the panels in each $F_\alpha$ ($\alpha = 1, 2, \ldots, q$) form a continuous surface, and consequently they have the same depth at the junction $s$. On the basis of this observation, we introduce $q$ vertices, $p$ elements of $R$, and $q$ elements of $T$ in the following way.

We first define $q$ new vertices, say $v_\alpha = (x_\alpha, y_\alpha, z_\alpha)$ ($\alpha = 1, 2, \ldots, q$), in such a way that $(x_1, y_1) = (x_2, y_2) = \cdots = (x_q, y_q) = u(s)$ and add them to $V$. We next generate, as new elements of R, $p$ pairs $(v_\alpha, f_j)$ such that $f_j$ is an element of $F_\alpha$ ($\alpha = 1, \ldots, q$, $j = 1, \ldots, p$). Last, we generate $q$ triples $(v_{\alpha-1}, v_\alpha, \delta_\alpha)$ ($\alpha = 1, 2, \ldots, q$), as elements of T, such that

$\delta_\alpha$ = BEHIND if $l_\alpha$ has an in-arrow,
$\delta_\alpha$ = FRONT if $l_\alpha$ has an out-arrow,

where we assume $v_0 \equiv v_q$.

If the junction $s$ does not have any occluding line (i.e., $q = 0$), then we simply add to $V$ one new vertex, say $v_1 = (x_1, y_1, z_1)$, such that $(x_1, y_1) = u(s)$, and add $p$ elements $(v_1, f_j)$ ($j = 1, \ldots, p$) to R.

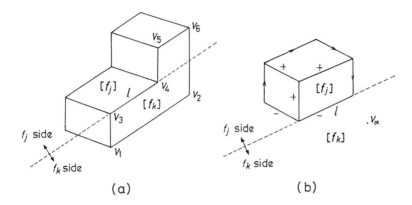

**Fig. 3.5.** Vertex on the $f_k$ side with respect to the line $l$.

We repeat the above procedure for all junctions of $D$. Then, we get the "basic part" of the spatial structure $S = (V,F,R,T)$. We call it the basic part, because $V$, $R$, and $T$ shall be furthermore augmented in the sequel.

For the spatial structure $S = (V,F,R,T)$ thus constructed from $D = (J,E,u,h)$, the following propositions are obvious.

**Proposition 3.1.** Let $l$ be any convex or concave line in $D$, and let $s$, $t$, $[f_j]$, $[f_k]$ be the initial junction, the terminal junction, the right side region, and the left side region, respectively, of $l$. Then, there exist $v_\alpha$ and $v_\beta$ in $V$ such that

$(x_\alpha,y_\alpha) = u(s)$, $(x_\beta,y_\beta) = u(t)$,
$(v_\alpha,f_j)$, $(v_\alpha,f_k)$, $(v_\beta,f_j)$, $(v_\beta,f_k) \in R$.

**Proposition 3.2.** Let $l$ be any occluding line in $D$, and let $s$, $t$, $[f_j]$, $[f_k]$ be the initial junction, the terminal junction, the right side region, and the left side region, respectively, of $l$. Then, there exist four vertices $v_\alpha$, $v_\beta$, $v_\gamma$, $v_\delta$ (not necessarily distinct) in $V$ such that

$(x_\alpha,y_\alpha) = (x_\beta,y_\beta) = u(s)$, $(x_\gamma,y_\gamma) = (x_\delta,y_\delta) = u(t)$,
$(v_\alpha,f_j)$, $(v_\beta,f_k)$, $(v_\gamma,f_j)$, $(v_\delta,f_k) \in R$,
$(v_\alpha,v_\beta,\text{FRONT})$, $(v_\delta,v_\gamma,\text{BEHIND}) \in T$.

We have constructed elements of $V$, $R$, and $T$ at junctions. Now we augment the sets at lines.

Let $l$ be any convex or concave line, and $[f_j]$ and $[f_k]$ be the right and left side regions, respectively, of $l$. The line $l$, when extended, divides the picture plane into two open half spaces, which shall be referred to as the $\bar{}\,f_j$ side$\bar{}$ and the $\bar{}\,f_k$ side$\bar{}$ with respect to $l$. The region $[f_k]$ often occupies part of the $f_j$ side (and *vice versa*) as shown in Fig. 3.5, but there is no ambiguity in naming the $f_j$ side and the $f_k$ side because the side name is defined according to which region occupies the side in the neighbor of the middle point of the line segment $l$. Then, we choose a vertex, say $v_\alpha$, such that $v_\alpha$ lies on $f_k$ but not on $f_j$, and that $v_\alpha$ is on the $f_k$ side with respect to $l$.

For example, out of the six vertices $v_1$, ..., $v_6$ on $f_k$ in Fig. 3.5(a), only $v_1$ and $v_2$ satisfy the condition. The other vertices do not, because $v_3$ and $v_4$ lie also on $f_j$, and $v_5$ and $v_6$ are on the $f_j$ side. Hence, we can choose as $v_\alpha$ either $v_1$ or $v_2$.

Sometimes we may not find any such vertex. For example, see Fig. 3.5(b). In this case we introduce a new vertex, say $v_\alpha$, which lies on $f_k$ and which is on the $f_k$ side, as shown in Fig. 3.5(b). Formally, we put $\alpha = |V| + 1$, choose an arbitrary point $(x_\alpha, y_\alpha)$ on the $f_k$ side with respect to $l$, introduce new unknown $z_\alpha$, and add new vertex $v_\alpha = (x_\alpha, y_\alpha, z_\alpha)$ to $V$ and the associated vertex-panel pair $(v_\alpha, f_k)$ to $R$.

If the line $l$ is convex, the vertex $v_\alpha$ chosen in this way should be behind the planar surface on which the panel $f_j$ lies. If, on the other hand, $l$ is concave, $v_\alpha$ should be in front of the surface containing $f_j$. Therefore, we add the triple $(v_\alpha, f_j, \delta)$ to $T$, where

$\delta$ = PROPERLY-BEHIND if $l$ is convex,
$\delta$ = PROPERLY-FRONT if $l$ is concave.

We generate similar triples for all convex and concave lines.

The above process directly results in the following proposition.

**Proposition 3.3.** Let $l$ be any convex or concave line of $D$, and $[f_j]$ and $[f_k]$ be the right side region and the left side region, respectively, of $l$. Then, there exists a vertex $v_\gamma$ in $V$ such that $(x_\gamma, y_\gamma)$ is on the $f_k$ side with respect to $l$, and

$$(v_\gamma, f_k) \in R, \quad \text{and} \quad (v_\gamma, f_j, \delta) \in T,$$

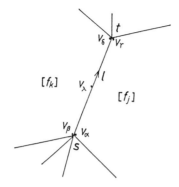

**Fig. 3.6.** Vertices generated around an occluding line.

where

$\delta$ = PROPERLY-BEHIND if $l$ is convex,
$\delta$ = PROPERLY-FRONT if $l$ is concave.

   Next, let $l$ be any occluding line, and let $[f_j]$ and $[f_k]$ be the right side region and the left side region, respectively, of $l$, as shown in Fig. 3.6. Furthermore, let $l^*$ be the three-dimensional counterpart of $l$; that is, $l^*$ is the line segment in the space that belongs to the boundary of the panel $f_j$ and its projection coincides with $l$. As stated in Proposition 3.2, we have already generated four vertices (i.e., $v_\alpha$, $v_\beta$, $v_\gamma$, $v_\delta$ in Proposition 3.2), four elements of R, and two elements of T, which altogether express that the panel $f_k$ does not pass in front of $l^*$. Indeed, this meets what is required by the occluding line $l$. Recall, however, that the occluding line $l$ also implies that $f_k$ should not touch $f_j$ at all points on $l^*$ (if $f_k$ touches $f_j$ at all points on $l^*$, $l$ must be categorized as a concave line). Since the panels are planar, $f_k$ can touch $f_j$, if possible, only either at the initial point or at the terminal point of $l^*$. In order to express this property, we generate a new vertex $v_\lambda = (x_\lambda, y_\lambda, z_\lambda)$ whose two-dimensional position $(x_\lambda, y_\lambda)$ coincides with the midpoint of $l$, a new vertex-panel pair $(v_\lambda, f_k)$, and a new triple $(v_\lambda, f_j, \text{PROPERLY-BEHIND})$, and add them to V, R, and T, respectively. We repeat the same process for all occluding lines.
   This directly leads us to the following proposition.

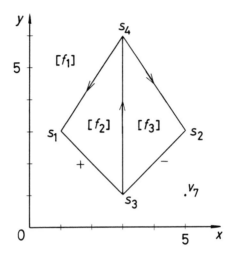

**Fig. 3.7.** Labeled picture considered in Example 3.1.

**Proposition 3.4.**   Let $l$ be any occluding line in $D$, and $[f_j]$ and $[f_k]$ be the right side region and the left side region, respectively, of $l$.   Then there exists a vertex $v_\lambda$ in $V$ such that $(x_\lambda, y_\lambda)$ is the midpoint of $l$, and

$(v_\lambda, f_k) \in R$,     and     $(v_\lambda, f_j, \text{PROPERLY-BEHIND}) \in T$.

Thus we have completely constructed the spatial structure $S = (V, F, R, T)$ from the labeled picture $D = (J, E, u, t)$.

**Example 3.1.**  Consider a labeled picture shown in Fig. 3.7.  This picture partitions the $x$-$y$ plane into three regions: two triangular regions and one surrounding region.  We name them $[f_1]$, $[f_2]$, and $[f_3]$ as shown in the figure.  Hence, $F = \{f_1, f_2, f_3\}$.

Since junction $s_1$ has exactly one occluding line, one vertex, say $v_1$, is generated at this junction:

$v_1 \in V$,   $(x_1, y_1) = (1, 3)$.

Two regions $[f_1]$ and $[f_2]$ share this junction, and hence we get

$(v_1,f_1)$, $(v_1,f_2)$ $\in$ $R$.

Moreover, the occluding line at $s_1$ has an in-arrow, and hence we get

$(v_1,v_1,\text{BEHIND})$ $\in$ $T$.

Similarly, at junction $s_2$ we get

$v_2$ $\in$ $V$, $(x_2,y_2)$ = $(5,3)$,
$(v_2,f_1)$, $(v_2,f_3)$ $\in$ $R$, $(v_2,v_2,\text{BEHIND})$ $\in$ $T$.

Junction $s_3$ also has exactly one occluding line, and therefore one vertex, say $v_3$, is generated at this junction:

$v_3$ $\in$ $V$, $(x_3,y_3)$ = $(3,1)$.

Since $s_3$ is shared by all of the three regions, we get

$(v_3,f_1)$, $(v_3,f_2)$, $(v_3,f_3)$ $\in$ $R$.

The occluding line at $s_3$ has an out-arrow, which generates

$(v_3,v_3,\text{FRONT})$ $\in$ $T$.

Junction $s_4$ has three occluding lines, and hence three vertices, say $v_4$, $v_5$, $v_6$, are generated at this junction in such a way that

$v_4$, $v_5$, $v_6$ $\in$ $V$, $(x_4,y_4)$ = $(x_5,y_5)$ = $(x_6,y_6)$ = $(3,6)$,
$(v_4,f_1)$, $(v_5,f_2)$, $(v_6,f_3)$ $\in$ $R$,
$(v_4,v_5,\text{FRONT})$, $(v_5,v_6,\text{BEHIND})$, $(v_6,v_4,\text{FRONT})$ $\in$ $T$.

Next consider the convex line $s_1s_3$ (assume that the direction of the line is defined to be from $s_1$ to $s_3$). This line has the right side region $[f_1]$ and the left side region $[f_2]$. The vertex $v_5$ is on the $f_2$ side (i.e., to the left of the line $s_1s_3$ in the picture plane) and lies on $f_2$ (i.e., $(v_5,f_2)$ $\in$ $R$), but not on $f_1$. Hence we get

$(v_5,f_1,\text{PROPERLY-BEHIND})$ $\in$ $T$.

The concave line $s_2s_3$ has the right side region $[f_3]$ and the left side region $[f_1]$. There is, however, no vertex that is to the left of $s_2s_3$ and that lies on $f_1$ but not on $f_3$. Hence we generate a new vertex, say $v_7$, at some point to the left of the line $s_2s_3$ so that

$v_7 \in V$, $(x_7,y_7) = (5,1)$, $(v_7,f_1) \in R$,
$(v_7,f_3,\text{PROPERLY-FRONT}) \in T$.

For the other three lines, occluding lines, we generate three vertices whose projections on the $x$-$y$ plane respectively coincide with the midpoints of these lines: say $v_8$ for the line $s_4s_1$, $v_9$ for $s_3s_4$, and $v_{10}$ for $s_4s_2$. Then, we get

$v_8$, $v_9$, $v_{10} \in V$,
$(x_8,y_8) = (2, 4.5)$, $(x_9,y_9) = (3, 3.5)$, $(x_{10},y_{10}) = (4, 4.5)$,
$(v_8,f_2) \in R$, $(v_8,f_1,\text{PROPERLY-BEHIND}) \in T$,
$(v_9,f_2) \in R$, $(v_9,f_3,\text{PROPERLY-BEHIND}) \in T$,
$(v_{10},f_1) \in R$, $(v_{10},f_3,\text{PROPERLY-BEHIND}) \in T$.

Thus, the spatial structure $S = (V,F,R,T)$ of the labeled picture in Fig. 3.7 consists of all the elements described above: $|V| = 10$, $|F| = 3$, $|R| = 14$, and $|T| = 11$.

In the definition of the triple $(v_\alpha,f_j,\delta)$ for a convex or concave line, we have chosen as $f_j$ the right side face and as $v_\alpha$ a vertex that is to the left of the line and is on the left side face. Since our aim is to represent convexedness or concaveness of the line, the range in choice of the triple can be widened. For example, we can adopt as $f_j$ the left side face and as $v_\alpha$ a vertex that is to the right of the line and is on the right side face (in this case $\delta$ is the same as above), or we can adopt as $f_j$ the right side face and as $v_\alpha$ a vertex that is to the right of the line and is on the left side face (in this case $\delta$ should be changed from PROPERLY-FRONT to PROPERLY-BEHIND or vice versa). Consider the line drawing in Fig. 3.7 again. For the line $s_2s_3$ we have generated the triple $(v_7,f_3,\text{PROPERLY-FRONT})$. Instead of this triple, however, we can choose any one of the following:

$(v_1,f_3, \text{PROPERLY-BEHIND})$,
$(v_4,f_3, \text{PROPERLY-BEHIND})$,

$(v_6, f_1, \text{PROPERLY-FRONT})$.

Thus we can save generating the pseudo-vertex $v_7$. This kind of modification is useful for computer implementation of the present method. We adopt the above definition of the spatial structure only because we want to describe our basic idea simply.

### 3.4.  Interpretation as a Planar-Panel Scene

Suppose that $S = (V, F, R, T)$ is the spatial structure of labeled picture $D = (J, E, u, h)$. Let $|V| = n$ and $|F| = m$. For each vertex $v_\alpha = (x_\alpha, y_\alpha, z_\alpha)$ in $V$, $x_\alpha$ and $y_\alpha$ are given constants whereas $z_\alpha$ is an unknown variable. Hence, we have $n$ unknowns $z_1, \ldots, z_n$. With each panel $f_j$ in $F$, we associate a planar surface

$$a_j x + b_j y + z + c_j = 0,$$

on which the panel $f_j$ should lie. This equation cannot represent a surface that is parallel to the $z$ axis. There is, however, no problem because we have assumed that such panels never occur (recall Assumption 2.4). Thus we further obtain $3m$ unknowns $a_1, b_1, c_1, \ldots, a_m, b_m, c_m$.

   An element $(v_\alpha, f_j)$ of $R$ represents the fact that $v_\alpha$ lies on the planar surface containing $f_j$, and hence we get

$$a_j x_\alpha + b_j y_\alpha + z_\alpha + c_j = 0. \tag{3.1}$$

Note that this equation is linear with respect to the unknowns. Gathering all such equations, one for each element of $R$, we get the system of linear equations

$$Aw = 0, \tag{3.2}$$

where $w = {}^t(z_1 \ \cdots \ z_n a_1 b_1 c_1 \ \cdots \ a_m b_m c_m)$ ($t$ denotes transpose) and $A$ is a constant matrix of size $|R| \times (3m+n)$.

   Next we consider relative depth constraints represented by $T$. A triple of the form $(v_\alpha, v_\beta, \text{FRONT})$ represents the fact that "vertex $v_\alpha$ is in front of vertex $v_\beta$." From the way we construct $S$, we can easily see that if $(v_\alpha, v_\beta, \text{FRONT})$ is an element of $T$, then the projection of $v_\alpha$ coincides with that of $v_\beta$, that is, $x_\alpha = x_\beta$ and $y_\alpha = y_\beta$. Therefore, the constraint represented by the triple can be paraphrased by

$$z_\alpha \geqq z_\beta,$$                                                                    (3.3a)

because we see the scene from the view point infinitely distant in the
positive direction of the $z$ axis. Similarly, for the triple $(v_\alpha, v_\beta, \text{BEHIND})$,
we get

$$z_\alpha \leqq z_\beta.$$                                                                    (3.3b)

A triple of the form $(v_\alpha, f_j, \text{PROPERLY-FRONT})$ represents that the vertex $v_\alpha$
is properly in front of the planar surface on which the panel $f_j$ lies, and
hence we get

$$a_j x_\alpha + b_j y_\alpha + z_\alpha + c_j > 0.$$                                          (3.3c)

Similarly, for the triple $(v_\alpha, f_j, \text{PROPERLY-BEHIND})$, we get

$$a_j x_\alpha + b_j y_\alpha + z_\alpha + c_j < 0.$$                                          (3.3d)

We can note that any element of $T$ belongs to one of the above four
types. Gathering all inequalities of the forms (3.3a), ..., (3.3d), we get

$$Bw > 0,$$                                                                                    (3.4)

where $B$ is a constant matrix of size $|T| \times (3m+n)$, and the inequality
symbol is an abbreviation of componentwise inequalities, some of which
allow equalities.

Thus, a labeled hidden-part-eliminated line drawing is associated with
the spatial structure $S$, and we consequently obtain (3.2) and (3.4)
uniquely. Now, we can state the next theorem.

**Theorem 3.1 (Correct pictures of planar-panel scenes).** A labeled line
drawing $D$ represents a planar-panel scene if and only if the system
consisting of (3.2) and (3.4) has a solution.

**Proof.** First suppose that $D$ represents a planar-panel scene. Then, from
this planar-panel scene we can construct a solution to (3.2) and (3.4) in
the following way. First, for each $j$ $(j = 1, ..., m)$ we define three reals

$a_j$, $b_j$, $c_j$ in such a way that $a_jx+b_jy+z+c_j = 0$ coincides with the surface on which the $j$th panel lies. Next, for each $\alpha$ ($\alpha = 1, \ldots, n$) we define a real $z_\alpha$ as the $z$ coordinate of the point of intersection of the line that goes through $(x_\alpha,y_\alpha,0)$ parallelly to the $z$ axis and a panel which $v_\alpha$ is to lie on. Finally, using the $n+3m$ reals, we construct column vector $^t(z_1 \cdots z_n a_1 b_1 c_1 \cdots a_m b_m c_m)$, which obviously satisfies (3.2) and (3.4). Thus, if $D$ represents a planar-panel scene, the system consisting of (3.2) and (3.4) has a solution.

Next suppose that we are given constants $z_1, \ldots, z_n, a_1, b_1, c_1, \ldots, a_m, b_m, c_m$ such that $w = {}^t(z_1 \cdots z_n a_1 b_1 c_1 \cdots a_m b_m c_m)$ satisfies (3.2) and (3.4). From $w$ we construct a planar-panel scene in the following way. For each $j$ ($1 \leq j \leq m$) we fix the planar surface $a_jx+b_jy+z+c_j = 0$ to a three-dimensional space, and scissor off some part of it in such a way that the projection of the remaining part coincides with the corresponding region $[f_j]$ on the picture plane. In this way we obtain the set of $m$ panels $f_j$ ($j = 1, \ldots, m$) in a three-dimensional space. These panels may touch each other, but do not penetrate one another because their projections on the picture plane do not overlap. Next we slightly extend them so that they overlap along occluding lines. We fix a sufficiently small positive constant $\varepsilon$. Let $l$ be any occluding line of $D$, and $[f_j]$ and $[f_k]$ be the right side region and the left side region, respectively, of $l$. We extend panel $f_k$ toward the outside of the boundary line segment corresponding to $l$ in such a way that the additional part forms an isosceles triangle whose base coincides with the boundary line segment and whose height equals to $\varepsilon$, as shown in Fig. 3.8. We execute the extension for all occluding lines and rename the resulting panels as $f_k$ ($k = 1, \ldots, m$).

Now we can show that the collection of the panels $f_j$ ($j =, \ldots, m$) form a planar-panel scene represented by $D$. First, the panels are all planar. Second, the physical properties of convex lines and concave lines are satisfied. Indeed, let $l$ be a convex or concave line, and $[f_j]$ and $[f_k]$ be the right and the left side regions. Then, Proposition 3.1 assures us that the depths of $f_j$ and $f_k$ coincide at the two end points of $l$ (strictly, we have to say "at the three-dimensional counterparts of the two end points of $l$," because $l$ is on the picture plane, neither on $f_j$ nor on $f_k$; the strict expression is, however, unnecessarily long, and hence we use the abbreviated expression), and hence the surface consisting of $f_j$ and $f_k$ is continuous at all points on $l$. Moreover, it follows from Proposition 3.3 that $f_j$ and $f_k$ form a ridge along $l$ if $l$ is convex, whereas they form a valley if concave.

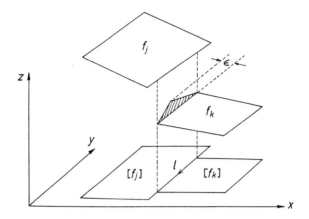

**Fig. 3.8.** Extension of a panel beyond an occluding line.

Third, the physical properties of occluding lines are satisfied for the following reason. Let $l$ be an occluding line, and $s$, $t$, $[f_j]$, $[f_k]$ respectively be the initial junction, the terminal junction, the right side region, and the left side region of $l$. Furthermore, let $l^*$ be the three-dimensional counterpart of $l$ that belongs to the boundary of the panel $f_j$. Then, Proposition 3.2 assures us that the panel $f_k$ passes behind the line segment $l^*$, and Proposition 3.4 further assures us that there is a net gap in depth between $f_k$ and the midpoint of $l^*$, which is what the occluding line means.

Last, the panels do not penetrate one another. As we have just seen, there is a net gap in depth between the occluded panel $f_k$ and the midpoint of the occluding boundary line segment $l^*$. Moreover, none of the panels is parallel to the $z$ axis. Therefore, if we choose a sufficiently small value as $\varepsilon$, we can execute the extension of panels without penetrating others.

**Example 3.1** (cont.). Let $S = (V,F,R,T)$ be the spatial structure obtained in the last section from the labeled picture in Fig. 3.7. As we have seen, $S$ satisfies $|V| = 10$, $|F| = 3$, $|R| = 14$, and $|T| = 11$. Hence, the associated system, (3.2) and (3.4), consists of 14 equations and 11 inequalities with respect to 19 $(= |V| + 3|F|)$ unknowns $z_1$, ..., $z_{10}$, $a_1$, $b_1$, $c_1$, ..., $a_3$, $b_3$, $c_3$. For example, since $(v_1, f_1) \in R$, we get

$a_1 + 3b_1 + z_1 + c_1 = 0$

(note that $x_1 = 1$ and $y_1 = 3$); since $(v_1, v_1, \text{BEHIND}) \in T$, we get

$z_1 \leqq z_1$ ;

since $(v_5, f_1, \text{PROPERLY-BEHIND}) \in T$, we get

$3a_1 + 6b_1 + z_5 + c_1 < 0$

(note that $x_5 = 3$ and $y_5 = 6$); and so on. This system of (3.2) and (3.4) has solutions. For example, we can easily see that

$z_1 = 0$, $z_2 = 0$, $z_3 = 0$, $z_4 = 0$, $z_5 = -10$, $z_6 = 10$, $z_7 = 0$, $z_8 = -5$, $z_9 = -5$, $z_{10} = 0$, $a_1 = 0$, $b_1 = 0$, $c_1 = 0$, $a_2 = 2$, $b_2 = 2$, $c_2 = -8$, $a_3 = 2$, $b_3 = -2$, $c_3 = -4$

satisfy the system, and hence from Theorem 3.1 the labeled picture in Fig. 3.7 represents a planar-panel scene correctly.

## 3.5. Interpretation as a Polyhedral Scene

We have restricted our consideration to planar-panel scenes, scenes consisting of thin objects. We now return to polyhedral objects, objects with finite thickness. We can prove the next theorem.

**Theorem 3.2 (Correct pictures of polyhedral scenes).** A labeled line drawing $D$ represents a polyhedral scene if and only if $D$ represents a planar-panel scene.

**Proof.** Assume that $D$ represents a polyhedral scene. From this polyhedral scene we can easily construct a planar-panel scene that $D$ can represent. For this purpose, we first collect all of the visible parts of the faces of the polyhedrons in the scene, which can be thought of as a collection of planar panels, and next, for each occluding line in $D$, we execute the extension shown in Fig. 3.8. Thus, if $D$ represents a polyhedral scene, $D$ represents a planar-panel scene.

Assume conversely that $D$ represents a planar-panel scene. From this planar-panel scene, we can construct a polyhedral scene by filling the rear side of the panels with material in the following way.

Let $z_0$ be a constant such that $z_0 < z_\alpha$ for any vertex $v_\alpha = (x_\alpha, y_\alpha, z_\alpha)$ in the scene. We first partition each panel into triangles in an arbitrary way. We call the resultant triangles *triangular panels*. For each triangular panel, we generate a new vertex, say $v_0$, such that the projection of $v_0$ on the $x$-$y$ plane coincides with that of the center of gravity of the triangular panel and that the $z$ coordinate of $v_0$ is equal to $z_0$, and generate a tetrahedron by packing material inside the convex hull defined by the triangular panel and the new vertex $v_0$. Since the scene is seen from the point that is infinitely far in the positive direction of the $z$ axis, $v_0$ is behind the triangular panel and hence the three new faces and the three new edges of the tetrahedron are all invisible. In this way we generate a tetrahedron for every triangular panel. Let $X_1$ be the set of all tetrahedrons thus generated.

The set-theoretical union of elements of $X_1$ may be considered as a polyhedral scene, but it is of no interest because tetrahedrons align accidentally and form "pathological" edges just like an edge shown in Fig. 2.1; it does not satisfy Assumption 2.2. We must construct a "normal" polyhedral scene. For this purpose, we next "weld" objects along these pathological edges.

Let $l$ be a convex edge (where an "edge" means a three-dimensional counterpart of a line in the line drawing) or a concave edge or a line segment generated by partitioning panels into triangles, let $v_1$ and $v_2$ be the two terminal points of $l$, and let $f_j$ and $f_k$ be the two triangular panels sharing $l$. Furthermore, let $v_3$ and $v_4$ be points on $f_j$ and $f_k$, respectively, such that $\{v_1, v_2, v_3\}$ and $\{v_1, v_2, v_4\}$ form isosceles triangles whose base coincides with $l$ and whose height is equal to $\varepsilon$, where $\varepsilon$ is a small positive constant. Next, let $v_0$ be a new vertex such that the projection of $v_0$ on the $x$-$y$ plane coincides with that of the midpoint of $l$ and the $z$ coordinate of $v_0$ equals $z_0$. We fill two tetrahedrons defined by $\{v_0, v_1, v_2, v_3\}$ and by $\{v_0, v_1, v_2, v_4\}$ with material, and glue them together along the triangular face $\{v_0, v_1, v_2\}$. Then we get a six-face object, of which only the two faces $\{v_1, v_2, v_3\}$ and $\{v_1, v_2, v_4\}$ are visible and the other four faces are invisible. We generate similar six-face objects for all convex edges, concave edges, and other line segments shared by two triangular panels. Let $X_2$ be the set of all such six-face objects.

Let $X$ be the set-theoretical union of all elements of $X_1$ and $X_2$. Then, $X$ is a polyhedral scene whose projection on the $x$-$y$ plane coincides with $D$.

Indeed, we fill the rear side of the panels with material in such a way that newly generated faces of tetrahedrons and of six-face objects are all invisible, and hence the line drawing of $X$ coincides with $D$. Moreover, $X$ satisfies Assumption 2.2 for the following reason. First, new vertices ($v_0$ in the above notation) generated in the rear side of the panels are distinct, and hence no pair of newly generated edges (invisible edges) align in the scene $X$. Second, "pathological" edges generated by the union of all the tetrahedrons are welded by six-face objects. Thus, if $D$ represents a planar-panel scene, $D$ represents a polyhedral scene.

### 3.6. Reducing to a Linear Programming Problem

Theorems 3.1 and 3.2 give us a theoretical answer to the problem of how to discriminate between correct and incorrect pictures. However, it is not very tractable in that the system of (3.4) contains proper inequalities (i.e., inequalities that do not allow equalities) such as (3.3c) and (3.3d). The equations (3.2) and inequalities (3.4) place linear constraints on the $n+3m$ unknowns, and hence the set of solutions to (3.2) and (3.4) form a polytope (i.e., a convex polyhedron) in the $(n+3m)$-dimensional space. It should be noted that this set is not necessarily closed, because some portions of the boundary of the polytope are defined by the proper inequalities. In general the judgment of nonemptiness of an open set is not so easy as that of a closed set. Fortunately, however, we can convert the system consisting of (3.2) and (3.4) to a more tractable one.

Let $e$ be any positive constant, and $e$ be a $|T|$-dimensional vector whose $i$th component is $e$ if the $i$th inequality in (3.4) is of the form (3.3c) or (3.3d), and is 0 if it is of the form (3.3a) or (3.3b). We construct an inequality system

$$Bw \geqq e. \tag{3.5}$$

Then, we get the following.

**Proposition 3.5.** The system consisting of (3.2) and (3.4) has a solution if and only if the system consisting of (3.2) and (3.5) has a solution.

**Proof.** A solution to (3.2) and (3.5) obviously satisfies (3.4). Conversely, let $w_1$ be a solution to (3.2) and (3.4). Then, we can find a sufficiently large positive constant $d$ such that $w_2 = dw_1$ satisfies (3.2) and (3.4).

From Theorems 3.1 and 3.2 and Proposition 3.5 we directly obtain the next theorem.

**Theorem 3.3** (Discrimination between correct and incorrect pictures). For any labeled picture $D$, the following four statements are equivalent:
(1)  $D$ represents a planar-panel scene.
(2)  $D$ represents a polyhedral scene.
(3)  the system consisting of (3.2) and (3.4) has a solution.
(4)  the system consisting of (3.2) and (3.5) has a solution.

Since all inequalities in (3.5) allow equalities, the solutions to the system composed of (3.2) and (3.5) form a closed set, and the judgment of nonemptiness of this set is equivalent to the judgment of the existence of a feasible solution to a linear programming problem whose constraint set is defined by (3.2) and (3.5). Moreover, methods for judging the existence of feasible solutions have been well established (Dantzig, 1963). Hence condition (4) in Theorem 3.3 can be checked efficiently. Thus the problem of discrimination between correct and incorrect line drawings is reduced to the problem of judging the existence of a feasible solution to the linear programming problem.

**3.7. Perspective Projection**

When the scene is at a finite distance from the observer, the picture is obtained as a perspective projection with the observer as the center of the projection. A perspective projection is different from an orthographic projection. However, as far as the realizability of a polyhedral scene is concerned, there is no difference between the perspective projection and the orthographic projection. This can be understood in the following way.

Without loss of generality suppose that the center of the projection (i.e., the observer) is at the origin $(0,0,0)$ and the picture plane is $z = 1$, as shown in Fig. 3.9. Let $p_\alpha = (x_\alpha, y_\alpha, 1)$ denote the position vector of the projection (onto the picture plane) of a vertex $v_\alpha$, and $x_\alpha = p_\alpha / t_\alpha$ denote the position vector of $v_\alpha$ itself, where $t_\alpha$ is unknown. Let $q_j \cdot x = -1$ denote the equation of the face $f_j$, where $q_j = (a_j, b_j, c_j)$. This equation cannot represent a plane that passes through the origin. There is, however, no problem because we have assumed that no face is coplanar with

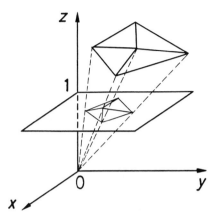

**Fig. 3.9.** Perspective projection.

the observer (recall Assumption 2.4).

If the vertex $v_\alpha$ is on the face $f_j$, we get $q_j \cdot p_\alpha + t_\alpha = 0$, that is,

$$a_j x_\alpha + b_j y_\alpha + c_j + t_\alpha = 0,$$

which has the same form as (3.1) (although the meaning of the unknowns is slightly different).

If the two vertices $v_\alpha$ and $v_\beta$ are projected on the same point (i.e., $p_\alpha = p_\beta$) and $v_\alpha$ is in front of $v_\beta$, then we get

$$\frac{1}{t_\alpha} \leq \frac{1}{t_\beta}, \quad \text{that is,} \quad t_\alpha \geq t_\beta.$$

This inequality is of the same form as (3.3a). If the vertex $v_\alpha$ is properly in front of the face $f_j$, we get

$$\frac{1}{t_\alpha} < \frac{-1}{q_j \cdot p_\alpha}, \quad \text{that is,} \quad a_j x_\alpha + b_j y_\alpha + c_j + t_\alpha > 0,$$

which is of the same form as (3.3c). Inequalities of the same forms as (3.3b) and (3.3d) can be obtained similarly. Therefore, we get the same system of linear equations and linear inequalities as in the case of the orthographic projection.

Thus, there is no difference between the algebraic structure of the orthographic projection and that of the perspective projection, and consequently we get the next theorem.

**Theorem 3.4** (Equivalence between the orthographic and perspective projections). Let $D$ be a labeled picture and $p$ be any three-dimensional point in the front side of the picture plane. Then $D$ is a perspective projection of a polyhedral scene with respect to the center of projection $p$ if and only if $D$ is an orthographic projection of a polyhedral scene.

**Proof.** Without changing the realizability of the picture $D$, we can translate the $(x,y,z)$ coordinate system and change the scale in such a way that $p$ coincides with the origin and the picture plane is on the surface $z = 1$. Hence the theorem follows from the above argument.

Therefore, the realizability of a scene depends on neither where the observer stands nor whether the picture is an orthographic projection or a perspective projection. We hereafter treat the pictures as the orthographic projections of the scenes, but because of Theorem 3.4 all the results in this book can be applied also to the case of perspective projections with, if necessary, only obvious modifications.

## 3.8. Pictures with Additional Information

We have concentrated our attention only on the information conveyed by a labeled picture itself. In practical situations, however, we are often given additional information.

One type of such additional information is about the occluded part of the objects. For example, consider the picture in Fig. 3.10(a). Some cue may tell us that $f_j$ and $f_k$ belong to the same panel, or at least it seems worth while to consider whether such an interpretation is possible. Our formulation can easily be generalized for these kinds of additional information. In the case of Fig. 3.10, the only thing we have to do is to add three more equations,

$$a_j = a_k, \ b_j = b_k, \ c_j = c_k,$$

to (3.2). Note that these additional equations are also linear and hence

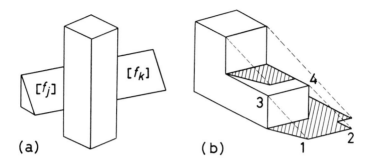

**Fig. 3.10.** Examples of additional information.

the linear programming methods are still applicable to this case.

Another type of additional information is given by shadows (Shafer and Kanade, 1983; Shafer, 1985). Suppose that pictures contain shadows and furthermore that the correspondences between edges and their shadows are given. Then, the system of equations (3.2) can be augmented by introducing virtual planes each of which should contain both an edge and the corresponding shadow line.

Consider for example a line drawing given in Fig. 3.10(b), which represents a polyhedral scene with shadows. Suppose that we know that the shadow line 1-2 is caused by the edge 3-4. Then, we introduce a new virtual plane, say $f_j$, and add to (3.2) the following four new equations:

$$a_j x_\alpha + b_j y_\alpha + z_\alpha + c_j = 0, \qquad \alpha = 1, 2, 3, 4.$$

Other pairs of edges and their shadows can be treated in a similar manner.

## 4. CORRECTNESS OF HIDDEN-PART-DRAWN PICTURES

We have presented in terms of linear algebra a necessary and sufficient condition for a labeled picture to represent a polyhedral scene, and have thus reduced the problem of judging the correctness of the picture to the problem of judging the existence of a solution to a certain system of linear equations and inequalities, which can be solved by linear programming techniques. However, the pictures have been restricted to hidden-part-eliminated ones. Here we shall generalize the condition so that it can be applied to hidden-part-drawn pictures.

### 4.1. Ambiguity in Interpretation

As has been seen, a labeled hidden-part-eliminated picture defines a unique spatial structure. If the hidden part is also drawn, on the other hand, a labeled picture cannot necessarily represent the spatial structure uniquely.

Let us consider the labeled picture in Fig. 4.1(a). The lines in the picture constitute two connected components, one representing a hexahedron, and the other representing a little more complicated object. The labels tell us that the bottom of the hexahedron should touch some other face. There are , however, two possible faces on which the hexahedron can lie, as shown in (b) and (c), where the objects are seen from the view angle indicated by the large arrow in (a).

Thus, even if a picture is labeled, the corresponding spatial interpretation is not unique. The correctness of a labeled picture should be judged for each of the spatial interpretations. While in the case of natural pictures a spatial structure is extracted automatically from a labeled picture, here we shall consider a spatial structure as new information. Assuming that we are given both a labeled picture and a spatial structure, we study how to judge whether the labeled picture represents the spatial structure correctly. This is the main reason why we treat hidden-part-drawn pictures in this new chapter.

In addition to the basic assumptions in Section 2.1, we make some more assumptions.

**Assumption 4.1.** Edges incident to a vertex are not collinear with each other.

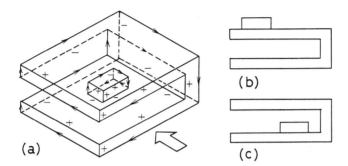

**Fig. 4.1.** Ambiguity in interpretation of a labeled hidden-part-drawn line drawing. The picture (a) admits the two interpretations (b) and (c).

**Assumption 4.2.** Every face is a simple polygon.

These two assumptions are about the objects themselves. Assumption 4.1 is helpful when we try to distinguish between projections of vertices and accidental crossings of distinct edges on the picture plane. Assumption 4.2 implies that a face has no holes and consequently the boundary of the face can be represented by a cyclic list of edges.

**Assumption 4.3.** Any pair of vertices is not collinear with the observer.

**Assumption 4.4.** The observer is outside the object.

**Assumption 4.5.** The whole part of the object is drawn in the picture plane.

These three assumptions state relationships between the object and the observer. Assumption 4.3 together with Assumptions 2.4 and 2.5 is usually paraphrased by saying that the observer is in "general position," which implies that interesting spatial features do not disappear in the picture. For example, if two edges are noncollinear in a space, the corresponding two lines are likewise noncollinear in the picture. Assumption 4.4 excludes a certain class of pathological interpretations. Assumption 4.5 reduces the number of possible interpretations, as was done in Chapter 2.

### 4.2.  Face–Layer Structure

In a way similar to the case of hidden–part–eliminated pictures, let $D$ = $(J,E,u,h)$ be a labeled line drawing, where $J$ is the set of junctions at which two or more lines meet, $E$ is the set of lines represented by ordered pairs of junctions, $u$ is a mapping from $J$ to $R^2$ so that $u(s)$ denotes the position of the junction $s$, and $h$ is a mapping from $E$ to the set of the eight categories of lines given in Fig. 2.6 so that $h(l)$ denotes the label assigned to the line $l$. Here again we assume that the lines in $E$ have been divided into as small fragments as possible, and hence lines do not meet each other except at their terminal points.

In hidden–part–drawn pictures, there often appear X–type junctions, that is, junctions composed of two pairs of collinear lines. X–type junctions usually occur when projections of two edges spatially apart cross each other on the picture plane. Since the objects are in general position with respect to the observer, it follows from Assumption 4.1 that X–type junctions never correspond to vertices of the objects. Let $J_2$ be the set of all X–type junctions, and let $J_1 = J - J_2$. Then, there is a one–to–one correspondence between the set $J_1$ and the set of all vertices of the object.

Since an X–type junction does not correspond to any vertex, line drawing $D$ should satisfy this condition: If $(s_1,s_2)$ and $(s_2,s_3)$ are mutually collinear lines meeting at the X–type junction $s_2$, then the two lines have the same line category, i.e., $h((s_1,s_2)) = h((s_2,s_3))$. This is what we observed in Rule 2.4.

For convenience, we also introduce another notation for the lines in the picture. While $E$ represents the set of all minimal line fragments connecting junctions, let $E^*$ denote the set of all line segments connecting junctions in $J_1$. Hence, an element of $E^*$ may have some X–type junctions midway. That is, an element of $E^*$ can be considered as a concatenation of one or more elements of $E$ of the form $((s_1,s_2), (s_2,s_3), \ldots, (s_{k-1},s_k))$ such that the $(s_\alpha,s_{\alpha+1})$'s $(\alpha = 1, 2, \ldots, k-1)$ are collinear and have the same label and that $s_1$ and $s_k$ belong to $J_1$ and all the other junctions $s_2$, $s_3$, $\ldots$, $s_{k-1}$ belong to $J_2$. From our assumptions there is a one–to–one correspondence between $E^*$ and the set of all edges of the object.

Unlike the case of natural pictures, we cannot extract a unique spatial structure directly from a labeled hidden–part–drawn picture because of the ambiguity we have seen in the last section. In order to avoid the ambiguity in interpretation we need some more information about the

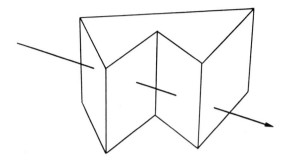

**Fig. 4.2.** Line of sight emanating from the viewer. It passes through faces facing the viewer and those facing opposite to the viewer alternatingly.

structure of the scene. For this purpose, we introduce a new concept, "face-layer structure."

A face-layer structure is an ordered triple $L = (F_1, F_2, g)$, whose intuitive meaning is the following. $F = F_1 \cup F_2$ is the set of all visible and invisible faces of the object, and it is partitioned into $F_1$ and $F_2$ ($F_1 \cap F_2 = \emptyset$) in such a way that outward normals to the faces in $F_1$ are in the direction of the observer, and those to the faces in $F_2$ are in the opposite direction. Since each face $f_j \in F_1 \cup F_2$ is a simple polygon in a space (recall Assumption 4.2), the projection of $f_j$ onto the picture plane, denoted by $[f_j]$, is a simple polygon on the picture plane.

The third constituent, $g$, represents how the faces overlap each other when seen by the observer. Consider a line of sight emanating from the observer and penetrating the object. If we travel along this line, we first pass through a face facing the observer, next pass through a face facing opposite to the observer, and similarly pass through these two kinds of faces alternatingly, as shown in Fig. 4.2. Hence, for each point $p$ on the picture plane there exist exactly an even number of faces whose projections contain $p$, half of which belong to $F_1$ and the other half to $F_2$. Let $(f_1, f_2, \ldots, f_{2k})$ be the list of faces that appear in this order when we travel along the line of sight passing through the picture point $p$. Then $f_{2j-1}$ ($j = 1, \ldots, k$) should belong to $F_1$ and $f_{2j}$ ($j = 1, \ldots, k$) to $F_2$. Moreover, even if $p$ moves on the picture plane, the associated list of faces does not change unless $p$ passes from one side of a boundary line of some polygon $[f_j]$ to the other side, because the faces should not penetrate each other. Hence, we need not specify the list of faces for each point $p$;

we need to specify it only for each region defined by the partition of the picture plane induced by all the boundary lines of the projections of the faces.

Keeping this in mind, we define the *face-layer structure* formally as the triple $L = (F_1, F_2, g)$ satisfying the next three conditions, (1), (2), and (3):

(1)  $F_1$ and $F_2$ are two disjoint sets (elements of $F_1 \cup F_2$ are called "faces").

(2)  With each face $f_j \in F_1 \cup F_2$ is associated a simple polygon on the picture plane (this polygon is called the "projection" of the face $f_j$ and is denoted by $[f_j]$).

(3)  Let $P$ be any picture region defined by the partition of the plane induced by all the boundary lines of the projections of the faces. Then, $g(P)$ is the list of an even number of faces, say $g(P) = (f_1, f_2, \ldots, f_{2k})$ , such that all the projections $[f_j]$ ($j = 1, 2, \ldots, 2k$) include $P$ and such that $f_{2j-1} \in F_1$ and $f_{2j} \in F_2$ for $j = 1, 2, \ldots, k$. Moreover, $P$ is not contained in a projection of any face that does not appear in the list $g(P)$.

The definition of the face-layer structure is independent of a labeled picture. Now we construct relationship between these two structures. A face-layer structure $L = (F_1, F_2, g)$ is said to be *consistent* with a labeled line drawing $D = (J, E, u, h)$ if they satisfy the following three conditions, (1), (2), and (3):

(1)  For any $f_j \in F_1 \cup F_2$ , the boundary of $[f_j]$ consists of lines in $E^*$ (i.e., the set of lines connecting non-X-type junctions).

(2)  Every line in $E^*$ belongs to the boundaries of exactly two of the projections $[f_j]$.

(3)  Let $l$ be any line in $E^*$, and let $[f_j]$ and $[f_k]$ be two polygons whose boundaries share $l$. Then: (3a) if $l$ is a solid line with + or − (i.e., the type (a) or (d) in Fig. 2.6), both $f_j$ and $f_k$ belong to $F_1$ and $[f_j]$ and $[f_k]$ are mutually in the opposite sides of $l$; (3b) if $l$ is a broken line with + or − (i.e., the type (e) or (h) in Fig. 2.6), both $f_j$ and $f_k$ belong to $F_2$ and $[f_j]$ and $[f_k]$ are mutually in the opposite sides of $l$; and (3c) if $l$ is a line with an arrow (i.e., the type (b), (c), (f), or (g) in Fig. 2.6), one of $f_j$ and $f_k$ belongs to $F_1$ and the other belongs to $F_2$, and both $[f_j]$ and $[f_k]$ are to the right of the

arrow.

These conditions are necessary for $F = F_1 \cup F_2$ to be a correct set of faces of the object represented by the picture $D$. This can be understood when we recall that all the corners of the projections of the faces should belong to the set $J_1$ (Assumptions 2.4, 2.5, and 4.1), every edge of the object should be shared by exactly two faces (Assumption 2.2), and the line categories in Fig. 2.6 depend only on local configurations of faces around the edges.

Since the boundary of every polygon $[f_j]$ is composed of lines in $E^*$, all the corners of the boundary belong to $J_1$. Hence, if we list the corners on the boundary of $[f_j]$ in the counterclockwise order, we get a cyclic list, say $(s_1, s_2, \ldots, s_k, s_1)$, where $s_i \in J_1$ $(i = 1, \ldots, k)$. This list specifies the polygonal region $[f_j]$ uniquely. We hereafter use the notation $[f_j] = (s_1, s_2, \ldots, s_k)$ in order to represent that $[f_j]$ is a polygon bounded by the lines $(s_1, s_2)$, $(s_2, s_3)$, $\ldots$, $(s_{k-1}, s_k)$, and $(s_k, s_1)$.

Note that the above definitions of $F_1$, $F_2$, and $g$ are not constructive; there may be more than one way to choose them. Thus a face-layer structure $L$ consistent with $D$ is not necessarily unique. This is why we call $L$ a face-layer structure "consistent with" $D$, but not the face-layer structure "of" $D$.

One problem here is how to get a face-layer structure. One of the main situations of machine interpretation of hidden-part-drawn pictures can be found in man-machine communication between a human designer and a computer-aided system for geometric design. In this situation it is the human designer who draws a line drawing, and hence he can also tell the system the face-layer structure of the object he intends by the line drawing. It is also possible to extract all consistent face-layer structures from a labeled line drawing automatically. The key point is how to choose efficiently the set of polygonal regions $[f_j]$ with the required properties. For this purpose, "cyclic order properties" of edges and vertices around faces can play an important role (Sugihara, 1978; Shapira and Freeman, 1979; Fukui et al., 1983). In what follows, however, we do not consider this problem any more, but merely assume that we are given a face-layer structure together with the labeled line drawing.

## 4.3.  Spatial Structure

Suppose that we are given a labeled line drawing $D$ = $(J,E,u,h)$ and a face-layer structure $L$ = $(F_1,F_2,g)$ consistent with $D$. Then we can construct the spatial structure $S$ = $(V,F,R,T)$ of $D$ and $L$. Like the spatial structure of a natural picture, $V$ is the set of vertices on the surface of the object, and $F$ is the set of faces. $R$ is the set of vertex-face pairs representing which vertices should be on which faces. $T$ is a set of ordered triples of the form $(\alpha,\beta,\delta)$ representing relative distances of parts of the object from the observer, where $\alpha$ and $\beta$ are taken from $V\cup F$ and $\delta$ is taken from the set {PROPERLY-FRONT, PROPERLY-BEHIND} .

The spatial structure $S$ = $(V,F,R,T)$ is defined in a constructive manner. $F$ is defined as $F$ = $F_1\cup F_2$ . The other three sets, $V$, $R$, and $T$, are initially set empty, and elements are added to them in the following way.

As has been seen, there is a one-to-one correspondence between $J_1$ and the set of vertices of the object. Hence, for each element $s_\alpha$ of $J_1$, we generate the corresponding vertex $v_\alpha$ = $(x_\alpha,y_\alpha,z_\alpha)$ , where $u(s_\alpha)$ = $(x_\alpha,y_\alpha)$ and $z_\alpha$ is an unknown, and add it to $V$. Next, for each polygon, say $[f_j]$ = $(s_1,s_2,\ldots,s_k)$ (where $s_1$, $s_2$, ..., $s_k$ are elements of $J_1$), we generate pairs $(v_1,f_j)$ , $(v_2,f_j)$ , ..., $(v_k,f_j)$ and add them to $R$. The three sets $V$, $F$, and $R$ generated by now represent the basic structure about which vertices should be on which faces. Since each line in $E^*$ belongs to the boundaries of the projections of exactly two faces, we get the following.

**Proposition 4.1.** Let $(s_1,s_2)$ be any line in $E^*$. Then, there are exactly two faces, say $f_j$ and $f_k$, such that $(s_1,s_2)$ belongs to the boundary of $[f_j]$ and that of $[f_k]$. Moreover, there exist $v_\alpha$ and $v_\beta$ in $V$ such that

$(x_\alpha,y_\alpha)$ = $u(s_1)$, $(x_\beta,y_\beta)$ = $u(s_2)$,
$(v_\alpha,f_j)$, $(v_\alpha,f_k)$, $(v_\beta,f_j)$, $(v_\beta,f_k)$ $\in$ $R$.

Next, we shall augment $V$, $R$, and $T$ in order to represent relative distances and the thickness of the object.

For each line in $E^*$ we generate one element of $T$ so that it may represent the physical category of the corresponding edge. Let $l$ be a line in $E^*$, and $[f_j]$ and $[f_k]$ be the two polygons whose boundaries contain $l$.

First suppose that $l$ is labeled with + or − (i.e., $l$ belongs to the category (a), (d), (e), or (h) in Fig. 2.6). Then, $[f_j]$ and $[f_k]$ are mutually on opposite sides of $l$ (recall condition (3) in the definition of the consistency of $L$ with $D$). Hence, as we have done in the construction of the spatial structure of a natural picture, we choose a vertex, say $v_\alpha$, such that $v_\alpha$ lies on $f_k$ but not on $f_j$ (i.e., $(v_\alpha, f_k)$ is an element of $R$ but $(v_\alpha, f_j)$ is not) and such that $v_\alpha$ is on the $f_k$ side with respect to $l$, and add the triple $(v_\alpha, f_j, \delta)$ to $T$, where

$\delta$ = PROPERLY-BEHIND if $l$ has the label +,
$\delta$ = PROPERLY-FRONT if $l$ has the label –.

Next suppose that $l$ is labeled with an arrow (i.e., $l$ belongs to the category (b), (c), (f), or (g) in Fig. 2.6). Then, both $[f_j]$ and $[f_k]$ are to the right of the arrow, and one of $f_j$ and $f_k$ belongs to $F_1$ and the other to $F_2$. Without loss of generality let $f_j$ belong to $F_1$ and $f_k$ belong to $F_2$. We choose a vertex, say $v_\alpha$, such that $v_\alpha$ lies on $f_k$ but not on $f_j$ and such that $v_\alpha$ is to the right of the arrow, and add the triple $(v_\alpha, f_j, \delta)$ to $T$, where

$\delta$ = PROPERLY-BEHIND if $l$ is a solid line (i.e., the category (b) or (c) in Fig. 2.6),
$\delta$ = PROPERLY-FRONT if $l$ is a broken line (i.e., the category (f) or (g) in Fig. 2.6).

Now we get the following.

**Proposition 4.2.** Let $l$ be any line in $E^*$, and $l$ be contained in the boundary of $[f_j]$ and that of $[f_k]$. Then we see, if necessary by interchanging $f_j$ and $f_k$, that there exists a vertex, say $v_\alpha$, such that $v_\alpha$ is on the $f_k$ side with respect to $l$ and

$(v_\alpha, f_k) \in R$, $(v_\alpha, f_j) \notin R$, $(v_\alpha, f_j, \delta) \in T$,

where $\delta$ = PROPERLY-BEHIND if $l$ has the label + or $l$ is a solid line with an arrow, and $\delta$ = PROPERLY-FRONT if $l$ has the label – or $l$ is a broken line with an arrow.

Finally, $V$, $R$, and $T$ are augmented in order to represent the relative distance information given by the mapping $g$. The picture plane is partitioned into regions by lines in $E$. Let $P$ be one of such regions, $p$ be an arbitrary interior point of $P$, and let $g(P) = (f_1, f_2, \ldots, f_{2k})$.

We first generate $2k$ new vertices, say $v_\alpha$ ($\alpha = 1, 2, \ldots, 2k$), whose $(x,y)$ coordinates coincide with those of $p$, generate $2k$ vertex-face pairs $(v_1, f_1)$, $(v_2, f_2)$, $\ldots$, $(v_{2k}, f_{2k})$, and generate $2k-1$ triples $(v_\alpha, v_{\alpha+1}, \text{PROPERLY-FRONT})$ ($\alpha = 1, 2, \ldots, 2k-1$). Thus we get the following.

**Proposition 4.3.** Let $P$ be any region defined by the partition of the picture plane induced by the lines in $E$. Then, there exists an interior point $p$ of $P$ such that, for any consecutive two faces $f_\alpha$ and $f_{\alpha+1}$ in the list $g(P)$, there exist two vertices, say $v_\alpha$ and $v_{\alpha+1}$, whose $(x,y)$ coordinates coincide with those of $p$ and

$(v_\alpha, f_\alpha)$, $(v_{\alpha+1}, f_{\alpha+1}) \in R$,
$(v_\alpha, v_{\alpha+1}, \text{PROPERLY-FRONT}) \in T$.

Next for each junction $s$ ($\in J_1 \cup J_2$) on the boundary of $P$ we do the following. We generate $2k$ new vertices, say $w_\beta$ ($\beta = 1, 2, \ldots, 2k$), whose $(x,y)$ coordinates coincide with $u(s)$, and generate $2k$ vertex-face pairs $(w_1, f_1)$, $(w_2, f_2)$, $\ldots$, $(w_{2k}, f_{2k})$. For each $\beta$ ($\beta = 1, 2, \ldots, 2k-1$), if the boundary of $[f_\beta]$ and that of $[f_{\beta+1}]$ share a common line and $s$ is on this common line (this occurs when $s$ is on a line, say $l$, in $E^*$ and $l$ belongs to both the boundary of $[f_\beta]$ and that of $[f_{\beta+1}]$), then we identify $v_\beta$ with $v_{\beta+1}$, and if otherwise we add the triple $(w_\beta, w_{\beta+1}, \text{PROPERLY-FRONT})$ to $T$. Hence, we get the next proposition.

**Proposition 4.4.** Let $P$ be any region defined by the partition of the picture plane induced by the lines in $E$. For any junction $s$ on the boundary of $P$ and for any consecutive two faces $f_j$ and $f_{j+1}$ in the list $g(P)$, there exist two vertices, say $v_\alpha$ and $v_\beta$, in $V$ such that

$(x_\alpha, y_\alpha) = (x_\beta, y_\beta) = u(s)$,
$(v_\alpha, f_j)$, $(v_\beta, f_{j+1}) \in R$,
$(v_\alpha, v_\beta, \text{PROPERLY-FRONT}) \in T$,

unless $s$ is on both the boundary of $[f_j]$ and that of $[f_{j+1}]$.

Thus we have completed the construction of the spatial structure $S = (V, F, R, T)$ of the line drawing $D = (J, E, u, h)$ and the face-layer structure $L = (F_1, F_2, g)$.

## 4.4. Example

Before presenting our main theorem, we will see by an example how the spatial structure can be constructed.

Let $D = (J,E,u,h)$ be the labeled line drawing shown in Fig. 4.3(a), where

$J = J_1 \cup J_2$, $J_1 = \{1,2,\ldots,10\}$, $J_2 = \{11,12,\ldots,15\}$,
$E = \{(1,2), (1,5), (1,6), (2,3), (2,12), (3,8), (3,12),$
$\qquad (4,5), (4,11), (4,13),$ etc.$\}$,

and $u$ and $h$ are as indicated in the figure (strictly, the labels should be assigned to elements of $E$, but in the figure the labels are assigned to elements of $E^*$; this is because, as we have seen in Rule 2.4, mutually collinear lines meeting at an X-type junction should have the same label). Since the junctions 11, 12, $\ldots$, 15 are of the X-type, the set of lines connecting non-X-type junctions, $E^*$, consists of 15 elements; for example, the line 5-10 belongs to $E^*$ whereas the lines 5-11, 11-14, and 14-10 belong to $E$.

Let us define the face set $F = F_1 \cup F_2$ by

$F_1 = \{f_1,f_2,f_3\}$, $F_2 = \{f_4,f_5,f_6,f_7\}$,
$[f_1] = (1,5,4,3,2)$, $[f_2] = (1,6,10,5)$, $[f_3] = (3,4,9,8)$,
$[f_4] = (1,6,7,2)$, $[f_5] = (2,7,8,3)$, $[f_6] = (4,9,10,5)$,
$[f_7] = (6,10,9,8,7)$.

The lines in $E$ partition the picture plane into one outer region, say $P_0$, and eleven polygons, say $P_1$, $P_2$, $\ldots$, $P_{11}$, as shown in Fig. 4.3(b). Let $g$ be defined by

$g(P_0) = \phi$, $\qquad\qquad\qquad$ $g(P_1) = (f_2,\ f_4)$,
$g(P_2) = (f_1,f_4)$, $\qquad\qquad$ $g(P_3) = (f_1,f_6,f_2,f_4)$,
$g(P_4) = (f_1,f_5)$, $\qquad\qquad$ $g(P_5) = (f_3,f_6,f_2,f_4)$,
$g(P_6) = (f_3,f_4)$, $\qquad\qquad$ $g(P_7) = (f_3,f_5)$,
$g(P_8) = (f_2,f_7)$, $\qquad\qquad$ $g(P_9) = (f_3,f_6,f_2,f_7)$,
$g(P_{10}) = (f_3,f_6)$, $\qquad\qquad$ $g(P_{11}) = (f_3,f_7)$.

Then, the triple $L = (F_1,F_2,g)$ is a face-layer structure, and we can easily see that $L$ is consistent with the line drawing $D$ given in Fig. 4.3(a).

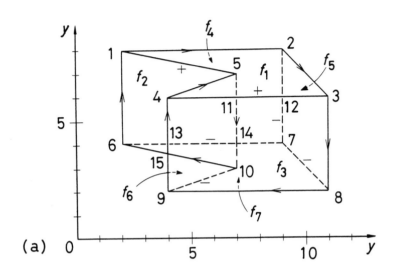

(a)

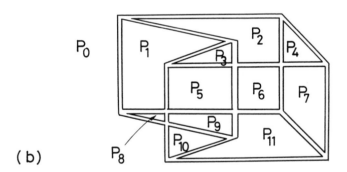

(b)

Fig. 4.3. Labeled line drawing, and the partition of the picture plane induced by all the lines.

Indeed, every line in $E^*$ belongs to the boundaries of the projections of exactly two faces (for example, the line 1-2 belongs to the boundaries of $[f_1]$ and $[f_4]$ and to them only), and these two faces possess the required properties (for example, $[f_1]$ and $[f_4]$ are both to the right of the arrow assigned to the line 1-2, and $f_1 \in F_1$ whereas $f_4 \in F_2$ ). Moreover, at each region $P_i$ ($i = 1, \ldots, 11$), $g(P_i)$ has an even number of faces, and the first and the third faces (if they exist) are taken from $F_1$ whereas the second and the fourth faces are taken from $F_2$.

From the above $D$ and $L$ we can generate the spatial structure $S = (V,F,R,T)$ systematically. The face set $F$ has already been defined in $L$. The other three sets $V$, $R$, and $T$ are initially made empty, and new elements are generated and added to them in the following way.

First, for each element of $J_1$ the associated vertex is generated and added to $V$:

$$v_1 = (2, 8, z_1), \quad v_2 = (9, 8, z_2), \quad v_3 = (11, 6, z_3), \quad v_4 = (4, 6, z_4),$$
$$v_5 = (7, 7, z_5), \quad v_6 = (2, 4, z_6), \quad v_7 = (9, 4, z_7), \quad v_8 = (11, 2, z_8),$$
$$v_9 = (4, 2, z_9), \quad v_{10} = (7, 3, z_{10}).$$

Second, for each face , say $f_j$, and each corner of the boundary of $[f_j]$, we generate the associated element of $R$. From $[f_1] = (1,5,4,3,2)$, we generate the five elements

$$(v_1,f_1), \ (v_5,f_1), \ (v_4,f_1), \ (v_3,f_1), \ (v_2,f_1) \in R.$$

New elements of $R$ are generated similarly for $f_2$, $f_3$, $\ldots$, $f_7$. At this point $|R| = 4 \times 5 + 5 \times 2 = 30$, because there are five quadrilateral faces and two pentagonal faces in $F$.

Third, new elements of $T$ are generated for lines in $E^*$. The line 1-2 is a solid line with an arrow from the junction 1 to the junction 2, and this line is shared by the boundary of $[f_1]$ and that of $[f_4]$. Since $f_4$ belongs to $F_2$, we choose one vertex which lies on $f_4$ but not on $f_1$ and whose projection on the picture plane is to the right of the arrow, say $v_6$ (or alternatively $v_7$), and generate

$$(v_6,f_1,\text{PROPERLY-BEHIND}) \in T.$$

Elements of $T$ are generated similarly for other lines in $E^*$, one for each line. Hence at this point the number of elements of $T$ is 15 ($= |E^*|$).

Finally, $V$, $R$, and $T$ are augmented for the polygonal regions bounded by the lines of the picture, that is, the regions $P_1$, $P_2$, $\ldots$, $P_{11}$ in Fig. 4.3(b) (since $g(P_0) = \emptyset$, we do nothing for $P_0$). In order to illustrate this process we consider the region $P_3$, because it is more informative than considering $P_1$. We choose an arbitrary point in $P_3$, say $p_3$ = (6, 6.33), which is the center of gravity of the three corners of $P_3$. Since $g(P_3) = (f_1, f_6, f_2, f_4)$ , we generate four new vertices,

$v_{11}$ = (6, 6.33, $z_{11}$),   $v_{12}$ = (6, 6.33, $z_{12}$) ∈ $V$,
$v_{13}$ = (6, 6.33, $z_{13}$),   $v_{14}$ = (6, 6.33, $z_{14}$) ∈ $V$,

four vertex-face pairs,

$(v_{11}, f_1)$,  $(v_{12}, f_6)$,  $(v_{13}, f_2)$,  $(v_{14}, f_4)$ ∈ $R$,

and three triples,

$(v_{11}, v_{12}, \text{PROPERLY-FRONT})$,  $(v_{12}, v_{13}, \text{PROPERLY-FRONT})$,  ∈ $T$,
$(v_{13}, v_{14}, \text{PROPERLY-FRONT})$ ∈ $T$.

The region $P_3$ has three corners, that is, the junctions 4, 11, and 5; new elements are further generated at these corners. At the junction 4, we generate four new vertices,

$v_{15}$ = (4, 6, $z_{15}$), $v_{16}$ = (4, 6, $z_{16}$)  ∈ $V$,
$v_{17}$ = (4, 6, $z_{17}$), $v_{18}$ = (4, 6, $z_{18}$)  ∈ $V$,

and four vertex-face pairs,

$(v_{15}, f_1)$,  $(v_{16}, f_6)$,  $(v_{17}, f_2)$,  $(v_{18}, f_4)$ ∈ $R$.

Since the boundary of $[f_1]$ and that of $[f_6]$ share the line 4–5 and the junction 4 is on this line, we identify $v_{15}$ with $v_{16}$; that is, we delete $v_{16}$ from $R$ and replace $(v_{16}, f_6)$ with $(v_{15}, f_6)$ . On the other hand, the junction 4 is neither on the boundary of $[f_2]$ nor on that of $[f_4]$, and hence we generate the two triples

$(v_{15}, v_{17}, \text{PROPERLY-FRONT})$,  $(v_{17}, v_{18}, \text{PROPERLY-FRONT})$ ∈ $T$.

Note that the first constituent of the left triple is not $v_{16}$ but $v_{15}$; this is because we have identified $v_{16}$ with $v_{15}$.

At the junction 5, we first generate four new vertices. However, the first and the second vertices are identified with each other because the boundary of $[f_1]$ and that of $[f_6]$ share the line 4-5. Similarly the second and third vertices are identified with each other because the boundary of $[f_6]$ and that of $[f_2]$ share the line 5-10 and the junction 5 is on this line. Hence, we eventually generate the two vertices

$$v_{19} = (7, 7, z_{19}), \quad v_{20} = (7, 7, z_{20}) \in V,$$

the four vertex-face pairs

$$(v_{19},f_1), \quad (v_{19},f_6), \quad (v_{19},f_2), \quad (v_{20},f_4) \quad \in R,$$

and the triple

$$(v_{19},v_{20},\text{PROPERLY-FRONT}) \in T,$$

where $v_{19}$ denotes the vertex resulting from the identification of the initially distinct three vertices, one of which was on $f_1$, another was on $f_6$, and still another was on $f_2$. Finally, at the junction 11, we generate

$$v_{21} = (7, 6, z_{21}), \quad v_{22} = (7, 6, z_{22}), \quad v_{23} = (7, 6, z_{23}) \in V,$$
$$(v_{21},f_1), \quad (v_{22},f_6), \quad (v_{22},f_2), \quad (v_{23},f_4) \in R,$$
$$(v_{21},v_{22},\text{PROPERLY-FRONT}), \quad (v_{22},v_{23},\text{PROPERLY-FRONT}) \in T.$$

For the other regions, $P_1$, $P_2$, $P_4$, ..., $P_{11}$, we generate new elements in a similar manner and thus complete the spatial structure $S$.

## 4.5. Realizability of a Polyhedral Scene

Let $D$ be a labeled line drawing, $L$ be a face-layer structure consistent with $D$, and $S = (V,F,R,T)$ be the spatial structure of $D$ and $L$. We can construct a system of linear equations and linear inequalities from $S$ in the same manner as we did in the case of natural pictures.

For each vertex $v_\alpha = (x_\alpha, y_\alpha, z_\alpha)$ ($\in V$), $x_\alpha$ and $y_\alpha$ are known constants and $z_\alpha$ is an unknown. With each face $f_j$ ($\in F$), we associate a planar surface $a_j x + b_j y + z + c_j = 0$ on which $f_j$ should lie, where $a_j$, $b_j$, and $c_j$ are unknowns. Thus, we have altogether $|V| + 3|F|$ unknowns. Since an element $(v_\alpha, f_j)$ of $R$ indicates that the vertex $v_\alpha$ should be on the face $f_j$, we get

$$a_j x_\alpha + b_j y_\alpha + z_\alpha + c_j = 0.$$

Collecting all such linear equations, one for each element of $R$, we obtain
the system of linear equations

$$Aw = 0, \qquad\qquad\qquad\qquad\qquad\qquad\qquad\qquad (4.1)$$

where $w = {}^t(z_1 \cdots z_n a_1 b_1 c_1 \cdots a_m b_m c_m)$, $m = |F|$, $n = |V|$, and $A$ is a
constant matrix of size $|R| \times (3m+n)$.

Elements of $T$ represent relative distances between parts of the
objects. From a triple of the form $(v_\alpha, v_\beta, \text{PROPERLY-FRONT})$ we get

$$z_\alpha > z_\beta,$$

from a triple of the form $(v_\alpha, f_j, \text{PROPERLY-FRONT})$ we get

$$a_j x_\alpha + b_j y_\alpha + z_\alpha + c_j > 0,$$

and from a triple of the form $(v_\alpha, f_j, \text{PROPERLY-BEHIND})$ we get

$$a_j x_\alpha + b_j y_\alpha + z_\alpha + c_j < 0.$$

Collecting all of the above three kinds of inequalities, one from each
element of $T$, we obtain the system of linear inequalities

$$Bw > 0, \qquad\qquad\qquad\qquad\qquad\qquad\qquad\qquad (4.2)$$

where $B$ is a constant matrix of size $|T| \times (3m+n)$.

Now we can prove the next theorem.

**Theorem 4.1 (Correctness of hidden-part-drawn pictures).** Let $D$ be a
labeled hidden-part-drawn line drawing, $L$ be a face-layer structure
consistent with $D$, and $S$ be the spatial structure of $D$ and $L$. $D$ represents
a polyhedral scene in which the faces are arranged along each line of sight
in the order as indicated by $L$ if and only if the system consisting of
(4.1) and (4.2) has a solution.

**Outline of the proof.** If $D$ represents a polyhedral scene in which the
faces are located in the way indicated by $L$, then from this scene we can
obviously obtain a solution to the system of (4.1) and (4.2).

Conversely, suppose that the system of (4.1) and (4.2) has a solution, say $w$. Then, we can construct a polyhedral scene from $w$ in the following way. First, for each face $f_j \in F$, we locate the planar surface $a_j x + b_j y + z + c_j = 0$ (where $a_j$, $b_j$, and $c_j$ are given in $w$), and scissor off some portion of it, forming a polygonal panel in such a way that the projection of the panel coincides with the polygon $[f_j]$. Next, we pack material between the panels. For this purpose, consider the partition of the picture plane induced by all the lines in $E$. Let $P$ be any one of such partitioned regions, and let $g(P) = (f_1, f_2, \ldots, f_{2k})$. If we translate the polygonal region $P$ in the direction perpendicular to the picture plane, the swept volume forms a prism extended infinitely in both the positive and negative directions of the $z$ axis. Now we pack material in the portion of the prism pinched by the two panels $f_{2j-1}$ and $f_{2j}$ for every $j = 1, 2, \ldots, k$ (recall that $f_{2j-1} \in F_1$ and $f_{2j} \in F_2$). We can indeed pack a nonzero volume of material in each portion because there are nonzero gaps between the faces (Proposition 4.3). We repeat the same process for every picture region, and thus construct a polyhedral scene.

It is not so difficult to see that this scene is what is represented by $D$ and $L$. Indeed, first, the polygonal panels are all planar, and for each partitioned region $P$ on the picture plane, the panels are arranged along the line of sight in the order in which they appear in $g(P)$ (Propositions 4.3 and 4.4). Second, from the definition of the face-layer structure, for each line $l$ in $E^*$ there exist exactly two panels, say $f_j$ and $f_k$, such that the boundaries of the two panels share a common edge in the space, whose projection on the picture plane coincides with $l$ (Proposition 4.1); each edge is shared by exactly two panels. Third, the panels do not penetrate each other, because for each picture region bounded by the lines in $E$ the corresponding panels do not touch each other except at the boundaries of the panels (Proposition 4.4). Fourth, exactly one side of each panel is filled with material; if the face belongs to $F_1$, material is packed in the rear side (i.e., the side with a smaller $z$ coordinate), and if it belongs to $F_2$, material is packed in the front side (i.e., the side with a larger $z$ coordinate). Finally, the configuration formed by material thus packed is the same as is required by the label assigned to each line (Proposition 4.2). Hence we get the theorem.

Thus we have obtained a necessary and sufficient condition for a hidden-part-drawn line drawing to represent a polyhedral scene. It should be noted that (4.1) and (4.2) have the same forms as those of (3.2) and

(3.4). Let $e$ be any positive constant and $\boldsymbol{e}$ be a $|T|$-dimensional vector whose components are all equal to $e$. Then, in the same way as in the last chapter, we can show that the existence of a solution to (4.1) and (4.2) is equivalent to the existence of a solution to (4.1) and

$$B w \geq \boldsymbol{e}. \tag{4.3}$$

Thus, the problem of judging the correctness of a hidden-part-drawn line drawing is also reduced to the problem of judging the existence of a feasible solution to the linear programming problem.

Moreover, we can show that Theorem 3.4 is valid also for hidden-part-drawn line drawings. That is, the correctness of a picture does not depend on whether it is considered as the orthographic projection or a perspective projection. However, we omit the proof because it is very similar to that for natural pictures.

## 5. ALGEBRAIC STRUCTURES OF LINE DRAWINGS

A necessary and sufficient condition for a labeled picture to be correct
has been given in terms of linear equations and inequalities. When a
picture is judged correct, the next problem is to reconstruct the
three-dimensional structure of the object represented there. However, the
structure is not unique; many different objects can yield the same picture.
Here we study how many and what kinds of degrees of freedom remain in the
choice of the object represented by a correct picture.

### 5.1. Degrees of Freedom in the Choice of Objects

In the last two chapters we considered natural pictures and
hidden-part-drawn pictures separately. In what follows, on the other hand,
we treat these two kinds of pictures in a unifying manner. Let $D$ be a
labeled line drawing and $S = (V,F,R,T)$ be a spatial structure associated
with $D$; $S$ is unique if $D$ is a natural picture, whereas $S$ depends on the
choice of a face-layer structure if $D$ is a hidden-part-drawn picture. Let

$$Aw = 0, \qquad\qquad\qquad\qquad\qquad\qquad\qquad (5.1)$$
$$Bw > 0 \qquad\qquad\qquad\qquad\qquad\qquad\qquad (5.2)$$

be the set of equations and that of inequalities obtained from the spatial
structure $S$, that is, (5.1) and (5.2) stand for (3.2) and (3.4),
respectively, if $D$ is a natural picture, and they stand for (4.1) and (4.2)
if $D$ is a hidden-part-drawn pictures. Furthermore, let

$$Bw \geq e \qquad\qquad\qquad\qquad\qquad\qquad\qquad (5.2')$$

denote (3.5) if $D$ is a natural picture and (4.3) if $D$ is a
hidden-part-drawn picture. As has been seen, for the picture $D$ to be
correct, for the system consisting of (5.1) and (5.2) to have a solution,
and for the system consisting of (5.1) and (5.2') to have a solution are
all equivalent.

    Suppose that the picture $D$ represents a polyhedral scene correctly.
Then, the picture itself does not specify the scene uniquely; an infinite
number of different scenes can be represented by $D$. Hence, we can determine
values of $z$ coordinates of some vertices and/or values of some face

parameters arbitrarily and can still obtain a polyhedral scene. Now, how many and what kinds of different scenes can the picture represent? We will answer this question in this chapter.

As we have seen, there is a one-to-one correspondence between a polyhedral scene that the picture $D$ can represent and a solution to the system consisting of (5.1) and (5.2). The number of possible scenes, therefore, is equal to the number of solutions to (5.1) and (5.2).

Recall that the unknown vector $w$ consists of the $z$ coordinates of vertices and the face parameters; that is, $w = {}^t(z_1 \cdots z_n a_1 b_1 c_1 \cdots a_m b_m c_m)$, where $n = |V|$ and $m = |F|$. Hence the total number of unknowns is $n+3m$; a solution to (5.1) and (5.2) can be considered as a point in an $(n+3m)$-dimensional Euclidean space. The set of solutions, therefore, forms a certain region in this space.

The dimension of this region depends mainly on (5.1). Indeed, each inequality in (5.2) represents an $(n+3m)$-dimensional half space, and hence the set of all inequalities in (5.2) defines an intersection of the half spaces. If this intersection is empty, the associated line drawing does not represent any polyhedral scene, which we are not interested in. Otherwise, it usually forms an $(n+3m)$-dimensional region, because the intersection of a finite number of $k$-dimensional half spaces in a $k$-dimensional space remains $k$-dimensional unless the half spaces are in some special position. In what follows, therefore, we assume that (5.2) form an $(n+3m)$-dimensional region, and concentrate our attention upon (5.1).

Each equation in (5.1) restricts the solutions to an $(n+3m-1)$-dimensional hyperplane in the $(n+3m)$-dimensional space. Since (5.1) contains rank$(A)$ independent equations, all the solutions to (5.1) form a region of dimension $(n+3m)-\text{rank}(A)$. This means that there are $n+3m-\text{rank}(A)$ degrees of freedom in the choice of a solution to (5.1); in other words, there exists a set of $n+3m-\text{rank}(A)$ unknowns such that we can specify the values of these unknowns independently, and once we do we get a unique solution to (5.1).

Let $u_i$ denote the $i$th component of the unknown vector $w$:

$$u_i = z_i \quad \text{if } 1 \leqq i \leqq n,$$
$$u_i = a_j \quad \text{if } i = n + 3j - 2, \ 1 \leqq j \leqq m,$$
$$u_i = b_j \quad \text{if } i = n + 3j - 1, \ 1 \leqq j \leqq m,$$
$$u_i = c_j \quad \text{if } i = n + 3j, \ 1 \leqq j \leqq m.$$

Furthermore, let $H$ denote the set of all unknowns: $H = \{z_1, \ldots, z_n, a_1, b_1, c_1,$

$\ldots, a_m, b_m, c_m\} = \{u_1, \ldots, u_{n+3m}\}$. Suppose that we give an arbitrary value to the $i$th unknown $u_i$, that is, $u_i = d_i$, where $d_i$ is an arbitrary constant. This equation can be rewritten as $e_i \cdot w = d_i$, where $e_i$ is an $(n+3m)$-dimensional row vector whose $i$th component is 1 and all the other components are 0's. It is obvious that we can choose an arbitrary value for $u_i$ and can still obtain a solution to (5.1) if and only if the system composed of $e_i \cdot w = d_i$ and (5.1) has a solution for any $d_i$. More generally, for any subset $X$ of the unknown set $H$, we can choose any values for the unknowns in $X$ and can still obtain a solution to (5.1) if and only if the system consisting of

$$e_i \cdot w = d_i \quad \text{for } u_i \in X \tag{5.3}$$

and (5.1) has a solution for any $d_i$.

Let $\{A\}$ denote the set of row vectors in the matrix $A$. Since the rank of $A$ is invariant under permutation of rows of $A$, the rank can be considered as a function of the row vector set $\{A\}$, rather than the matrix $A$ itself. Hence we can write rank($\{A\}$) = rank($A$). Using this notation, we define a nonnegative integer-valued function $\rho_H$ on $2^H$ (where $2^H$ represents the family of all subsets of $H$) by

$$\rho_H(X) = \text{rank}(\{A\} \cup \{e_i \mid u_i \in X\}) - \text{rank}(\{A\}), \tag{5.4}$$

where $X \subseteq H$. Then, we get the following.

**Theorem 5.1 (Degrees of freedom in the choice of objects).** Let $X$ be any subset of the unknown set $H$. Then, $\rho_H(X)$ is the maximum cardinality of the subset $Y$ of $X$ such that even if we fix values of the unknowns in $Y$ arbitrarily, the system of (5.1) still has a solution.

**Proof.** We have $n+3m-\text{rank}(A)$ degrees of freedom in the choice of a solution to (5.1). If we are given values of the unknowns in $X$, we have the additional constraints of the equations given by (5.3), and hence the degrees of freedom in the choice of a solution decrease to

$$n + 3m - \text{rank}(\{A\} \cup \{e_i \mid u_i \in X\}),$$

which corresponds to the degrees of freedom in the choice of a solution to the system composed of (5.1) and (5.3). The value $\rho_H(X)$ represents the

difference of these two kinds of the degrees of freedom; that is, $\rho_H(X)$
represents how much the degrees of freedom decrease when values of the
unknowns in $X$ are given. Thus, $\rho_H(X)$ represents the maximum number of
unknowns in $X$ whose values can be chosen arbitrarily.

We call $\rho_H(X)$ the *degrees of freedom* of the unknown set $X$. The unknown
set $X$ is said to be *independent* if $|X| = \rho_H(X)$, and *dependent* otherwise. A
maximal independent set is called a *base*. From Theorem 5.1 we see that we
can choose values of the unknowns in $X$ arbitrarily if and only if $X$ is
independent, and that we can specify a solution to (5.1) uniquely by giving
arbitrary values to the unknowns in $X$ if and only if $X$ is a base. Thus, the
function $\rho_H$ tells us how the degrees of freedom in the choice of a solution
to (5.1) are distributed over the unknowns, or in other words, it tells us
how the degrees of freedom in the choice of a polyhedral scene are
distributed over the vertices and the faces.

Let us partition the unknown set $H$ into the set of the $z$ coordinates
of the vertices $H_V = \{z_1, \ldots, z_n\} = \{u_1, \ldots, u_n\}$ and the set of the face
parameters $H_F = \{a_1, b_1, c_1, \ldots, a_m, b_m, c_m\} = \{u_{n+1}, \ldots, u_{n+3m}\}$, and let $\rho_H$
denote also the function obtained by restricting the domain to the family
of subsets of $H_V$ or to the family of subsets of $H_F$. Then, for any $X \subseteq H_V$,
$\rho_H(X)$ represents the maximum number of $z$ values in $X$ that can be chosen
independently. Similarly, for any $X \subseteq H_F$, $\rho_H(X)$ represents the maximum
number of face parameters in $X$ that can be chosen independently. The use of
the same symbol $\rho_H$ for the functions on the three different sets $H$, $H_V$, and
$H_F$ does not cause confusion because we can easily understand from context
what set is under consideration. Thus, the function $\rho_H$ also represents,
when the domain is restricted, the distribution of the degrees of freedom
in the choice of a polyhedral scene over the vertices or over the faces.

Since there is a natural one-to-one correspondence between the vertex
set $V$ and the $z$ coordinate set $H_V$, we can introduce from $\rho_H$ naturally a
function $\rho_V$ on $2^V$; that is, for any $X \subseteq V$, we can define

$$\rho_V(X) = \rho_H(\{z_\alpha \mid v_\alpha \in X\}). \tag{5.5}$$

For any subset $X$ of $V$, $X$ is said to be *independent* if $|X| = \rho_V(X)$ and
*dependent* otherwise, and a maximal independent set is called a *base*.

In the spatial structure $S$ every vertex is at least on one face and
every face has at least three vertices, and hence all the degrees of
freedom can be removed by specifying $z$ coordinates of some vertices, and so

can be removed by specifying some face parameters. Thus we get

$$\rho_V(V) = \rho_H(H_F) = \rho_H(H) = n + 3m - \text{rank}(A). \tag{5.6}$$

**Example 5.1.** Consider the labeled hidden-part-eliminated line drawing shown in Fig. 5.1(a). This picture has six junctions, and they are numbered as shown in the figure. Let $v_\alpha$ ($\alpha = 1, \ldots, 6$) be the vertex of the object that gives rise to the junction $\alpha$. (Formally, there are some other vertices that are on the background surface, but we now concentrate our attention on the vertices on the object at the center of the scene.) There are exactly four degrees of freedom in the choice of the object represented by the picture, because we can arbitrarily locate three vertices on one face and one more vertex that is not on this face. For example, if we give $z$ values to $v_1$, $v_3$, and $v_4$, the left quadrilateral face is fixed in a space and consequently the spatial position of $v_6$ is also determined. Hence we get $\rho_V(\{v_1, v_3, v_4\}) = \rho_V(\{v_1, v_3, v_4, v_6\}) = 3$, and consequently $\{v_1, v_3, v_4\}$ is independent whereas $\{v_1, v_3, v_4, v_6\}$ is dependent. Next if we specify one more vertex, say $v_2$, then the other two quadrilateral faces are fixed and eventually $v_5$ is also fixed in the space. Thus, we can give arbitrarily $z$ values to the vertices $v_1$, $v_2$, $v_3$, $v_4$ (provided that they do not violate the line labels), and once we do the object is determined uniquely. Hence $\{v_1, v_2, v_3, v_4\}$ is a base.

We have 4 degrees of freedom in the choice of the scene, but 1 degree of freedom is due to the translation of the whole scene along the $z$ axis. We therefore have 3 degrees of freedom in the choice of the object shape itself. In Fig. 5.1, (b) and (c) illustrate how the object deforms if we give different $z$ values to the base $\{v_1, v_2, v_3, v_4\}$. In (b), we choose the $z$ coordinates of the three vertices $v_1$, $v_2$, $v_3$ in such a way that they are on a plane parallel to the picture plane, and see how the object changes for different values of the $z$ coordinate of $v_4$. In (c), on the other hand, the three vertices $v_1$, $v_3$, $v_4$ are fixed, and $v_2$ is changed.

**Example 5.2.** Let us consider the labeled hidden-part-eliminated line drawing in Fig. 5.2. The picture has five junctions, which are numbered 1, 2, ..., 5, as shown in the figure. For a junction $\alpha$ ($\alpha = 1, 2, \ldots, 5$), let $v_\alpha$ be the corresponding vertex on the surface of the object at the center of the scene. Furthermore, let the four faces of the object be $f_1$, $f_2$, $f_3$, $f_4$, as shown in the figure (here again we exclude the surrounding background surface from our consideration). This picture can represent a

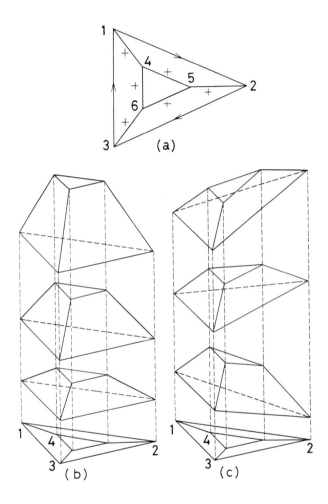

**Fig. 5.1.** Ambiguity in the quantitative interpretation of a labeled line drawing; a picture can represent many different objects.

pyramid seen from above, but it can also represent many other objects because the four vertices $v_1$, $v_2$, $v_3$, and $v_4$ need not be coplanar.

The parameter set $\{a_1, b_1, c_1, a_2\}$, for example, is independent. This can be understood in the following way. We first choose any values for $a_1$, $b_1$, and $c_1$ in order to fix the face $f_1$ in the three-dimensional space. When

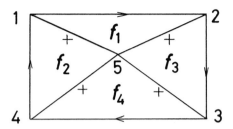

**Fig. 5.2.** Picture of a four-face object.

$f_1$ is fixed, the three vertices on it are also fixed, and hence the face $f_2$, which shares the vertices $v_1$ and $v_5$ with $f_1$, has only one degree of freedom due to rotations around the line connecting $v_1$ to $v_5$. To remove this degree of freedom, we can specify any one of the three parameters $a_2$, $b_2$, and $c_2$ arbitrarily (provided that the edge $v_1$–$v_5$ be convex). Thus, $\{a_1, b_1, c_1, a_2\}$ is independent; that is,

$$\rho_H(\ \{a_1, b_1, c_1, a_2\}\ ) = 4.$$

The parameter set $\{a_1, b_1, a_2, b_2\}$, on the other hand, is dependent, for the following reason. Recall that the $j$th surface is represented by the equation $a_j x + b_j y + z + c_j = 0$, which is perpendicular to the vector $(a_j, b_j, 1)$ and which intersects the $z$ axis at $(0, 0, -c_j)$. Hence, the pair of parameters $a_j$ and $b_j$ represents the normal to the surface, and if the normal has been given, the other parameter $c_j$ corresponds to the degree of freedom due to the translation along the $z$ axis. Therefore, if the values of $a_1$ and $b_1$ are given, the normal to the face $f_1$ is determined, and consequently the direction of the line $v_1$–$v_5$ is determined. Since the face $f_2$ should be parallel to this line, the normal to $f_2$ cannot be chosen arbitrarily; if one of $a_2$ and $b_2$ is given, the other is automatically determined. Thus, we have seen

$$\rho_H(\ \{a_1, b_1, a_2, b_2\}\ ) = 3.$$

The parameter set $\{a_1, b_1, c_1, a_2, a_3\}$ is a base. Indeed, giving any values to $a_1$, $b_1$, $c_1$, $a_2$, we can fix the two faces $f_1$ and $f_2$ in the space, and consequently fix the edge $v_2$–$v_5$. The face $f_3$, therefore, has only one degree of freedom corresponding to rotations around the line $v_2$-$v_5$. This degree of freedom can be removed if we give a value to $a_3$. Then, since both the edges $v_3$-$v_5$ and $v_4$-$v_5$ have been fixed, the face $f_4$ is also determined uniquely. Thus, the shape of the whole object is specified when the values of $a_1$, $b_1$, $c_1$, $a_2$, $a_3$ are given; there are five degrees of freedom in the choice of the object. This implies that if we want to determine the object shape by specifying $z$ values of vertices, we have to specify the $z$ values of all the five vertices. This can also be understood by noting that the faces are all triangular, and consequently a spatial position of any vertex is not determined by the spatial positions of the other vertices.

The unknown set $\{z_1, z_3, z_4, a_1, b_1\}$ is an example of a base containing both elements of $H_V$ and those of $H_F$. This is because the pair of $a_1$ and $b_1$ determines the normal to the face $f_1$, $z_1$ determines where the face $f_1$ intersects the $z$ axis (thus $a_1$, $b_1$, $z_1$ define $f_1$ uniquely), and $z_3$ and $z_4$ determine the remaining part of the object.

In the above two examples we were able to find at a glance how many degrees of freedom we have in the choice of the objects; we need not calculate the rank of the matrix $A$. This is because we could find a "convenient" base in the sense that once values of the unknowns in the base are fixed, all the other unknowns are determined in a step-by-step manner. In the case of Fig. 5.1(a), for example, if we give values to $v_1$, $v_2$, $v_3$, $v_4$, the left quadrilateral face and the right upper quadrilateral face are determined first, consequently $v_6$ and $v_5$, and finally the right lower quadrilateral face and the triangular face at the center are determined. This corresponds to the fact that if values of the unknowns in the base are given, the solution to (5.1) can be obtained by substitution; we need not solve all of (5.1) simultaneously. Sometimes, however, we cannot find such a convenient base. If there is no such convenient base, we have to solve (5.1) "simultaneously" in order to reconstruct a polyhedral scene from the line drawing on one hand, and we must give nontrivial consideration (or must calculate the rank of the matrix $A$ directly) in order to understand how many degrees of freedom we have in the choice of the object on the other hand. This case is illustrated in the next example.

**Example 5.3.** Let us consider the line drawing shown in Fig. 5.3(a), which represents an object composed of four quadrilateral planar panels connected in a cyclic manner along the four edges $v_1$-$v_5$, $v_2$-$v_6$, $v_3$-$v_7$, and $v_4$-$v_8$ (where $v_i$ denotes the vertex arising at junction $i$).

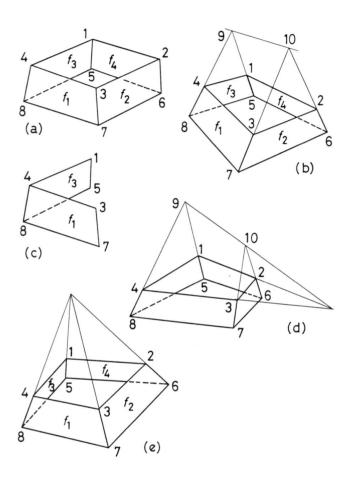

**Fig. 5.3.** Picture of an object composed of four planar panels.

The vertex set $\{v_1, v_2, v_3, v_5\}$ is a base. This can be understood as follows. Let junction 9 be the intersection of the lines 1-5 and 4-8, and junction 10 be the intersection of the lines 2-6 and 3-7, as shown in (b). Then, the line 9-10 represents the intersection of the two panels $f_1$ and $f_4$, where the surface on which the panel $f_j$ lies is also referred to as the "panel" $f_j$. Thus we can say that the vertex $v_9$, which corresponds to junction 9, is on the panels $f_1$, $f_3$, $f_4$, and the vertex $v_{10}$ is on the panels $f_1$, $f_2$, $f_4$. Now suppose that we give $z$ values to the vertices

$v_1$, $v_2$, $v_3$, $v_5$ . Then, since $v_1$, $v_2$, $v_5$ are fixed in the space, the panel $f_4$ is fixed and consequently $v_6$, $v_9$, $v_{10}$ are also fixed. Next from $v_2$, $v_3$, $v_6$ , the panel $f_2$ is fixed and so is $v_7$. Finally from $v_3$, $v_9$, $v_{10}$ , the panel $f_1$ is fixed and hence $v_4$ , $v_8$ , $f_3$ are all fixed. Therefore $\{v_1, v_2, v_3, v_5\}$ is a base.

The above consideration tells us that if $f_2$ and $f_4$ are fixed in the space, $f_1$ and $f_3$ are also determined uniquely. In other words, the determination of spatial positions of $v_1$, $v_3$, $v_5$, $v_7$ results in the determination of spatial positions of $f_1$ and $f_3$, because the substructure composed of $f_1$ and $f_3$ touches the substructure composed of $f_2$ and $f_4$ only at these four vertices. This implies that the vertex set $\{v_1, v_3, v_5, v_7\}$ is a base for the two-panel object shown in (c). Moreover, the substructure composed of $f_2$ and $f_4$ has essentially the same structure as that of $f_1$ and $f_3$, and hence $\{v_1, v_3, v_5, v_7\}$ is also a base for this substructure. Thus, the vertex set $\{v_1, v_3, v_5, v_7\}$ is a base for the original picture (a). Note that the two virtual panels $(v_1, v_2, v_{10}, v_9)$ and $(v_4, v_3, v_{10}, v_9)$ in (b) form the same configuration as the object in (c). We see therefore that $\{v_1, v_2, v_3, v_4\}$ is also a base of the original picture (a).

We must note, however, that the distribution of the degrees of freedom may change when the junctions are drawn in some ˙special˙ position. For example, if picture (b) is drawn in such a way that the three lines 1-2, 3-4, and 9-10 have a common point of intersection as shown in (d), then the four vertices $v_1$, $v_2$, $v_3$, $v_4$ are coplanar in any object represented by the picture and consequently the vertex set $\{v_1, v_2, v_3, v_4\}$ is dependent, whereas the vertex set $\{v_1, v_2, v_3, v_5\}$ still remains a base.

On the other hand, consider the case in which the four lines 1-5, 2-6, 3-7, and 4-8 have a common point of intersection, as shown in (e) (note that if any three out of the four lines have a common point of intersection, the other should also pass through the point because otherwise the picture is incorrect). We can easily see that in any object that can be represented by picture (e) the four vertices $v_1$, $v_3$, $v_5$, $v_7$ and the four vertices $v_2$, $v_4$, $v_6$, $v_8$ are respectively coplanar. Therefore, when the $z$ values of the vertices $v_1$, $v_2$, $v_3$, $v_5$ are given, the panels $f_2$ and $f_4$ only are fixed while $f_1$ and $f_3$ are not. We must give a $z$ value to one more vertex (for example, the vertex $v_4$), in order to fix the whole structure. Thus, there are 5 degrees of freedom in the choice of the object from picture (e), and the vertex set $\{v_1, v_2, v_3, v_4, v_5\}$ is an example of a base.

**Remark 5.1**   In Example 5.3 we have introduced two new conventions.  First, though our object world is that of polyhedrons, we also consider planar-panel scenes. This is because (5.1) essentially represents the configuration composed of planar surfaces and points on them; it does not depend on which sides of the surfaces are filled with material (whereas (5.2) depends on them). We can present a polyhedron whose degrees-of-freedom structure is essentially the same as the planar-panel object in Fig. 5.3(a). Indeed, if we add four triangular faces $(v_1,v_2,v_3)$, $(v_1,v_3,v_4)$, $(v_5,v_6,v_7)$, $(v_5,v_7,v_8)$ to Fig. 5.3(a), the resultant object is a polyhedron and the distribution of the degrees of freedom of this new object is the same as that of the original planar-panel object (note that addition of triangular faces does not change the essential structure of the degrees of freedom). Here we take up the planar-panel object because otherwise the triangular faces will make the picture unnecessarily complicated.

The second convention is that though we are considering labeled pictures, we sometimes treat unlabeled pictures as if they were labeled. We shall use this convention when the most natural spatial structure that the original picture evokes in our mind seems unambiguous, or when we can express the associated spatial structure more simply by words than by labels. Fig. 5.3(a) seems to evoke in our mind two kinds of objects; one is composed of the four panels $f_1$, $f_2$, $f_3$, $f_4$, and the other has one more panel at the bottom, that is, the panel $(v_5,v_6,v_7,v_8)$. We are now considering the former because we stated so at the beginning of Example 5.3.

We will hereafter adopt these two conventions whenever we can avoid treating unnecessarily messy figures.

As we have seen in the last example, the distribution of the degrees of freedom in the choice of objects depends on both which faces have which vertices in the spatial structure and where the junctions are drawn in the picture plane. Hence, if we treat line drawings in a purely geometrical manner, we have to perform complicated figure-construction tasks (which usually requires heuristic and analogical skills) in order to tell what sets of vertices form bases. The function $\rho_H$ defined by (5.4), on the other hand, gives us a very powerful tool, by which a computer can tell the distribution of the degrees of freedom in an analytical and systematic manner.

While in this section we have defined the degrees of freedom in terms of the ranks of some row vector sets, we will present in the next chapter a

counting theorem by which we can find the degrees of freedom by integer
calculation only.

## 5.2. Matroids

Let $E$ be a finite set and $\rho$ be an integer-valued function on $2^E$. A pair
$(E,\rho)$ is called a *matroid* if the following three conditions are satisfied
for any $X, Y \subseteq E$ (Welsh, 1976):

$$0 \le \rho(X) \le |X|, \tag{5.7a}$$

$$X \subseteq Y \text{ implies } \rho(X) \le \rho(Y), \tag{5.7b}$$

$$\rho(X \cup Y) + \rho(X \cap Y) \le \rho(X) + \rho(Y). \tag{5.7c}$$

$E$ and $\rho$ are called a *support set* and a *rank function*, respectively, of the
matroid $(E,\rho)$. A subset $X$ of $E$ is called *independent* if $\rho(X) = |X|$ and
*dependent* otherwise. A maximal independent set is called a *base* of the
matroid.

The function $\rho_H$ defined by (5.4) satisfies the above conditions
(5.7a), (5.7b), and (5.7c). For the proof we refer to textbooks such as the
one by Welsh (1976), but we can understand it intuitively in the following
manner. First, for any set $X$ of unknowns, the value of the degrees of
freedom is neither negative nor greater than the size of $X$; hence $\rho_H$
satisfies condition (5.7a). Next, if $X \subseteq Y$, then $Y$ can admit the same
degrees of freedom as, or greater degrees of freedom than, $X$ can, and thus
condition (5.7b) is satisfied. Finally, let us consider how many degrees of
freedom remain in $X$-$Y$ when values of some unknowns outside $X$-$Y$ are given.
If values of the unknowns in $Y$ are given, there remain in $X$-$Y$ only
$\rho_H(X \cup Y)-\rho_H(Y)$ degrees of freedom; see Fig. 5.4. If on the other hand
values of the unknowns in $X \cap Y$ are given, then the degrees of freedom left
to $X$-$Y$ amount to $\rho_H(X)-\rho_H(X \cap Y)$. Less degrees of freedom remain in $X$-$Y$ if
values of more unknowns outside $X$-$Y$ are given (for example, less degrees of
freedom are left for us to choose $z$ values of vertices in $X$-$Y$ when we fix $z$
values of the vertices in $Y$ than when we fix $z$ values of the vertices in
$X \cap Y$. ) Thus we get

$$\rho_H(X \cup Y) - \rho_H(Y) \le \rho_H(X) - \rho_H(X \cap Y),$$

which is equivalent to the condition (5.7c).

Thus, the pairs $(H,\rho_H)$, $(H_V,\rho_H)$, and $(H_F,\rho_H)$ are matroids, and

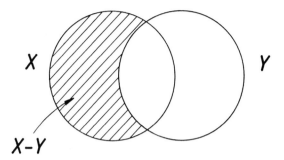

**Fig. 5.4.** Third axiom in the definition of the matroid; smaller degrees of freedom remain in $X$-$Y$ if the degrees of freedom are removed from a larger set outside $X$-$Y$.


consequently so is the pair $(V, \rho_V)$.

One of the salient properties of a matroid $(E, \rho)$ is that $\rho(X) = \rho(E)$ holds for any base $X$ ($\subseteq E$); that is, every base has the same cardinality $\rho(E)$. This can be seen in the following way. Let $X$ be any subset of $E$, and suppose that there exist $Y_1$ and $Y_2$ such that $\rho(X) = \rho(Y_1) = \rho(Y_2)$, $X \subseteq Y_1 \subseteq E$, and $X \subseteq Y_2 \subseteq E$. Then, on one hand, from (5.7b) we get $\rho(Y_1 \cap Y_2) = \rho(X)$ and $\rho(Y_1 \cup Y_2) \geq \rho(X)$. On the other hand, from (5.7c) we get $\rho(Y_1 \cup Y_2) + \rho(Y_1 \cap Y_2) \leq \rho(Y_1) + \rho(Y_2)$, and consequently, using $\rho(Y_1) = \rho(Y_2) = \rho(Y_1 \cap Y_2) = \rho(X)$, we get $\rho(Y_1 \cup Y_2) \leq \rho(X)$. Therefore, we see $\rho(Y_1 \cup Y_2) = \rho(X)$, which implies that for any $X \subseteq E$ there exists a unique maximal subset $Y$ such that $\rho(X) = \rho(Y)$ and $X \subseteq Y \subseteq E$. We call this $Y$ the *closure* of $X$, and denote it by $Y = \text{cl}(X)$. $X$ is called a *flat* if $\text{cl}(X) = X$. Now suppose that $X$ is independent and $\rho(X) < \rho(E)$. Then, $E$-$\text{cl}(X)$ is not empty, and moreover, it follows from the definition of the closure that $\rho(X \cup \{x\}) = \rho(X) + 1$ for any $x \in E - \text{cl}(X)$. Thus, $X \cup \{x\}$ is also independent. In other words, any independent set can be augmented without violating the independence until it becomes a base. Therefore, every base has the same cardinality $\rho(E)$.

This property is important from the viewpoint of computational complexity, because we can obtain a base of a matroid efficiently in the following way. Initially let $X$ be an empty set. Next, choose and delete elements $e$ from $E$ one by one, and add them to $X$ if $X \cup \{e\}$ is independent and discard them otherwise. Eventually $X$ becomes large enough to satisfy

$\rho(X) = \rho(E)$, and thus we get a base. This procedure is called a "greedy algorithm" (Edmonds, 1971).

The greedy algorithm can also find a minimum-weight base. Suppose that each element of $E$ has a nonnegative value called a *weight*. If the element with the minimum weight is taken at every stage of the greedy algorithm, the resultant base attains the minimum sum of the weight among all the bases.

One application of a minimum-weight base arises in the use of a spot range finder. A spot range finder is a device for measuring a range to a point on the object from the observer. One method for this purpose is triangulation; that is, a spot light is projected onto the object, the image of the spot is observed from another angle, and the triangle formed by the light source, the observer, and the point on the object is determined (Ishii and Nagata, 1976). Another method is the measurement of time of flight; that is, an amplitude modulated laser beam is projected on the object, the reflected light is detected, and the phase difference is observed (Nitzan et al., 1977). The measurement of range data is time consuming because a range of only one point can be obtained at a time and the direction of the projection of the light is usually changed by a mechanical manner (for example, by the rotation of a mirror). It is therefore desired that a range finder be used as few times as possible. Suppose that we have already obtained a line drawing from an image originated with a real polyhedral object, and that we want to measure ranges of a minimum number of points in order to recover the three-dimensional shape of the object. Suppose, furthermore, that we can estimate an expected error of measurement for each vertex of the object. Then, the problem can be reduced to the problem of finding a base of the matroid $(V, \rho_V)$ with the minimum sum of weights, where the weights denote the expected errors. Hence, we can solve the problem by the greedy algorithm.

## 5.3. Pictures with Four Degrees of Freedom

Given a correct line drawing $D$ and its spatial structure $S$, we have at least four degrees of freedom in the choice of a polyhedral scene represented by $D$ and $S$ unless the scene consists of only one face. This can be intuitively understood when we note that we have to specify three parameters in order to fix one face in the space and at least one more parameter to fix another face. More formally, we get the following.

**Theorem 5.2** (**Lower bound of the degrees of freedom**). Let $D$ be a labeled line drawing and $S$ be a spatial structure associated with $D$. If $D$ together with $S$ represents a polyhedral scene and $S$ has two or more faces, then there are at least four degrees of freedom in the choice of a polyhedral scene from $D$ and $S$.

**Proof**. Let $P$ denote a set of three-dimensional points forming a polyhedral scene represented by $D$ and $S$, and $P'$ denote the set of all points $(x',y',z')$ obtained by the affine transformation

$$\begin{bmatrix} x' \\ y' \\ z' \end{bmatrix} = \begin{bmatrix} 1 & 0 & 0 \\ 0 & 1 & 0 \\ \alpha & \beta & \gamma \end{bmatrix} \begin{bmatrix} x \\ y \\ z \end{bmatrix} + \begin{bmatrix} 0 \\ 0 \\ \delta \end{bmatrix}, \tag{5.8}$$

where $\alpha$, $\beta$, and $\delta$ are any real numbers, $\gamma$ is a positive real number, and $(x,y,z)$ moves over $P$. Since the transformation is affine, the edges and the faces of $P$ are transformed to some edges and faces, respectively, of $P'$, and hence $P'$ also is a polyhedral scene. Moreover, $P'$ admits the same line drawing $D$ and the same spatial structure $S$ as $P$ does, because, first, the transformation does not change the $x$ and $y$ coordinates of the points, and second, the determinant of the coefficient matrix of the transformation (5.8) is positive (recall $\gamma > 0$) and hence the transformation does not change the spatial orientation; that is, the outer normals to the faces are never reversed. Thus, $P'$ is a polyhedral scene represented by $D$ and $S$. The transformation (5.8) has the four parameters, and their values are determined uniquely if the destinations of noncoplanar four points on $P$ are specified. These noncoplanar four points can always be chosen because the scene has two or more faces. Therefore, $z$ values of at least four vertices can be chosen arbitrarily when we want to reconstruct a polyhedral scene from $D$ and $S$.

It may be interesting to note that if $\gamma < 0$, the transformation (5.8) applied to a polyhedral scene $P$ generates a polyhedral scene, say $P'$, that has the reversed orientation in the sense that any set of three noncoplanar vectors forming a right hand system in $P$ is transformed to the one forming a left hand system. In terms of the labels, the category (a) in Fig. 2.6 is transformed to the category (h), the category (d) to the category (e). Particularly, if $\alpha = \beta = 0$ and $\gamma = -1$, then $P'$ is a mirror image of $P$ with respect to a mirror parallel to the $x$-$y$ plane. For (unlabeled) hidden-part-drawn pictures whose hidden lines are also represented by solid lines, a pair of interpretations that are mirror images of each other usually occurs in human visual perception, and this phenomenon is called Necker's reversal (Gregory, 1971). In the case of hidden-part-eliminated pictures, on the other hand, this phenomenon does not occur. This is probably because the transformation (5.8) with a negative $\gamma$ brings rear invisible faces to the front, so that the corresponding line drawings must also be changed.

We have shown that there are at least four degrees of freedom when we reconstruct a polyhedral scene from a correct line drawing. If the degrees of freedom are exactly four, the corresponding polyhedral scenes possess the following remarkable property.

**Theorem 5.3 (Collinearity-coplanarity property).** Let $D$ and $S$ be a line drawing and the associated spatial structure, respectively, and $\mathcal{P}(D,S)$ be the set of all polyhedral scenes that can be represented by $D$ and $S$. If $\rho_V(V) = 4$ (that is, there are exactly four degrees of freedom in the choice of a polyhedral scene), then a vertex set $X$ ($\subseteq V$) that is collinear (resp. coplanar) in some scene $P$ in $\mathcal{P}(D,S)$ is also collinear (resp. coplanar) in any scene $P'$ in $\mathcal{P}(D,S)$.

**Proof.** Let us choose from $\mathcal{P}(D,S)$ an arbitrary scene, say $P$, and fix it. Without loss of generality, let $\{v_1, v_2, v_3, v_4\}$ be a base of the matroid $(V, \rho_V)$ (note that the cardinality of every base is 4 because $\rho_V(V) = 4$), and let $z_1$, $z_2$, $z_3$, $z_4$ be the real numbers representing the $z$ coordinates of the associated four vertices in the scene $P$. Any scene, say $P'$, in $\mathcal{P}(D,S)$ is specified uniquely if we choose four real numbers, say $z_1'$, $z_2'$, $z_3'$, and $z_4'$, for the $z$ coordinates of the vertices $v_1$, $v_2$, $v_3$, and $v_4$. On the other hand, we can uniquely determine the transformation of the form (5.8) that transforms the four points $(x_i, y_i, z_i)$ ($i = 1, \ldots, 4$) to $(x_i', y_i', z_i')$. Let $P''$ be the result of the transformation applied to $P$. However, since $P''$ is a polyhedral scene and $\{v_1, v_2, v_3, v_4\}$ is a base, it follows that $P'$ and $P''$ represent the same scene. Thus, any two scenes in $\mathcal{P}(D,S)$ can be transformed to each other by a transformation of the form (5.8). Since the transformation (5.8) preserves both collinearity and coplanarity, we get the theorem.

Theorem 5.3 enables us to judge whether some classes of figure-construction problems have unique solutions or not. Let $D$ be a correct line drawing, $S$ be the associated spatial structure, and $\mathcal{P}(D,S)$ be the set of all polyhedral scenes $D$ and $S$ can represent. Let us consider the following figure-construction problems.

**Problem 5.1.** Given $S$ and $D$, find the intersection of a planar surface passing through the three vertices $v_1$, $v_2$, $v_3$ ($\in V$) and a straight line passing through the two vertices $v_4$, $v_5$ ($\in V$), and draw it on the picture plane.

**Problem 5.2.** Given $S$ and $D$, find the intersection of a planar surface passing through the vertices $v_1$, $v_2$, $v_3$ ($\in V$) and a planar surface passing through the vertices $v_4$, $v_5$, $v_6$ ($\in V$), and draw it on the picture plane.

These kinds of problems do not always make sense, because the intersection to be found usually depends on a polyhedral scene chosen from $\mathcal{P}(D,S)$, and so does its projection on the picture plane. However, if $\rho_V(V)$ = 4, the result of the figure construction is unique because collinearity and coplanarity of any vertex set do not depend on the choice of a polyhedral scene in $\mathcal{P}(D,S)$. Thus, we get the following.

**Corollary 5.3.1 (Unique solvability of figure-construction problems).** If $\rho_V(V)$ = 4, figure-construction problems of the types given by Problems 5.1 and 5.2 admit unique solutions.

Note that we have obtained Theorem 5.3 and Corollary 5.3.1 by considering the pictures as orthographic projections of polyhedral objects. However, as we saw in Section 3.7, the algebraic structure of pictures does not depend on whether we consider the pictures as orthographic projections or perspective projections. The above theorem and corollary are therefore valid also for perspectively drawn pictures.

Theorem 5.3 also gives us a general principle for solving the figure-construction problems.

**Principle 5.1.** Choose any one polyhedral scene the picture can represent, find the intersection in a three-dimensional space, and project the result on the picture plane.

Theorem 5.3 assures us that the result does not depend on the choice of the polyhedral scene. This principle will also play an important role in the correction of incorrect pictures.

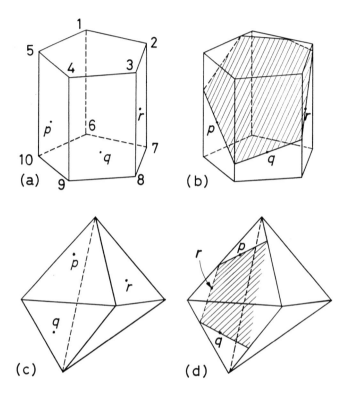

**Fig. 5.5.** Unique    solvability    of    figure-construction    problems:    the
figure-construction    problem    (a)    admits the unique solution shown in (b),
whereas the problem (c) does not and the problem (d) does only partially.

**Example 5.4.** Let us consider this figure-construction problem: "Find  the
intersection of the object represented in Fig. 5.5(a) and the plane passing
through the three points $p$, $q$, $r$ on the visible faces of the object  (here
again we assume that the picture evokes a common spatial structure in every
reader, and hence we omit the labels; recall Remark 5.1)." Since this  line
drawing  can  be  a  picture of a pentagonal prism, the picture is correct.
Moreover, if we specify $z$ values of some  noncoplanar  four  vertices  (for
example,  $v_1$, $v_2$, $v_3$ ,  and  $v_6$), the whole structure is located uniquely in
the space, and therefore there are exactly four degrees  of  freedom.   The
above  problem  can  be  decomposed  into  several  problems of finding the

intersections between the object edges and the cutting plane (i.e., the plane passing through $p$, $q$, $r$), that is, the problem of finding the intersection between the cutting plane and the edge $v_2$-$v_7$, that between the cutting plane and the edge $v_3$-$v_8$, and so on. Hence from Corollary 5.3.1, the original figure-construction problem admits a unique solution. The solution is shown in (b).

Next consider this problem: "Find the intersection between the object represented in Fig. 5.5(c) and the cutting plane passing through the three points $p$, $q$, $r$ on the visible faces." Since all the faces are triangular, the degrees of freedom in the choice of the object amount to the number of vertices, 5. Hence the solution is not unique. If, on the other hand, the point $r$ is on the left rear invisible face as shown in (d), then the problem can be partially solved. This is because the left three triangular faces form a substructure with exactly 4 degrees of freedom, so that the intersection between the cutting plane and the three faces can be determined uniquely. The partial solution is shown in (d).

**Example 5.5.** The last observation in Example 5.4 leads to an extreme case. Consider this problem: "Find the intersection of the corner of a polyhedron shown in Fig. 5.6(a) and the cutting plane passing through the three points $p$, $q$, $r$ on the surface." Without changing the degrees of freedom, we can consider the picture as the picture of a tetrahedron, and hence there are exactly 4 degrees of freedom in the choice of this partial structure. Therefore, the problem has a unique solution.

We can easily obtain the solution by employing Principle 5.1, but figure construction on a purely two-dimensional plane is also possible in the following way (see also Crapo, 1981).

Let the three lines be $l_1$, $l_2$, and $l_3$, and the three faces be $f_1$, $f_2$, and $f_3$, as shown in (b). First, choose an arbitrary point, say $a$, on the line $l_1$, and let $b$ be the intersection of the line $l_2$ and the line $ap$ (here by $ap$ we denote the line passing through $a$ and $p$), and $c$ be the intersection of the line $l_3$ and the line $aq$. Then, the triangle $abc$ can be interpreted as the intersection of the three-dimensional corner and the plane passing through $p$, $q$, and $a$. Next, let $d$ be the intersection of the line $pq$ and the line $bc$. Since in the space the points $b$ and $c$ are on the face $f_1$, the point $d$ can be interpreted as the intersection of the line $pq$ and the face $f_1$. Hence, the line $dr$ is also in the face $f_1$. Finally, let $b'$ be the intersection of the line $dr$ and the line $l_2$, $c'$ be the intersection of $dr$ and $l_3$, and $a'$ be the intersection of $b'p$ and $l_1$. In the space the

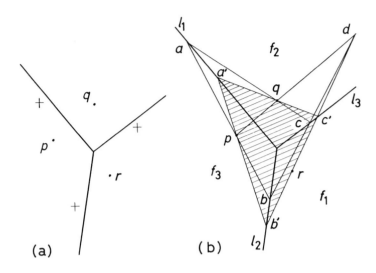

**Fig. 5.6.** Simplest example of a uniquely solvable figure-construction problem.

point $d$ is both on the line $pq$ and on the face $f_1$, and consequently the plane determined by the two lines $pq$ and $dr$ passes through the three points $p$, $q$, and $r$, and this plane cuts the three edges corresponding to $l_1$, $l_2$, $l_3$ at $a'$, $b'$, $c'$, respectively. Thus, the triangle $a'b'c'$ is the intersection of the corner and the plane passing through $p$, $q$, $r$.

It may be interesting to note that the result does not change even if we change the interpretation from a convex corner to a concave corner such as a corner of a room, that is, even if we change all the labels + in the picture (a) to −. This is because the change of the interpretation merely corresponds to the application of the transformation (5.8) with a negative $\gamma$, and hence the collinearity and coplanarity are still preserved.

**Example 5.6.** Another class of figure-construction problems is shown in Fig. 5.7. Line drawings (a), (b), and (c) are hidden-part-eliminated pictures, and all three objects admit exactly four degrees of freedom. Suppose that the rear side of the object represented in (a) consists of three faces, one having the vertices $v_1$, $v_2$, $v_3$, another having $v_3$, $v_4$, $v_5$, and the still other having $v_5$, $v_6$, $v_1$. Then, from Corollary 5.3.1 the pairwise intersections of the three invisible faces are determined uniquely

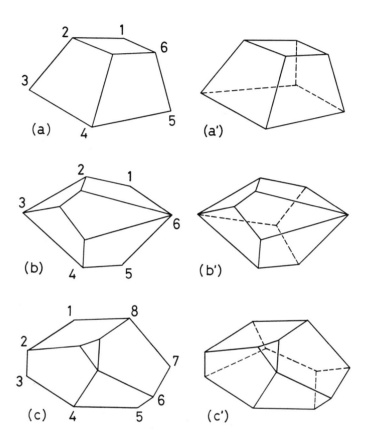

**Fig. 5.7.** Uniqueness of figure construction of the hidden parts of the objects.

on the picture plane, and hence all the hidden lines can be recovered from the visible part, as shown in (a'). Similarly if each rear face of the objects in (b) and (c) has at least three visible vertices and we know them, we can uniquely recover all the hidden lines, as shown in (b') and (c'). The hidden lines in Fig. 5.7 were found by a computer program, which employed Principle 5.1.

Pictures with exactly four degrees of freedom admit another important property, which gives us a simple way to judge the correctness of the pictures. As has been seen in Theorem 3.3, the problem of judging the correctness of a picture can be reduced to a problem of judging the existence of a feasible solution to some linear programming problem. Though efficient methods (such as the simplex method; see Dantzig, 1963) have been developed to deal with linear programming problems, the time required is not negligible, particularly when the complexity of the pictures grows. However, if the pictures have exactly four degrees of freedom, we need not solve the linear programming problem; instead we need to examine only two solutions to (5.1).

   In order to see this, let us first recall that a labeled picture is correct if and only if a solution exists to the associated system of the equations $Aw = 0$ and the inequalities $Bw > 0$ defined by (5.1) and (5.2). Let $Bw < 0$ denote the set of inequalities obtained from $Bw > 0$ by replacing every occurrence of $\geq$ with $\leq$ and $>$ with $<$, and let $Bw = 0$ denote the set of equations obtained by replacing all the inequalities with equalities. Then, we get the next theorem.

**Theorem 5.4.** Let $D$ be a labeled line drawing representing a polyhedral scene correctly, and let $Aw = 0$ and $Bw > 0$ be the associated equations and the inequalities defined by (5.1) and (5.2). If $D$ admits exactly four degrees of freedom in the choice of the scene (i.e., $\rho_V(V) = 4$), any solution $w$ to $Aw = 0$ satisfies $Bw > 0$ or $Bw < 0$ or $Bw = 0$.

**Proof.** For any solution $w = {}^t(z_1 \cdots z_n a_1 b_1 c_1 \cdots a_m b_m c_m)$ to $Aw = 0$, let $P(w)$ be the corresponding configuration composed of the planes in the space; that is,

$$P(w) = \{(x,y,z) \mid a_j x + b_j y + z + c_j = 0 \text{ for some } f_j \in F\}.$$

Because of the same discussion as given in the proofs of Theorems 5.2 and 5.3, it can be shown that, for any solution $w_1$ to $Aw = 0$, $w_2$ is a solution to $Aw = 0$ if and only if $P(w_1)$ is transformed to $P(w_2)$ by a transformation of the form (5.8).

   Recall that, if the line drawing $D$ is a hidden-part-eliminated one, an inequality in $Bw > 0$ is of the form (3.3a), (3.3b), (3.3c), or (3.3d). In the former two cases, the inequality represents the constraint that one of the two vertices $v_\alpha$ and $v_\beta$ having the same $x$ and $y$ coordinates should have a greater $z$ coordinate than the other. In the latter two cases, it represents the constraint that the vertex $v_\alpha$ should be in one of the two half spaces defined by the face $f_j$. Similarly, as we have seen in Chapter 4, $Bw > 0$ driven from a hidden-part-drawn picture also consists of the same two types of constraints as above. These two kinds of constraints are preserved by the transformation (5.8) if $\gamma > 0$, and are reversed if $\gamma < 0$ (note that the spatial orientation is preserved if the determinant of the matrix in (5.8) is positive, and is reversed if negative).

Now, since $D$ is a correct line drawing, there exists a solution, say $w_1$, to $Aw = 0$ and $Bw > 0$. Let $w_2$ be any vector that satisfies $Aw = 0$. Then, $P(w_2)$ is obtained from $P(w_1)$ by some transformation of the form (5.8). According to whether the parameter $\gamma$ in the transformation is positive, zero, or negative, $w_2$ satisfies $Bw_2 > 0$, $Bw_2 = 0$, or $Bw_2 < 0$, respectively. Thus we get the theorem.

From this theorem, we can construct a simple method for finding a solution to $Aw = 0$ and $Bw > 0$. Suppose that there are exactly four degrees of freedom in the choice of the solution to $Aw = 0$. Then, there exist four vertices, say $v_1$, $v_2$, $v_3$, and $v_4$, such that their $z$ values $z_1$, $z_2$, $z_3$, and $z_4$ uniquely specify the solution $w$ to $Aw = 0$ (a method for finding them will be given in the next chapter). If we choose the $z$ values in such a way that the four vertices are coplanar, then the corresponding $w$ satisfies $Bw = 0$. Otherwise, we have these three cases: (1) $w$ satisfies $Bw > 0$, (2) $w$ satisfies $Bw < 0$, or (3) $w$ satisfies neither of them. In case (1), $w$ is a solution we want to get. In case (2), we can get a desired solution from $w$ by the transformation (5.8) with a negative $\gamma$. In case (3), there exists no solution. Hence, we get the following algorithm for finding a solution to $Aw = 0$ and $Bw > 0$.

**Method 5.1 (Recovery of a polyhedral scene from a line drawing with exactly four degrees of freedom).**
Input: a labeled line drawing having four degrees of freedom in the choice of the polyhedral scene. (Without loss of generality, let $\{z_1, z_2, z_3, z_4\}$ form a base of the matroid $(V, \rho_V)$; that is, specification of the values of these four unknowns determines a solution to $Aw = 0$ uniquely.)
Output: a polyhedral scene represented by the line drawing.
Procedure:
Step 1. Assign any real numbers to $z_1$, $z_2$, and $z_3$.
Step 2. Find the intersection of the plane passing through the three vertices $v_\alpha = (x_\alpha, y_\alpha, z_\alpha)$, $\alpha = 1$, 2, 3, and the line that is parallel to the $z$ axis and that passes through the point $(x_4, y_4)$.

Let the intersection be $(x_4, y_4, z_4^{(0)})$.

Step 3. Choose any real numbers $z_4^{(1)}$ and $z_4^{(2)}$ such that $z_4^{(1)} < z_4^{(0)} < z_4^{(2)}$. (Then, the orientation of $(v_1, v_2, v_3, v_4^{(1)})$ is opposite to that of $(v_1, v_2, v_3, v_4^{(2)})$, where $v_4^{(k)} = (x_4, y_4, z_4^{(k)})$, $k = 1, 2$.)

Step 4. If the vector, say $w^{(1)}$, specified by $(z_1, z_2, z_3, z_4^{(1)})$ satisfies $Bw > 0$, then return $w^{(1)}$. If the vector, say $w^{(2)}$, specified by $(z_1, z_2, z_3, z_4^{(2)})$ satisfies $Bw > 0$, then return $w^{(2)}$. Otherwise return ˙false.˙

By this method, we can judge the correctness of the picture $D$ quickly. If it returns ˙false,˙ $D$ is incorrect, and otherwise $D$ is correct.

## 5.4. Axonometric Projection

The line drawings we have considered so far give no quantitative information about the thickness of the objects; they describe qualitative structures of the objects, but do not specify lengths of edges or orientations of faces. There is, however, an exceptional class of engineering line drawings called axonometric drawings. The axonometric drawings are the orthographic projection of objects, and they contain scales in certain principal directions, so that we can read real lengths of edges that are parallel to the scale axes. Thus they specify objects more definitely than usual pictures. In this section we study how many degrees of freedom are left to the objects represented by the axonometric drawings.

Let $(X, Y, Z)$ be a three-dimensional Cartesian coordinate system fixed to an object. This coordinate system is supposed to be chosen in such a way that a large number of the edges of the object are parallel to the coordinate axes. Let $e_X$, $e_Y$, and $e_Z$ denote the unit vectors along the $X$, $Y$, and $Z$ axes, respectively.

As before, we consider another Cartesian coordinate system, say $(x, y, z)$, whose $x$-$y$ plane is regarded to be a picture plane. The object and the unit vectors $e_X$, $e_Y$, $e_Z$ are projected orthographically on this plane, as shown in Fig. 5.8. Contrary to the $(X, Y, Z)$ coordinate system, the $(x, y, z)$ coordinate system is chosen in general position with respect to the object so that no accidental alignment occurs in the picture plane. The projection of the object together with that of the unit vectors $e_X$, $e_Y$, $e_Z$ is called an *axonometric drawing* of the object.

Let $l_X$, $l_Y$, $l_Z$ be the projection on the $x$-$y$ plane of the unit vectors $e_X$, $e_Y$, $e_Z$, respectively. Since $l_X$ is the image of the unit vector, $|l_X|$

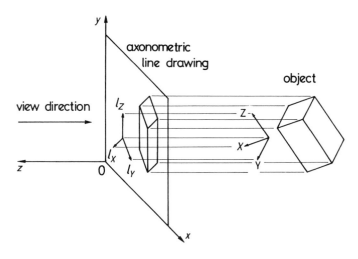

**Fig. 5.8.** Axonometric projection.

denotes the ratio of the projected length to the real length (where $|l|$ denotes the length of the vector $l$). This ratio is common to all edges that are parallel to the $X$ axis in the space. Similarly, $|l_Y|$ and $|l_Z|$ denote the ratios of the projected lengths to the real lengths of edges that are parallel to the $Y$ axis and the $Z$ axis, respectively. Moreover, since we have assumed that the $(x,y,z)$ coordinate system is in general position, we can easily find edges that are parallel to the coordinate axes:

**Heuristic 5.1.** If a line segment is parallel to the projected axis $l_X$ [resp. $l_Y$ or $l_Z$], then the corresponding edge in the scene is also parallel to the $X$ axis [resp. the $Y$ axis or the $Z$ axis].

Using this heuristic together with ratios $|l_X|$, $|l_Y|$, $|l_Z|$, we can determine real lengths of edges that are parallel to the coordinate axes. For example, if there is a line segment in a picture that is parallel to $l_X$ and of length $t$, then the line segment is an image of an edge that is parallel to the $X$ axis and of length $t/|l_X|$.

In many practical line drawings, $l_X$, $l_Y$, $l_Z$ are not drawn explicitly. This is because, first, for engineering objects such as mechanical parts and buildings, the directions of the vectors $l_X$, $l_Y$, $l_Z$ can often be found easily as the directions of the three- prevailing groups of mutually parallel edges, and second, once the directions of $l_X$, $l_Y$, $l_Z$ (on the picture plane) are found, the ratios $| l_X |$, $| l_Y |$, $| l_Z |$ can be calculated in a systematic manner (see, for example, Kanatani, 1986). However, we assume for simplicity that the three vectors $l_X$, $l_Y$, $l_Z$ are given explicitly in the line drawing.

Note that from the vector $l_X$ in the picture we can determine the direction of the corresponding spatial vector $e_X$ up to the mirror-image reversal with respect to a mirror parallel to the $x$-$y$ plane. The ambiguity due to the mirror-image reversal may be removed if we analyze the line drawing globally; in particular, important information is given by the distinction between solid lines (visible edges) and broken lines (invisible edges) at junctions having three lines that are respectively parallel to $l_X$, $l_Y$, and $l_Z$ (Kanatani, 1986). In what follows, however, we simply assume that all of the three spatial vectors $e_X$, $e_Y$, $e_Z$ face toward the viewer. Hence, given $l_X$, $l_Y$, $l_Z$, we can determine the directions of $e_X$, $e_Y$, $e_Z$ uniquely. Thus, if all the edges are connected and are parallel to $e_X$, $e_Y$, or $e_Z$, then the spatial structure of the edges (i.e., the skeleton of the object) can be determined uniquely from its axonometric drawing.

Let $D$ be a labeled axonometric line drawing and $S = (V,F,R,T)$ be a spatial structure associated with $D$. As we have seen, the associated three-dimensional structure should satisfy (5.1). Also, the axonometric axes give additional constraints to the three-dimensional structure in the following way.

Let $E_X$, $E_Y$, and $E_Z$ be the sets of edges that are parallel to the $X$ axis, the $Y$ axis, and the $Z$ axis, respectively. Suppose that each edge in $E_X$, $E_Y$, $E_Z$ is represented by an ordered pair of the terminal vertices in which the order coincides with the positive direction of the associated axis. Hence, for example, "$(v_\alpha, v_\beta) \in E_X$" implies that there is an edge connecting $v_\alpha$ with $v_\beta$ and that the direction from $v_\alpha$ to $v_\beta$ coincides with the positive direction of the $X$ axis.

Now suppose that $(v_\alpha, v_\beta)$ is in $E_X$. Recall that the ratio of the length of the edge to the length of its image is $1/| l_X |$, which implies that if a point moves along the image of the edge in the $l_X$ direction by distance $| l_X |$, then the corresponding spatial point moving along the edge itself increases its $z$ coordinate by $\sqrt{1 - | l_X |^2}$. Thus we get

$$z_\beta - z_\alpha = \frac{\sqrt{1 - | l_X |^2} \sqrt{(x_\beta - x_\alpha)^2 + (y_\beta - y_\alpha)^2}}{| l_X |}. \qquad (5.9a)$$

The right hand side of (5.9a) is a constant determined by the line drawing $D$, and hence (5.9a) is linear in the unknowns $z_\alpha$ and $z_\beta$. In a similar way, for an element $(v_\alpha, v_\beta)$ in $E_Y$ we get

$$z_\beta - z_\alpha = \frac{\sqrt{1 - |l_Y|^2}\sqrt{(x_\beta - x_\alpha)^2 + (y_\beta - y_\alpha)^2}}{|l_Y|}, \tag{5.9b}$$

and for an element $(v_\alpha, v_\beta)$ in $E_Z$ we get

$$z_\beta - z_\alpha = \frac{\sqrt{1 - |l_Z|^2}\sqrt{(x_\beta - x_\alpha)^2 + (y_\beta - y_\alpha)^2}}{|l_Z|}. \tag{5.9c}$$

Collecting all the equations of the above three types (i.e., (5.9a), (5.9b), and (5.9c)), we get a system of linear equations,

$$Cw = d, \tag{5.10}$$

where $w$ is the unknown vector $w = {}^t(z_1 \cdots z_n a_1 b_1 c_1 \cdots a_m b_m c_m)$, $C$ is a constant matrix of size $|E_X \cup E_Y \cup E_Z| \times (n+3m)$, and $d$ is a $|E_X \cup E_Y \cup E_Z|$ – dimensional constant vector.

Thus, the object represented by the axonometric drawing $D$ is constrained by (5.1) and (5.10). Hence, we have

$$n + 3m - \mathrm{rank}(\{A\} \cup \{C\})$$

degrees of freedom in choosing the object and locating it in the space.

For any subset $X$ of the set of the unknowns $H = \{z_1, \ldots, z_n, a_1, b_1, c_1, \ldots, a_m, b_m, c_m\}$, let us define a function $\sigma_H(X)$ by

$$\sigma_H(X) = \mathrm{rank}(\{A\} \cup \{C\} \cup \{e_i \mid u_i \in X\}) - \mathrm{rank}(\{A\} \cup \{C\}), \tag{5.11}$$

where $e_i$ denotes an $(n+3m)$-dimensional vector whose $i$th component is 1 and the other components are 0's. Then, by the same discussion as in Sections 5.1 and 5.2, we see that $(H, \sigma_H)$ is a matroid and $\sigma_H(X)$ is the maximum cardinality of a subset $Y$ of $X$ such that if we give values to the unknowns in $Y$ arbitrarily, the system consisting of (5.1) and (5.10) still admits a solution. In other words, we can remove $\sigma_H(X)$ degrees of freedom in the choice of the object by selecting appropriate values for the unknowns in $X$. Thus, the matroid $(H, \sigma_H)$ represents how the degrees of freedom in the

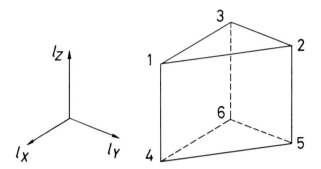

**Fig. 5.9.** Axonometric line drawing representing a unique shape.

choice of the object are distributed in the set $H$ of the unknowns.    We call $\sigma_H(X)$ the *degrees of freedom* of the set $X$.

Since one degree of freedom is due to the translation along the $z$ axis, the object shape itself admits $\sigma_H(H)-1$ degrees of freedom.    That is, $\sigma_H(H)-1$ additional data (such as lengths of edges and angles between faces) are required in order to specify the shape of the object uniquely.

**Example 5.7.**    Consider the axonometric line drawing $D$ shown in Fig. 5.9 together with the spatial structure

$V = \{v_1, \ldots, v_6\}$ ,
$F = \{f_1, \ldots, f_5\}$ ,
$R = \{(v_1,f_1), (v_2,f_1), (v_3,f_1), (v_1,f_2), (v_2,f_2), (v_4,f_2),$
$\quad\quad (v_5,f_2), (v_1,f_3), (v_3,f_3), (v_4,f_3), (v_6,f_3), (v_2,f_4),$
$\quad\quad (v_3,f_4), (v_5,f_4), (v_6,f_4), (v_4,f_5), (v_5,f_5), (v_6,f_5)\}$ ,
$E_X = \{(v_3,v_1), (v_6,v_4)\}$ ,
$E_Y = \{(v_3,v_2), (v_6,v_5)\}$ ,
$E_Z = \{(v_4,v_1), (v_5,v_2), (v_6,v_3)\}$ .

In the figure, the vertex $v_\alpha$ ($\alpha = 1, \ldots, 6$) is denoted by the number $\alpha$. The face $f_1$ corresponds to the top face of the object, $f_2$ the front face, $f_3$ the left rear face, $f_4$ the right rear face, and $f_5$ the bottom face. From this line drawing, we get the system of linear equations (5.1) and (5.10), whose coefficient matrices satisfy rank( $\{A\} \cup \{C\}$ ) = 20. Hence

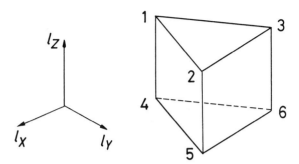

**Fig. 5.10.** Axonometric line drawing admitting two degrees of freedom.

$\sigma_H(H) - 1 = 6 + 3 \times 5 - 20 - 1 = 0$;

that is, the shape is uniquely represented by this picture.

This result is reasonable for the following reason. First, note that, for any edge in $E_X \cup E_Y \cup E_Z$, if we specify the spatial position of one terminal vertex, then the position of the other terminal vertex is determined uniquely. Second, note that the graph composed of the node set $V$ and the arc set $E_X \cup E_Y \cup E_Z$ is connected. Therefore, if we specify the position of any one vertex of the object (this corresponds to the removal of the degree of freedom of the translation along the $z$ axis), then the whole structure is uniquely located in a three-dimensional space, which coincides with our result $\sigma_H(H) - 1 = 0$.

**Example 5.8.** Next consider the line drawing $D$ shown in Fig. 5.10, where $V$, $F$, $R$, $E_Z$ are the same as those in Example 5.7, but $E_X = \phi$ and $E_Y = \phi$ (note that the object has the same topological structure as that in Fig. 5.9, but unlike Fig. 5.9 no line segment is parallel to $l_X$ or $l_Y$). The system consisting of (5.1) and (5.10) satisfies rank( $\{A\} \cup \{C\}$ ) = 18, and hence we get

$\sigma_H(H) - 1 = 6 + 3 \times 5 - 18 - 1 = 2$;

that is, two more data are necessary to specify the shape uniquely. This can be understood in the following way. Since the three side edges are parallel to the $Z$ axis, the three side faces are all parallel to the $Z$

axis. The three edges on the top face are respectively parallel to the
three edges on the bottom face, and consequently the top face is parallel
to the bottom face. However, no edge is parallel to the $X$ axis or the $Y$
axis, and hence there is no information about the angles between the top
face and the side faces. The gradient of the top face (or, in other words,
the direction of the normal to the top face) has two degrees of freedom,
and once these degrees of freedom are removed, the shape is determined
uniquely. This is what our result $\sigma_H(H) - 1 = 2$ means.

For example, $U = \{z_1, z_2, z_3\}$ is a base of the matroid $(H, \sigma_H)$. Hence,
if we specify values of $z_1$, $z_2$, $z_3$, then the shape and the position is
determined. Giving the first value, say the value of $z_1$, corresponds to the
removal of the degree of freedom of the translation along the $z$ axis, and
consequently we can give any value to $z_1$ without affecting the shape of the
object. We put $z_1 = 0$. Then, the shape of the object can be specified by
selecting appropriate values for $z_2$ and $z_3$.

# 6. COMBINATORIAL STRUCTURES OF LINE DRAWINGS

We have presented the two modules, the module for finding candidates for spatial interpretations of a line drawing, and the module for discriminating between correct and incorrect interpretations. Indeed, they constitute a theoretical solution to the problem of line drawing interpretation. In a practical sense, however, they alone cannot enable a machine to interpret line drawings as human beings do, because the algebraic treatment of pictures in the second module is too strict to mimic flexible human perception; some pictures are judged to be incorrect only because they contain slight errors in the vertex positions. In order to overcome this difficulty we shall in this and the succeeding two chapters present the third module, which makes a machine more flexible in that it can extract the three-dimensional structures even if the pictures contain vertex position errors and hence are incorrect in a strict sense. For this purpose we study in this chapter some combinatorial structures of line drawings that will play main roles in the third module.

## 6.1. Difficulties in the Algebraic Approach

Using Theorem 3.3 (or Theorem 4.1 in the case of hidden-part-drawn pictures), we can judge whether an assignment of labels to a picture is a correct interpretation of the picture or not. Indeed the theorem represents a necessary and sufficient condition for a picture to be correct in terms of linear algebra. However, this algebraic condition is too sensitive to numerical errors in the following two points.

First, the system of equations (5.1) is not necessarily linearly independent. When it is linearly dependent, even small errors in numerical computation cause the rank of $A$, the coefficient matrix of (5.1), to change, so that it is not easy to judge the existence of a solution to (5.1) and (5.2) in a stable manner. Therefore, before applying the linear programming method, we have to check linear independence of the matrix $A$; if it is not linearly independent, redundant equations should be deleted from the system of equations (5.1) in order to make it independent.

Second, even if the system of equations (5.1) is linearly independent, the theorem is too strict to be applied to practical data, which usually contain numerical errors due to digitization, etc.

The superstrictness of the theorem can be illustrated by the typical

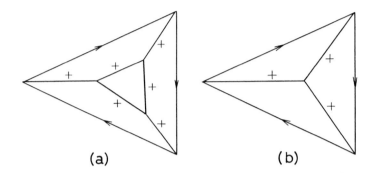

**Fig. 6.1.** Sensitivity of correctness to vertex positions: the correctness of picture (a) is sensitive to vertex-position errors, whereas that of (b) is not.

example shown in Fig. 6.1(a). This labeled line drawing corresponds to the interpretation of the picture as a top view of a truncated pyramid. In a strict sense, however, it does not represent any polyhedron; indeed, if it were a truncated pyramid, the three quadrilateral faces would have a common point of intersection in the three-dimensional space (when they were extended), and hence the three lines of pairwise intersections should meet at a common point on the picture plane, but they do not, as has been shown in Fig. 1.3. This implies that there is no solution to the system consisting of (3.2) and (3.4) associated with this picture. Thus, Theorem 3.3 judges that the picture is incorrect.

It should be noted that this difficulty is not the same as the first point. Indeed the system of equations (5.1) associated with the line drawing in Fig. 6.1(a) is linearly independent, as will be shown later (see Example 6.1).

What is important is that though the judgment based on Theorem 3.3 is correct, it is quite different from what we want. Line drawings drawn by human beings or extracted from light intensity images almost always contain vertex position errors, and in order to extract three-dimensional structures from these line drawings, a machine should be tolerant of such inevitable errors. Indeed the labeling scheme discussed in Chapter 2 is much tolerant of quantitative errors; it treats line drawings in a symbolic manner. However, recall that the labeling scheme alone is not enough for the picture interpretation, because pictures of impossible objects often admit consistent assignments of the labels (recall the pictures (e) and (f) in Fig. 2.15). Thus, we have to search for some intelligent mechanism in order to make a machine flexible in the sense that, like human beings, it can accept pictures even if they contain errors in their vertex positions.

## 6.2. Generically Reconstructible Incidence Structures

We have seen that a picture of a truncated pyramid like Fig. 6.1(a) becomes incorrect when vertices (and consequently the lines incident to them) are moved slightly on the picture plane. However, not all pictures are so sensitive to the vertex positions. A picture of a tetrahedron shown in Fig. 6.1(b), for example, represents a polyhedral object correctly even if the vertex positions are perturbed. Thus, some pictures are sensitive to vertex position errors, while others are not. Here we shall distinguish between these two kinds of pictures more precisely. For this purpose we concentrate our attention upon the equations (5.1), and introduce some new concepts.

Let $D$ be a labeled line drawing, and let $S = (V,F,R,T)$ be its spatial structure. Recall that an element of $R$ is of the form $(v_\alpha, f_j)$, representing the constraint that the vertex $v_\alpha$ should be on the face $f_j$. In what follows we call elements of $R$ *incidence pairs*, and the triple $I = (V,F,R)$ composed of the first three constituents of $S$ the *incidence structure* associated with the line drawing $D$. In a more formal manner, we can say that a triple $I = (V,F,R)$ is an incidence structure, if $V$ and $F$ are mutually disjoint finite sets and $R$ is a subset of $V \times F$, where $V \times F$ denotes the set of all ordered pairs whose first elements are taken from $V$ and second elements from $F$. The incidence structure $I = (V,F,R)$ can also be regarded as a bipartite graph having the two node sets $V$ and $F$ and the arc set $R$. If $(v,f) \in R$, we say that "the vertex $v$ is on the face $f$" and "the face $f$ has the vertex $v$."

For an incidence structure $I = (V,F,R)$, we use the following notation. For any subset $X$ of $V$, let $F(X)$ be the set of faces that has at least one vertex in $X$, and let $R(X)$ be the set of incidence pairs whose first components belong to $X$; that is,

$$F(X) = \{f \mid (v,f) \in R, \text{ for some } v \in X\} \quad (X \subseteq V),$$
$$R(X) = \{(v,f) \mid (v,f) \in R \text{ and } v \in X\} \quad (X \subseteq V).$$

Similarly, for any subset $X$ of $F$, let $V(X)$ be the set of vertices that are on at least one face in $X$, and let $R(X)$ be the set of incidence pairs whose second components belong to $X$; that is,

$$V(X) = \{v \mid (v,f) \in R \text{ for some } f \in X\} \quad (X \subseteq F),$$
$$R(X) = \{(v,f) \mid (v,f) \in R \text{ and } f \in X\} \quad (X \subseteq F).$$

Furthermore, for any subset $X$ of $R$, let $V(X)$ and $F(X)$ be the set of vertices and that of faces, respectively, that appear in some elements of $X$; that is,

$$V(X) = \{v \mid (v,f) \in X\} \quad (X \subseteq R),$$
$$F(X) = \{f \mid (v,f) \in X\} \quad (X \subseteq R).$$

The above notation may seem ambiguous. Indeed $V(X)$, for example, is used both for $X \subseteq F$ and for $X \subseteq R$. In what follows, however, we use the notation only when we can say from the context which it means; the notation can save many symbols.

A triple $I' = (V',F',R')$ is called a *substructure* of the incidence structure $I = (V,F,R)$ if $V' \subseteq V$, $F' \subseteq F$, and $R' \subseteq R \cap (V' \times F')$. For any subsets $X \subseteq V$, $Y \subseteq F$, and $Z \subseteq R$, the substructures $(X,F(X),R(X))$, $(V(Y),Y,R(Y))$, and $(V(Z),F(Z),Z)$ are called the substructures *induced by* $X$, $Y$, and $Z$, respectively.

Though the system of the equations (5.1) was originally introduced for a polyhedral scene, it represents the constraints placed by the incidence structure $I$, that is, the constraints placed by which vertices should be on which planes. Other properties of the polyhedral scene (such as properties of edges and thickness of objects) are all represented by the inequalities (5.2). Hence, it seems natural to interpret a solution to (5.1) not as a polyhedral scene itself but as a collection of planes in the space. That is, with any solution $w = {}^t(z_1 \cdots z_n a_1 b_1 c_1 \cdots a_m b_m c_m)$ to (5.1), we associate the collection, say $P(w)$, of the planes defined by

$$P(w) = \{(x,y,z) \mid a_j x + b_j y + z + c_j = 0 \text{ for some } f_j \in F\}. \tag{6.1}$$

A solution $w = {}^t(z_1 \cdots z_n a_1 b_1 c_1 \cdots a_m b_m c_m)$ to (5.1) is said to be *nondegenerate* if $a_j \neq a_k$ or $b_j \neq b_k$ or $c_j \neq c_k$ holds for any $j$ and $k$ $(1 \leq j < k \leq m)$, and *degenerate* otherwise. In other words, $w$ is nondegenerate if and only if no two distinct elements of $F$ correspond to the same plane in $P(w)$. The system of equations (5.1) always has a degenerate solution; for example, the $(n+3m)$-dimensional null vector $w =$ $^t(0 \cdots 0)$ is a solution to (5.1). On the other hand, the system does not necessarily have a nondegenerate solution.

Whether or not the system of equations (5.1) admits a nondegenerate solution depends on the vertex positions $(x_1, y_1), \ldots, (x_n, y_n)$, and the incidence structure $I = (V, F, R)$ because they define the system (recall that $A$, the coefficient matrix of (5.1), contains $x_1, y_1, \ldots, x_n, y_n$ as its components). For example, it seems at least intuitively obvious that the picture of a tetrahedron in Fig. 6.1(b) admits a nondegenerate solution, whereas any solution is degenerate for the picture of an "impossible truncated pyramid" in Fig. 6.1(a); this picture has a nondegenerate solution only when it is drawn in the way that the three edges have a common point of intersection.

What is important is that if the picture is sensitive to vertex positions, the associated system of equations (5.1) has nondegenerate solution only when the vertices are drawn in some special position. From this observation we can introduce the following definition.

The $n$ points $(x_1, y_1), \ldots, (x_n, y_n)$ are said to be *in generic position* if the $2n$ real numbers $x_1, y_1, \ldots, x_n, y_n$ are algebraically independent over the rational field. By the definition of the algebraic independence, if the points are in generic position, any polynomial of $x_1, y_1, \ldots, x_n, y_n$ with coefficients being rational numbers is 0 if and only if it is identically 0 when we consider $x_1, y_1, \ldots, x_n, y_n$ as indeterminate symbols. Roughly speaking, therefore, the vertices being in generic position means that there is no special dependence among the vertex positions; for example, no three points are on a common straight line or no three lines meet at a common point. In practical situations the vertices can almost always be regarded as being in generic position because any special dependence, if exists, will be lost by digitization errors, computation errors, and so on.

In particular, if the vertices are in generic position, a subdeterminant of the coefficient matrix $A$ in (5.1) does not vanish unless it is identically 0 when $x_1, y_1, \ldots, x_n, y_n$ are considered as indeterminate symbols, and hence the existence of nondegenerate solutions depends on $I$ only. Thus, we can introduce the next definition.

The incidence structure $I = (V, F, R)$ is said to be *generically reconstructible* if and only if the system of the equations (5.1) has a nondegenerate solution when the vertices are in generic position. In other words, the incidence structure $I$ is generically reconstructible if and only if for any picture whose incidence structure is $I$ and whose vertices are in generic position, the associated system of equations (5.1) admits a solution $w$ such that the planar surfaces corresponding to elements of $F$ are mutually distinct in the configuration $P(w)$. Therefore, if $I$ is generically reconstructible, the correctness of the picture is not affected by small errors in vertex positions. Note, however, that being generically reconstructible does not imply that the corresponding picture represents a polyhedral scene, because the generic reconstructibility depends only on (5.1) whereas the correctness of the picture depends on both (5.1) and (5.2).

Now we can state the following theorems, which will play the most important role in the third module.

**Theorem 6.1 (Linear independence of the equations (5.1)).** Let $D$ be a labeled line drawing whose vertices are in generic position, and let $I = (V,F,R)$ be its incidence structure. Then, the equations (5.1) associated with $D$ are linearly independent if and only if, for any nonempty subset $X$ of $R$,

$$| V(X) | + 3 | F(X) | \geq | X | + 3. \qquad (6.2)$$

**Theorem 6.2 (Recognition of the generic reconstructibility).** For any incidence structure $I = (V,F,R)$, the following three statements are equivalent.
(1) $I$ is generically reconstructible.
(2) For any subset $X$ of $F$ such that $| X | \geq 2$,

$$| V(X) | + 3 | X | \geq | R(X) | + 4. \qquad (6.3)$$

(3) For any subset $X$ of $R$ such that $| F(X) | \geq 2$,

$$| V(X) | + 3 | F(X) | \geq | X | + 4. \qquad (6.4)$$

**Corollary 6.2.1.** Let $D$ be a labeled line drawing, and let $I$ be the associated incidence structure. If the vertices of $D$ are in generic position and $I$ is generically reconstructible, the equations (5.1) associated with $D$ are linearly independent.

Theorem 6.2 and Corollary 6.2.1 were first conjectured by Sugihara and proved by him for special cases, including pictures of trihedral objects and pictures of convex objects (Sugihara, 1979c, 1984c). Quite recently they were proved completely by Whiteley (1984a). The proofs will be given in the next section.

The important point of the theorems is that both the linear independence and the generic reconstructibility can be recognized by integer calculation only.

**Example 6.1.** Let us consider the labeled line drawing in Fig. 6.1(a) again. If we regard it as a natural picture (i.e., a picture representing only visible part of the object), the object has six vertices and four faces: $|V| = 6$ and $|F| = 4$. Since the three faces are quadrilateral and the other is triangular, there are altogether 15 $(= 3 \times 4 + 1 \times 3)$ incidence pairs: $|R| = 15$. Therefore, substituting $X = F$ in the inequality (6.3), we see that the left hand side amounts to $|V| + 3|F| = 6 + 3 \times 4 = 18$, whereas the right hand side to $|R| + 4 = 15 + 4 = 19$, falsifying the inequality. Hence, from Theorem 6.2 the incidence structure associated with this picture is not generically reconstructible, and consequently this picture does not represent a polyhedral scene when the vertices are in generic position.

However, the incidence structure satisfies the inequality (6.2) in Theorem 6.1, and hence the equations (5.1) are linearly independent when the vertices are in generic position. This shows that the two difficulties discussed in Section 6.1 are not equivalent.

In the above counting we do not consider the background plane corresponding to the surrounding region in the picture. Even if the background plane and the vertices on it are added to the incidence structure, it is still generically unreconstructible. We can see this from Theorem 6.2, because the inequality (6.3) is falsified if we adopt as $X$ the subset consisting of the four visible faces of the truncated pyramid.

The generic unreconstructibleness can be seen also when we regard the picture as a hidden-part-drawn one (i.e., when we count the invisible face forming the base triangle of the truncated pyramid).

On the other hand, the object represented in Fig. 6.1(b) has four visible vertices and three visible faces, which are all triangular, and hence has 9 $(= 3 \times 3)$ incidence pairs. Putting $X = F$, the left hand side of the inequality (6.3) equals $|V| + 3|F| = 4 + 3 \times 3 = 13$ and the right hand side also equals $|R| + 4 = 9 + 4 = 13$. Thus, the inequality (6.3) is satisfied. In a similar manner we can see easily that the inequality holds for any two-element subset $X$ of $F$. Hence the incidence structure associated with the picture in Fig. 6.1(b) is generically reconstructible.

From the viewpoint of time complexity, Theorem 6.2 in its original form is not very practical. If we check statement (2) in the theorem in a straightforward manner, we have to check the inequality (6.3) for almost all subsets of the face set $F$; it will require $O(2^m)$ time in the worst case, where $m$ denotes the number of the faces. The check of statement (3) also requires $O(2^{|R|})$ time. Fortunately, however, the check can be done in $O(|R|^2)$ if we modify the theorem. An efficient algorithm will be given in Chapter 8.


**6.3. Proofs of the Main Theorems**

Here we shall prove Theorems 6.1 and 6.2. The proofs below are due to Whiteley (1984a).

Let $M = \{1,2,\ldots,p\}$ and $N = \{1,2,\ldots,q\}$, respectively, be the sets of the first $p$ and the first $q$ natural numbers, and let $W$ be a subset of $M \times N$. The triple $G = (M,N,W)$ can be regarded as a *bipartite graph* having the *left node* set $M$, the *right node* set $N$, and the *arc* set $W$. We call an element $i$ of $M$ the $i$th left node and an element $j$ of $N$ the $j$th right node. An element $(i,j)$ of $W$ is called the arc connecting the $i$th left node with the $j$th right node, and $i$ and $j$ are called the left terminal node and the right terminal node, respectively, of the arc $(i,j)$. For any subset $M'$ of $M$, let $N(M')$ denote the set of right nodes that are connected to some elements of $M'$; that is,

$$N(M') = \{j \mid (i,j) \in W \text{ for some } i \in M'\} \quad (M' \subseteq M).$$

Then, the triple $(M',N(M'),W \cap (M' \times N(M')))$ also forms a bipartite graph, which we call the *subgraph of $G$ induced by* the left node set $M'$.

A subset $W'$ of $W$ is called a *matching* of $G = (M,N,W)$ if the terminal nodes of arcs in $W'$ are all distinct. A matching $W'$ of $G$ is said to be *complete* if any element of $M$ is a terminal node of some arc in $W'$. A subset $M'$ of $M$ is said to *have a complete matching* if the subgraph induced by $M'$ has a complete matching.

Let $G = (M,N,W)$ be a bipartite graph having $p$ left nodes and $q$ right nodes, and let $X$ be a $p$ by $q$ matrix of indeterminates $x_{ij}$ $(1 \leq i \leq p,$

$1 \leqq j \leqq q$ ). We define the $p$ by $q$ matrix $\Theta(G,X)$ with entities $\theta_{ij}$ by

$\theta_{ij} = x_{ij}$ if $(i,j) \in W$,
$\theta_{ij} = 0$ otherwise.

The next proposition is a well-known theorem.

**Proposition 6.1.** Let $G = (M,N,W)$ be a bipartite graph. For any subset $M'$ of $M$, the following three statements are equivalent.
(1) $M'$ has a complete matching.
(2) Any subset $Z$ of $M'$ satisfies $|Z| \leqq |N(Z)|$.
(3) The rows of $\Theta(G,X)$ corresponding to the elements of $M'$ are linearly independent.

The equivalence of (1) and (2) was proved by Hall (1935), and the equivalence of (1) and (3) was proved by Edmonds (1967) and Mirsky and Perfect (1967) (see also Mirsky, 1971).

For a bipartite graph $G = (M,N,W)$ having $p$ left nodes and $q$ right nodes and a $p$ by $q$ matrix $X$ of indeterminates, we consider the following system of linear equations:

$$\Theta(G,X)u = 0, \tag{6.5}$$

where $u$ is a $q$-dimensional unknown vector. For any solutions $u_1$ and $u_2$ to (6.5), $\alpha u_1 + \beta u_2$ also is a solution to (6.5). Thus the solutions to (6.5) form a linear space of the dimension $q$-rank$(\Theta(G,X))$; the space is called the *kernel* of $\Theta(G,X)$ and its dimension the *nullity* of $\Theta(G,X)$. If the nullity equals $k$, we can choose $k$ out of $q$ entities of the unknown vector $u$ in such a way that any entity of the solution vector to (6.5) can be expressed as a linear combination of these $k$ entities; the $k$-element subset of $N$ corresponding to these $k$ entities is said to *span* the kernel.

Then, we get the next proposition.

**Proposition 6.2.** For a bipartite graph $G = (M,N,W)$ and a nonnegative integer $k$, the following two statements are equivalent.
(1) $|M| = |N| - k$ and, for any nonempty subset $M'$ of $M$, $|M'| \leqq |N(M')| - k$.
(2) The nullity of $\Theta(G,X)$ is $k$ and, for any $k$-element subset $N'$ of $N$, $N'$ spans the kernel of $\Theta(G,X)$.

**Proof.** Assume that statement (1) is true. Then, any subset $M'$ of $M$ obviously satisfies $|M'| \leq |N(M')|$, and from Proposition 6.1 the rows of $\Theta(G,X)$ are linearly independent. Thus, the nullity of $\Theta(G,X)$ equals $|N| - \text{rank}(\Theta(G,X)) = |N| - |M| = k$. Next, for any $k$-element subset $N' = \{j_1, j_2, \ldots, j_k\}$ of $N$, let $G^* = (M^*, N^*, W^*)$ be the bipartite graph obtained by adding to $G$ $k$ new left nodes $p+i$, $i = 1, \ldots, k$ (where $p = |M|$), and $k$ new arcs $(p+i, j_i)$, $i = 1, 2, \ldots, k$; that is,

$M^* = M \cup \{p+1, \ldots, p+k\}$,

$N^* = N$,

$W^* = W \cup \{(p+1, j_1), \ldots, (p+k, j_k)\}$.

Then, $|M^*| = |N^*|$ and, for any subset $M'$ of $M^*$, $|M'| \leq |N^*(M')|$. Hence from Proposition 6.1 the rows of $\Theta(G^*, X^*)$ are linearly independent, where $X^*$ is a $p+k$ by $p+k$ matrix of indeterminates. Since the $k$ rows corresponding to the added $k$ left nodes have nonzero entities only on the $k$ columns corresponding to elements of $N'$, $N'$ spans the kernel.

Conversely, assume that statement (2) is true. Suppose, contrary to the theorem, that there exists a nonempty subset $M'$ of $M$ such that $|M'| > |N(M')| - k$; let $M'$ be minimal with this property. Then, we get $|M'| = |N(M')| - (k - l)$ for some $l > 0$. Because of the minimalness of $M'$, any proper nonempty subset $Z$ of $M'$ satisfies $|Z| \leq |N(Z)| - k \leq |N(Z)| - (k - l)$. Hence, from the former half of the proof, the nullity of $\Theta(G', X')$ is $k - l$, where $G'$ is the subgraph of $G$ induced by $M'$ and $X'$ is the submatrix of $X$ composed of the $|M'|$ rows corresponding to $M'$ and the $|N(M')|$ columns corresponding to $N(M')$. Thus, $N(M')$ spans the kernel of $\Theta(G', X')$, which is of dimension $k - l$. Since $\Theta(G', X')$ is a subgraph of $\Theta(G, X)$, $N(M')$ spans an at most $(k-l)$-dimensional subspace of the kernel of $\Theta(G, X)$. However, $N(M')$ has at least $k-l+1$ elements. Hence, any $k$-element subset of $N$ containing $N(M')$ can span at most $(k-1)$-dimensional subspace of the kernel of $\Theta(G, X)$. This contradicts the assumption.

A bipartite graph is said to be *of degree* $k+1$ if every left node is connected with exactly $k+1$ right nodes. Let $M = \{1, 2, \ldots, p\}$ and $N = \{1, 2, \ldots, q\}$, and let $G = (M, N, W)$ be a bipartite graph of degree $k+1$. Note that in our notation the left nodes and the right nodes are ordered. For an element $(i, j)$ of $W$, we define $\text{sign}(i, j)$ to be $(-1)^{l-1}$ if the right node $j$ is the $l$th node connected with the left node $i$. Let $Y$ be a $k$ by $q$ matrix

With entities $y_{ij}$ such that $y_{k1} = y_{k2} = \cdots = y_{kq} = 1$ and the other entities are distinct indeterminates, and, for any $(i,j) \in W$, let $Y(i/j)$ denote the $k$ by $k$ matrix composed of the columns of $Y$ corresponding to the right nodes in $N(\{i\})$ except the right node $j$. Now, we define the $p$ by $q$ matrix $\Phi(G,Y)$ with entities $\varphi_{ij}$ by

$\varphi_{ij} = \text{sign}(i,j)\det(Y(i/j))$ if $(i,j) \in W$,

$\varphi_{ij} = 0$ otherwise.

Then, we get the next proposition.

**Proposition 6.3.** Let $G = (M,N,W)$ be a degree $k+1$ bipartite graph having $p$ left nodes and $q$ right nodes, and let $Y$ be a $k$ by $q$ matrix whose last row is $(1 \cdots 1)$ and whose other rows are composed of indeterminate entities. For any subset $M'$ of $M$, the following two statements are equivalent.
(1) For any nonempty subset $Z$ of $M'$, $|Z| \leq |N(Z)| - k$.
(2) The rows of $\Phi(G,Y)$ corresponding to $M'$ are linearly independent.

**Proof.** Note that whether statement (1) and/or (2) is true depends only on the subgraph induced by $M'$; it does not depend on the other part of the underlying bipartite graph. Therefore, without loss of generality we can assume that the left node set of $G$ has been augmented so that, for any $k+1$ right nodes, there exists the left node that is connected to all of them and to them only; hence $p = \binom{q}{k+1}$.

First we assume that $M'$ satisfies statement (1) and derive statement (2). Since our goal here is to show linear independence of the corresponding rows, it suffices to consider $M'$ that is maximal with the required property. Thus, without loss of generality we assume that $|M'| = |N(M')| - k$. Let $G'$ be the subgraph induced by $M'$, and let us renumber the nodes in $G'$ in such a way that $M' = \{1,2, \ldots, |M'|\}$ and $N(M') = \{1,2, \ldots, |N(M')|\}$. Furthermore, let $X$ be an $|M'|$ by $|N(M')|$ matrix of indeterminates $x_{ij}$. Then, by Proposition 6.2, the nullity of $\Theta(G',X)$ is exactly $k$ (and hence the rows of $\Theta(G',X)$ are linearly independent), and the kernel is spanned by any $k$-element subset of $N(M')$. We choose as a basis for the kernel the rows of a $k$ by $|N(M')|$ matrix $U$ with entities $u_{ij}$ ($i = 1,\ldots,k$; $j = 1,\ldots,|N(M')|$).

Without loss of generality we can choose $(1 \cdots 1)$ as the $k$th row of $U$ in the following way. First, since the row vectors of $U$ span the kernel of $\Theta(G',X)$, any column of $U$ has a nonzero entities in some row. Hence, making

an appropriate linear combination of the rows, we obtain a row whose
entities are all nonzero, and replace some row of $U$ with this new row; let
us put this new row at the bottom (i.e., the $k$th row) of $U$. Next, without
changing the linear independence of the rows of $\Theta(G',X)$, we multiply the
$j$th column of $\Theta(G',X)$ by $u_{kj}$ and the $j$th column of $U$ by $1/u_{kj}$. In what
follows let us denote the resultant two matrices by $\Theta(G',X)$ and $U$,
respectively. It is obvious that thus modified matrix $U$ has $(1 \cdots 1)$ as
the $k$th row and the set of rows of $U$ still form a basis for the kernel of
$\Theta(G',X)$.

Now, let $u_j$ denote the $j$th column of $U$. Then, for any left node $i$ in
$M'$, we have $\sum_j x_{ij} u_j = 0$, where the summation is taken over all right nodes
$j$ connected with the left node $i$. For simplicity, if we assume that the
left node $i$ is connected with the first $k+1$ right nodes $1$, $2$, $\ldots$, $k+1$,
then the equation can be expressed by

$$\left[ u_1 \ u_2 \ \cdots \ u_{k+1} \right] \begin{bmatrix} x_{i1} \\ x_{i2} \\ \cdot \\ \cdot \\ \cdot \\ x_{i,k+1} \end{bmatrix} = 0.$$

In other words,

$$\left[ u_1 \ \cdots \ u_k \right] \begin{bmatrix} x_{i1} \\ \cdot \\ \cdot \\ \cdot \\ x_{ik} \end{bmatrix} = - x_{i,k+1} \left[ u_{k+1} \right].$$

Since the coefficient matrix in the left hand side is nonsingular, by
Cramer's formula we get

$$x_{ij} = \frac{(-1)^{k-j} \det[u_1 \cdots u_{j-1} u_{j+1} \cdots u_{k+1}]}{\det[u_1 \cdots u_k]} x_{i,k+1} \quad (i = 1, \ldots, k).$$

If we put

$$x_{i,k+1} = (-1)^{k+1} \det[u_1 \cdots u_k],$$

then we get

$$x_{ij} = (-1)^{j-1}\det[u_1 \cdots u_{j-1}u_{j+1} \cdots u_{k+1}] \quad (j = 1, \ldots, k).$$

Thus $(x_{i1} \cdots x_{i,k+1} \ 0 \ \cdots \ 0)$, the row of $\Theta(G',X)$, coincides with the corresponding row of the matrix $\Phi(G',X)$, which is a specialization of $\Phi(G',Y)$. Since these rows associated with $M'$ are linearly independent in $\Theta(G',X)$, they remain independent in $\Phi(G',Y)$. The corresponding rows in $\Phi(G,Y)$ can be obtained from the rows of $\Phi(G',Y)$ by inserting $0$'s in some columns; they still remain independent in $\Phi(G,Y)$. Thus we get statement (2).

Conversely, assume that $M'$ satisfies statement (2). For each left node $i$ in $M'$ and each row, say the $l$th row, of $Y$, we have

$$\sum_j y_{lj}(-1)^{j-1}\det(Y(i/j)) = 0,$$

where the summation is taken over all the right nodes connected with the left node $i$. This is because the left hand side is the determinant of a $(k+1)$ by $(k+1)$ matrix with two rows the same. Thus, the kernel of the submatrix of $\Phi(G,Y)$ composed of the rows corresponding to $M'$ contains all the $k$ rows of $Y$. Hence, the kernel of the submatrix forms a $k$ or more dimensional space, which together with statement (2) implies that $|M'| \leq |N(M')| - k$. Since any subsets of a linearly independent set of rows are also linearly independent, we get, for any nonempty subset $Z$ of $M'$, $|Z| \leq |N(Z)| - k$.

Let $I = (V,F,R)$ be an incidence structure. Recall that an element $(v_\alpha, f_j)$ of $R$ represents the constraint that the $\alpha$th vertex should be on the $j$th plane, and hence corresponds to a linear equation of the form (3.1). If the plane $f_j$ has exactly three vertices in $I$ (that is, $|V(\{f_j\})| = 3$), the plane places no essential constraint on the three-dimensional position of the vertices; indeed we can construct the planar surface in the space for any given position of the three vertices. If, on the other hand, the plane $f_j$ has four vertices, say $v_1$, $v_2$, $v_3$, and $v_4$, then it constrains the vertices in such a way that they should be coplanar in the space. This constraint can be expressed by

$$
\begin{vmatrix}
x_1 & x_2 & x_3 & x_4 \\
y_1 & y_2 & y_3 & y_4 \\
1 & 1 & 1 & 1 \\
z_1 & z_2 & z_3 & z_4
\end{vmatrix} = 0,
$$

and consequently

$$
\begin{vmatrix}
x_2 & x_3 & x_4 \\
y_2 & y_3 & y_4 \\
1 & 1 & 1
\end{vmatrix} z_1 -
\begin{vmatrix}
x_1 & x_3 & x_4 \\
y_1 & y_3 & y_4 \\
1 & 1 & 1
\end{vmatrix} z_2 +
\begin{vmatrix}
x_1 & x_2 & x_4 \\
y_1 & y_2 & y_4 \\
1 & 1 & 1
\end{vmatrix} z_3 -
\begin{vmatrix}
x_1 & x_2 & x_3 \\
y_1 & y_2 & y_3 \\
1 & 1 & 1
\end{vmatrix} z_4 = 0. \quad (6.6)
$$

Thus, a set of four vertices on a common plane imposes one linear constraint upon the $z$ coordinates $z_1, \ldots, z_n$ of the vertices. Keeping this in mind, we introduce the following definition.

For any incidence structure $I = (V,F,R)$, we define a degree 4 bipartite graph $G(I)$ whose right nodes correspond to the elements of $V$ and whose left nodes correspond to the sets of four coplanar vertices specified as below, that is, $G(I) = (\cup M_j, V, \cup W_j)$ where, for each face $f_j$ with $3+l$ vertices, say $v_1, v_2, \ldots, v_{3+l}$,

$M_j = \{ t_{j1}, \ldots, t_{jl} \}$ ,
$W_j = \{ (t_{ji}, v_1), (t_{ji}, v_2), (t_{ji}, v_3), (t_{ji}, v_{3+i}) \mid i = 1, \ldots, l \}$ ,

and for $f_j$ with three or less vertices, both $M_j$ and $W_j$ are empty.

Then, each left node of $G(I)$ corresponds to an equation of the form (6.6), and the coefficients of the equation are the entities of the corresponding row of the matrix $\Phi(G(I),Y)$, where

$$
Y = \begin{bmatrix}
x_1 & x_2 & \cdots & x_n \\
y_1 & y_2 & \cdots & y_n \\
1 & 1 & \cdots & 1
\end{bmatrix} . \tag{6.7}
$$

**Proposition 6.4.** Let $D$ be a labeled line drawing having $v$ vertices drawn at $(x_i, y_i)$, let $I = (V,F,R)$ and $G(I) = (M,N,W)$ be the associated incidence structure and the degree 4 bipartite graph, and let $Y$ be a 3 by $n$ matrix of the form (6.7). If the vertices are in generic position, the following four statements are equivalent.

(1) The rows of the coefficient matrix $A$ in the equations (5.1) are linearly independent.
(2) For any nonempty subset $R'$ of $R$, $|R'| \le |V(R')| + 3|F(R')| - 3$.
(3) The rows of $\Phi(G(I),Y)$ are linearly independent.

(4) For any nonempty subset $M'$ of $M$, $|M'| \leq |N(M')|-3$.

**Proof.** Without loss of generality we can assume that in $I$ any face has at least three vertices and any vertex is at least on one face. This can be understood in the following way. First, deletion of an isolated vertex from $I$ does not affect linear independence of the rows of $A$ or the inequality in statement (2). Second, if some face has less than three vertices, we can add new vertices that are only on this face until the face has exactly three vertices. The addition does not affect the linear independence of the rows of $A$ because it does not place any new constraint on the original vertices and faces. It does not affect the inequality in statement (2) either, because at each time one vertex and one incidence pair are added simultaneously. Third, the above change of $I$ does not concern faces having four or more vertices; it does not change $G(I)$ and consequently does not affect statement (3) or (4).

Under this assumption we get $|M| = |R|-3|F|$, and from the definition we get $|N| = |V|$.

For each solution $w = {}^t(z_1 \cdots z_n a_1 b_1 c_1 \cdots a_m b_m c_m)$ to (5.1), the vector $u = {}^t(z_1 \cdots z_n)$ composed of the first $n$ entities of $w$ is a solution to $\Phi(G(I),Y)u = 0$. Conversely, from each solution to $\Phi(G(I),Y)u = 0$, we can construct the unique solution $w$ to (5.1), because every face has at least three vertices and they determine the planar surface uniquely. Hence, the two solution spaces have the same dimensionality, say $d$. Then we get $d = |V|+3|F|-\text{rank}(A) = |V|-\text{rank}(\Phi(G(I),Y))$, and consequently $\text{rank}(A) = \text{rank}(\Phi(G(I),Y))+3|F|$. Since $A$ has $|M|+3|F|$ $(= |R|)$ rows and $\Phi(G(I),Y)$ has $|M|$ rows, the rows of $A$ are linearly independent if and only if the rows of $\Phi(G(I),Y)$ are linearly independent. Thus, statements (1) and (3) are equivalent.

Next suppose that statement (2) is true. This implies that no two faces have four vertices in common, because if $v_1$, $v_2$, $v_3$, and $v_4$ are all on both $f_j$ and $f_k$, then $R' = \{(v_\alpha,f_j), (v_\alpha,f_k) | \alpha = 1,2,3,4\}$ falsifies the inequality in statement (2). Therefore, any left node in $M$ corresponds to the unique face that generates the node. For any left node $t$ in $M$, let $f(t)$ be the corresponding unique face and $\widetilde{N}(t)$ be the set of all left nodes generated by the face $f(t)$. By the definition of $G(I)$, if $f(t)$ has $l$ vertices, $\widetilde{N}(t)$ contains $l-3$ elements, one of which is $t$. Assume, contrary to the theorem, that some subset $M'$ of $M$ satisfies $|M'| > |N(M')|-3$. Then, $\widetilde{M}'$ defined by $\cup\widetilde{N}(t)$ where the union is taken over all $t$ in $M'$ also satisfies $|\widetilde{M}'| > |N(\widetilde{M}')|-3$, because the extension from $M'$ to $\widetilde{M}'$ adds at most one right node for each added left node. Let $F' = \{f(t) \mid t \in M'\}$ and $R' = R(F')$. Then, we get

$$
|\tilde{M}'| = \sum_{f_j \in F'} (|V(\{f_j\})| - 3) = |R'| - 3|F'| = |R'| - 3|F(R')|
$$
$$
\leq |V(R')| - 3 = |N(\tilde{M}')| - 3.
$$

This is a contradiction. Thus, statement (2) implies statement (4).

Conversely, suppose that statement (4) is true, but that some subset $R'$ of $R$ satisfies $|R'| > |V(R')| + 3|F(R')| - 3$. Let $R_1 = R(F(R'))$. Then $R_1$ also satisfies $|R_1| > |V(R_1)| + 3|F(R_1)| - 3$, because the extension from $R'$ to $R_1$ adds at most one vertex but no face for each added incidence pair. Next let $F_0$ be the set of faces in $F(R')$ that have exactly three vertices, and let $R_2 = R_1 - R(F_0)$. Then $R_2$ also satisfies $|R_2| > |V(R_2)| + 3|F(R_2)| - 3$, because the shrinkage from $R_1$ to $R_2$ deletes exactly three incidence pairs for each deleted face in $F_0$. Let $F_2 = F(R') - F_0$ and $M_2$ be the set of left nodes in $G(I)$ generated by faces in $F_2$. Then

$$
|R_2| = \sum_{f_j \in F_2} |V(\{f_j\})| = \sum_{f_j \in F_2} (|V(\{f_j\})| - 3 + 3) = |M_2| + 3|F_2|
$$
$$
\leq |N(M_2)| + 3|F_2| - 3 = |V(R_2)| + 3|F(R_2)| - 3,
$$

which is a contradiction. Thus statement (4) implies statement (2).

Hence, we get equivalence of statements (2) and (4). Since the equivalence of statements (3) and (4) is a direct consequence of Proposition 6.3, we have completed the proof.

**Proof of Theorem 6.1.** Theorem 6.1 is nothing but a paraphrase of the equivalence of statements (1) and (2) in Proposition 6.4.

**Proof of Theorem 6.2.** Assume that statement (3) in the theorem is true. From Proposition 6.4 the equations (5.1) are linearly independent and have a solution space of dimension $|V| + 3|F| - |R|$. If we take any two faces $f_j$ and $f_k$ and add a new common vertex $v$, this creates a new incidence structure $I^* = (V^*, F, R^*)$ with one more vertex and two more incidence paris. Hence, for any nonempty subset $X$ of $R^*$, $|V(X)| + 3|F(X)| \geq |X| + 3$. From Proposition 6.4 again, the equations (5.1) associated with $I^*$ are also linearly independent and have a solution space of dimension $|V| + 3|F| - |R| - 1$. If $f_j$ and $f_k$ generate the same plane in $P(w)$ for any solution $w$ to (5.1), this is impossible. So we conclude that, for some solution $w$, the two faces are distinct in $P(w)$. This is true for any pair of faces, and hence some appropriate linear combination of these solutions gives a nondegenerate solution to (5.1). This implies that statement (1) is true.

Next assume that statement (3) is false. Then, for some subset $X$ of $R$ with $|F(X)| \geqq 2$, we have $|V(X)| + 3|F(X)| \leq |X| + 3$. Without loss of generality we choose as $X$ a minimal subset with this property. Then, $|V(X)| + 3|F(X)| = |X| + 3$ and, for every nonempty subset $X'$ of $X$, $|V(X)| + 3|F(X)| \geqq |X| + 3$ (note that if $|F(X)| = 1$, the equality holds). From Proposition 6.4, the equations (5.1) associated with the substructure $(V(X), F(X), X)$ have a solution space of dimension 3, and hence the faces in $F(X)$ must be identical in $P(w)$ for any solution $w$. Hence statement (1) is false as well.

Thus we have shown equivalence of statements (1) and (3).

Assume that statement (2) is true. For any subset $X$ of $R$, let us define $g(X)$ by $g(X) = |X| - |V(X)|$. Suppose that $r = (v, f)$ is an element of $R$–$X$. Then we get $g(X \cup \{r\}) = |X| + 1 - |V(X) \cup \{v\}|$, and hence

$g(X \cup \{r\}) = g(X) + 1$ if $v \in V(X)$,
$g(X \cup \{r\}) = g(X)$ if $v \in V - V(X)$.

Therefore, $g(X)$ is monotonically nondecreasing; that is, $X_1 \subseteqq X_2 \subseteqq R$ implies $g(X_1) \leq g(X_2)$. Now suppose that $X$ is any subset of $R$ with $|F(X)| \geqq 2$, and let $Y = F(X)$. Since $X \subseteqq R(Y)$, we get

$g(X) = |X| - |V(X)| \leq g(R(Y)) = |R(Y)| - |V(R(Y))|$.

From $V(R(Y)) = V(Y)$, we get $|V(X)| - |X| \geqq |V(Y)| - |R(Y)|$. Hence,

$|V(X)| + 3|F(X)| - |X| - 4 \geqq |V(Y)| + 3|Y| - |R(Y)| - 4 \geqq 0$,

which implies that statement (3) is true.

Conversely, assume that statement (3) is true. Suppose that $Y$ is any subset of $F$ such that $|Y| \geqq 2$, and let $Z = R(Y)$. Then, $Y = F(Z)$ and $V(Y) = V(Z)$. Therefore, we get

$|V(Y)| + 3|Y| - |R(Y)| - 4 = |V(Z)| + 3|F(Z)| - |Z| - 4 \geqq 0$, which means that statement (2) is true. Hence, statements (2) and (3) are equivalent.

**Proof of Corollary 6.2.1.** An incidence structure that satisfies the inequality (6.4) obviously satisfies the inequality (6.2). Hence, the corollary is an immediate consequence of Theorems 6.1 and 6.2.

### 6.4. Generic Degrees of Freedom

In Sections 5.1 and 5.2 we defined two functions $\rho_H$ and $\rho_V$, the degrees of freedom in the choice of the object represented by a line drawing, in terms of ranks of some matrices (recall (5.4) and (5.5)). When the vertices are in generic position, the functions are determined by the associated incidence structure only, and hence the distribution of the degrees of freedom is characterized by the combinatorial structures of line drawings. Here we study the combinatorial aspects of the functions, which will be used in the fourth module.

**Theorem 6.3 (Combinatorial characterization of the matroid $(V, \rho_V)$).** Suppose that the vertices of a labeled line drawing $D$ are in generic position and its incidence structure $I = (V, F, R)$ is generically reconstructible. Then, a subset $Y$ of $V$ is an independent set of the matroid $(V, \rho_V)$ if and only if

$$| V(X) | + 3 | F(X) | \geq | X | + | V(X) \cap Y |  \tag{6.8}$$

is satisfied for any subset $X$ of $R$.

**Proof.** Recall that the set of rows of the coefficient matrix $A$ in (5.1) is in one-to-one correspondence with the incidence pair set $R$. For any subset $X$ of $R$, let $A(X)$ denote the submatrix of $A$ composed of the rows corresponding to $X$. From the hypothesis and Corollary 6.2.1 the rows of $A$ are linearly independent, and hence, for any subset $X$ of $R$, the rows of $A(X)$ are also independent.

First, assume that a subset $Y$ of $V$ is an independent set of the matroid $(V, \rho_V)$ but $| V(X_0) | + 3 | F(X_0) | < | X_0 | + | V(X_0) \cap Y |$ for some subset $X_0$ of $R$. The solutions to (5.1) associated with the substructure $S_0 = (V(X_0), F(X_0), X_0)$ form a linear space of dimension $| V(X_0) | + 3 | F(X_0) | - \mathrm{rank}(A(X_0))$, because it has $| V(X_0) | + 3 | F(X_0) |$

unknowns. Since the rows of $A(X_0)$ are linearly independent, we get

$$|V(X_0)|+3|F(X_0)|-\text{rank}(A(X_0)) = |V(X_0)|+3|F(X_0)|-|X_0| < |V(X_0)\cap Y| ;$$

that is, $|V(X_0)\cap Y|$ is greater than the dimension of the linear space formed by the solutions to (5.1) associated with $S_0$. This contradicts the assumption that $Y$ is an independent set. Thus, if $Y$ is independent, the inequality (6.8) is satisfied for any subset $X$ of $R$.

Next, suppose that a subset $Y$ of $V$ is a minimal dependent set and $v \in Y$. Let $V_0$ and $F_0$ be the set of vertices and that of faces, respectively, that are located uniquely in the space when the $z$ coordinates of vertices in $Y-\{v\}$ are given. Obviously $Y \subsetneqq V_0$ and $V(F_0) \subsetneqq V_0$ .

Assume that there exists a vertex $v_0$ in $V_0-V(F_0)$ . Then, since $v_0$ is not on any face in $F_0$, the $z$ coordinate of $v_0$ must be specified directly when we specify the $z$ coordinates of the vertices in $Y-\{v\}$ , and hence $v_0 \in Y-\{v\}$ . However, since $v_0$ is not on any face in $F_0$, the specification of the $z$ coordinate of $v_0$ does not constrain other variables. Thus, $Y-\{v_0\}$ must also be dependent. This contradicts the minimalness of $Y$. Therefore, $V_0-V(F_0) = \emptyset$ , that is, $V_0 = V(F_0)$ .

Let $X_0 = (V_0 \times F_0)\cap R$. Because $V(F_0) = V_0$ (that is, each vertex in $V_0$ is on some face in $F_0$), we get $V_0 = V(X_0)$ and $F_0 = F(X_0)$ . Because the system of equations (5.1) associated with $(V(X_0),F(X_0),X_0)$ is linearly independent and every variable in it can be expressed by a linear combination of the variables in $\{z_i | v_i \in Y-\{v\} \}$ , the matrix $A(X_0)$ can be transformed by elementary transformations of rows and permutations of columns into $[A_0 | A_1]$ , where $A_0$ is an $|X_0|$ by $|Y-\{v\}|$ matrix whose columns correspond to the unknowns in $\{z_\alpha | v_\alpha \in Y-\{v\})\}$ , and $A_1$ is the $|X_0|$ by $|X_0|$ identity matrix whose columns correspond to the unknowns in $\{z_\alpha | v_\alpha \in V_0-(Y_0-\{v\})\} \cup \{a_j,b_j,c_j | f_j \in F_0\}$ . Hence we get

$$|V(X_0)|+3|F(X_0)|-|X_0| = |Y-\{v\}| ,$$

and consequently

$$|V(X_0)|+3|F(X_0)|-|X_0| < |Y| = |Y\cap V(X_0)| .$$

Thus, if $Y$ is not independent, $X_0$ defined as above does not satisfy the inequality (6.8).

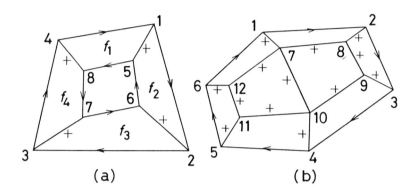

**Fig. 6.2.** Pictures requiring nontrivial consideration in order for us to tell how many degrees of freedom they have and which sets of vertices form bases for the associated matroids.

**Corollary 6.3.1.** Suppose that the vertices of a labeled line drawing $D$ are in generic position and its incidence structure $I = (V,F,R)$ is generically reconstructible. Then, for any subset $Y$ of $V$, the matroid function $\rho_V$ satisfies

$$\rho_V(Y) = \max \{ \, |Y'| : Y' \subseteq Y, \; |V(X)| + 3|F(X)|$$
$$\geq |X| + |V(X) \cap Y'| \; \text{ for any } X \subseteq R \} . \qquad (6.9)$$

**Proof.** From the definition of $\rho_V$, $\rho_V(Y)$ is the size of a maximal independent subset of $Y$, and hence from Theorem 6.3 we get (6.9).

**Example 6.2.** Fig. 6.2 shows pictures for which intuitive consideration is not very helpful in telling how many degrees of freedom there are or which sets of vertices form bases. However, these questions can be answered easily if we employ Theorem 6.3.

Let us consider the hidden-part-eliminated picture in Fig. 6.2(a). In a strict sense it is not easy to judge whether the vertices are in generic position. However, we can expect that they are almost always in generic position, particularly when the coordinates of the vertices are represented by the floating point representation. So we assume that the vertices of the picture are in generic position.

The object represented here has eight visible vertices ($|V| = 8$) and four visible faces ($|F| = 4$), forming a ring structure. In the picture the $\alpha$th vertex $v_\alpha$ is represented simply by the number $\alpha$. Since the faces are all quadrilateral, it has $4\times4 = 16$ incidence pairs ($|R| = 16$). Thus we get $|V|+3|F| = |R|+4 = 20$. Since any set of two or more faces satisfies the inequality (6.3), the incidence structure is generically reconstructible and the equations (5.1) are linearly independent. Consequently, there are $|V|+3|F|-|R| = 4$ degrees of freedom in the choice of the object in the space. By elementary counting we can see from Theorem 6.3 that any four vertices, unless they all are on a common face, form a base of the matroid $(V, \rho_V)$. Hence the object is specified and fixed to the space if we give some values to the $z$ coordinates of the vertices in, for example, $\{v_1, v_2, v_3, v_4\}$ or $\{v_1, v_3, v_5, v_7\}$. Note that the incidence structure of this picture is the same as that of the picture in Fig. 5.3(a). As we saw in Example 5.3, it requires nontrivial consideration if we want to find the degrees of freedom of the incidence structure intuitively. In contrast, Theorems 6.1, 6.2, and 6.3 give us a systematic way of finding the degrees of freedom and of finding a base.

The hidden-part-eliminated picture in Fig. 6.2(b) also has a generically reconstructible incidence structure and four degrees of freedom. Here again the elementary counting leads to the conclusion that any four vertices that are not all on the same face form a base. Hence, if we specify the $z$ coordinates of the vertices in, for example, $\{v_1, v_4, v_7, v_{10}\}$ or $\{v_1, v_3, v_5, v_8\}$, then the object shape and its spatial position are determined uniquely.

## 7.  OVERCOMING THE SUPERSTRICTNESS

We have found a counting method for judging whether an incidence structure is reconstructible in a generic sense, that is, reconstructible when the vertices are in generic position. If the incidence structure is generically reconstructible, the reconstructibility is not disturbed by small movements of vertices on the picture plane, and hence the correctness of the picture can be judged without worrying about digitization errors. If it is not generically reconstructible, on the other hand, the superstrictness of the algebraic method prevents us from judging the correctness of the picture. The purpose of this chapter is to remove the superstrictness. We shall first construct a method for correcting vertex position errors automatically, and next, using it, establish a mechanism that can judge the correctness of the picture flexibly in the sense that, even if it is mathematically incorrect, it is judged "practically correct" if the incorrectness is only due to a small deviation of vertex positions.

### 7.1.  Correction of Vertex Position Errors

From the definition of generic reconstructibility it follows that if a picture has a generically reconstructible incidence structure and the vertices are in generic position, the associated spatial structure composed of planar surfaces can be realized without any degeneracy. Because we use a digital computer, we can regard the vertices as being almost always in generic position; any special relationships among the vertices, if they exist, will be canceled out by digitization and numerical computation. Therefore, if the incidence structure is generically reconstructible, the reconstructibility is not disturbed by small errors in vertex position, so that we can apply our algebraic method (i.e., Theorem 3.3 or Theorem 4.1) directly to the judgment of the correctness of the picture.

In this sense, our problem, the problem of discriminating between correct and incorrect pictures flexibly, has been solved partially. Using Theorem 6.2, we first judge whether the associated incidence structure is generically reconstructible or not. If it is, we next check directly the existence of a feasible solution to the linear programming problem stated in Theorem 3.3 or 4.1. Thus, our next problem is how we should deal with pictures whose incidence structures are not generically reconstructible.

If the incidence structure is not generically reconstructible, it can

be realized in the space only when the vertices are in some special
position. This means that the vertex positions are not independent;
positions of some vertices constrain the others. Using this kind of
constraint, we can determine the correct position of the vertices. This is
the basic idea of the following method for automatic correction of
incorrect pictures.

Suppose that an incidence structure $I = (V,F,R)$ is not generically
reconstructible. Then, the inequality (6.3) is falsified by some subset $X$
of $F$. However, if we delete incidence pairs one by one from $R$, the
resultant substructure eventually satisfies statement (2) in Theorem 6.2.
This can be understood if we note, first, that deletion of an element, say
$(v,f)$, from $R$ causes the left hand side of (6.3) to decrease by 1 if and
only if $f \in X$ and $v$ is not on other faces in $X$ whereas, it causes the
right hand side to decrease by 1 if $f \in X$, and second, that, if $R$ is
empty, the inequality (6.3) holds trivially. Thus, from any incidence
structure $I = (V,F,R)$, we can extract a maximal subset, say $R^*$, of $R$ such
that the substructure $I^* = (V,F,R^*)$ is generically reconstructible. If $I$
itself is generically reconstructible, we get $R^* = R$, but in general $R^*$ is
not unique.

At least in principle, a maximal generically reconstructible
substructure can be found by applying Theorem 6.2 to all substructures of
the incidence structure $I$, but this is obviously impractical because the
number of substructures is of the exponential order of $|R|$. In Chapter 8
we shall present a more practical method, which can find a maximal
generically reconstructible substructure in $O(|R|^2)$ time.

Let $D$ be a labeled line drawing, and let $I = (V,F,R)$ be its incidence
structure. Suppose that $I$ is not generically reconstructible, and hence it
is practically meaningless to judge its correctness directly by Theorem 3.3
(or Theorem 4.1). Let $R^*$ be a maximal subset of $R$ such that the
substructure $I^* = (V,F,R^*)$ is generically reconstructible, and let

$$A(R^*)w = 0 \qquad\qquad\qquad\qquad (7.1)$$

be the system of the equations of the form (5.1) generated from the
elements of $R^*$, where $A(R^*)$ represents the submatrix of $A$ composed of the
rows corresponding to elements of $R^*$. Thus, (7.1) is a subsystem of (5.1).
Since $I^*$ is generically reconstructible, we can find a nondegenerate
solution, say $w^*$, to the system (7.1) and construct the associated
configuration $P(w^*)$ of the surfaces in the space. Note that the projection

on the picture plane of the points of intersection of the surfaces in $P(w^*)$ coincides with the vertices of the original picture $D$ except for the vertices in $V(R-R^*)$, where, for any $Y \subseteq R$, $V(Y)$ denotes the set of vertices appearing in some elements of $Y$. If vertices in $V(R-R^*)$ are incident to three or fewer faces in the original incidence structure $I$, their correct position in a three-dimensional space can be found as intersections of the associated surfaces in $P(w^*)$. Projecting them on the picture plane, we obtain the correct position of the vertices on the picture plane. Thus we get the following method.

**Method 7.1 (Correction of vertex position errors).**
Input:  A labeled line drawing $D$ and its incidence structure $I = (V,F,R)$.
Output: A corrected line drawing.
Procedure:
Step 1.  Find a maximal subset $R^*$ of $R$ such that $I^* = (V,F,R^*)$ is generically reconstructible.
Step 2.  Find a solution $w^*$ to (7.1) and (5.2'). If there is no solution, return "false."
Step 3.  Find correct spatial positions of the vertices in $V(R-R^*)$ as intersections of the surfaces in the configuration $P(w^*)$.
Step 4.  Project the corrected positions onto the picture plane.
Step 5.  See whether the corrected picture obeys the labeling rules. If it does not, return "false."
Step 6.  Regenerate the system of inequalities (5.2) using the corrected positions of the vertices. If the new system of inequalities is satisfied by $w^*$, return the corrected picture. Otherwise return "false."

If there is no solution to (7.1) and (5.2') in Step 2, it implies that the system of inequalities (5.2') contains contradictory propositions (note that the system of the equations (7.1) always has a nondegenerate solution because $I^*$ is generically reconstructible). In this case it is usually impossible to correct the picture by movements of vertices. So the method returns "false."

Step 3 is not always possible. Let $F_0$ be the set of faces in $F$ that have four or more vertices on them in $I$. Then, Step 3 is impossible if a vertex in $V(R-R^*)$ is on four or more faces in $F_0$. This is because four or more faces in general do not have any common point. Note that we need not consider faces in $F-F_0$, because a face with three or less vertices does not

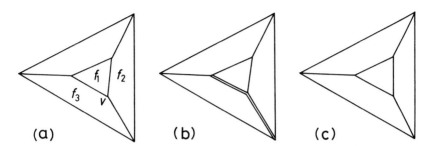

**Fig. 7.1.** Correction of vertex position errors: (a) is an incorrect picture, (b) is a generically reconstructible substructure of the incidence structure of (a), and (c) is a corrected picture.

place any essential constraint on $I^*$; that is, we can always add the faces in $F-F_0$ after we construct a three-dimensional configuration of the other part of $I^*$. In order to make Step 3 possible, therefore, we have to delete from $R$ those incidence pairs that contain vertices which are on at most three faces when we construct $R^*$ in Step 1. In other words, Step 3 is possible only when $|(\{v\} \times F_0) \cap R| \leq 3$ for any $v \in V(R-R^*)$. An efficient method of constructing $R^*$ with this property will be presented in Chapter 8.

Steps 5 and 6 are necessary because displacement of the junctions on the picture plane may disturb the labeling rules or the system of inequalities (5.2). The labeling rules are usually kept undisturbed if the displacement is small. However, if it is not so small, the rules may be disturbed. Displacement of a junction sometimes cause the change of a junction type, for example, from Y-type to W-type, and as a result the labels assigned to the lines around the junction may violate the rules (recall Rules 2.5 and 2.5'). The system of inequalities (5.2) may also be disturbed because the coefficient matrix $B$ depends on the position of the junctions. Thus, the check in Steps 5 and 6 is necessary.

**Example 7.1.** Consider the picture of the truncated pyramid in Fig. 7.1(a). As we have seen, the incidence structure $I = (V,F,R)$ of this picture is not generically reconstructible. Let $v$ be a vertex incident to three faces $f_1$, $f_2$, $f_3$, as illustrated in the figure, and define $R^*$ as $R^* = R - \{(v,f_3)\}$. That is, we delete from $I$ the constraint that the vertex $v$ must be on the face $f_3$, as shown in (b), where the double lines mean that the side faces may form a gap along these lines. Since the substructure $I^* = (V,F,R^*)$ is generically reconstructible, we find a nondegenerate solution $w^*$ and obtain the correct position of $v$ as the intersection of the three surfaces $f_1$, $f_2$, $f_3$ in $P(w^*)$. Projecting it onto the picture plane, we correct the picture; the result of the correction is as shown in (c).

It seems interesting to note that the result of the correction does not depend on the choice of the solution $w^*$. This can be understood in the following way. The picture in Fig. 7.1(b) has exactly four degrees of freedom in the choice of the spatial structure. Hence from Corollary 5.3.1 there exists a unique solution to the figure construction problem: "Find the intersection of the plane $f_3$ and the line shared by $f_1$ and $f_2$," which is a problem of the type given by Problem 5.1 (see Section 5.3).

**Example 7.2.** Let $I = (V,F,R)$ be an incidence structure of the hidden-part-drawn picture shown in Fig. 7.2(a). The picture has eight vertices, six faces, and 24 incidence pairs (because each of the six faces has exactly four vertices on it). Consequently, if we put $X = F$, the left hand side of (6.3) amounts to $|V|+3|F| = 8+3\times6 = 26$ whereas the right hand side to $|R|+4 = 24+4 = 28$. Thus, $I$ is not generically reconstructible, and indeed the picture is incorrect. If we remove any two incidence pairs associated with an arbitrary vertex, the structure becomes generically reconstructible. Therefore, we can correct this picture by the displacement of any one vertex. Examples of the correction are shown in Fig. 7.2(b), (c), (d), where the circles denote the vertices that were displaced for the correction. The system of equations (7.1) associated with this picture admits exactly four degrees of freedom in the choice of the solution, and hence it follows from Corollary 5.3.1 that, once we choose a vertex to be displaced, the result of the correction is unique.

**Remark 7.1.** Method 7.1 contains a great deal of arbitrariness in Steps 1, 2, and 3. We have to refine these steps in order to obtain a precise computer algorithm.

There is almost no problem in Steps 2 and 3. As we have seen in Examples 7.1 and 7.2, usually the arbitrariness in Step 2 does not affect the result of the correction. The arbitrariness in Step 3 is easily resolved by a natural criterion: "Move each vertex to the nearest correct position."

On the contrary, it is not so easy to resolve the arbitrariness in

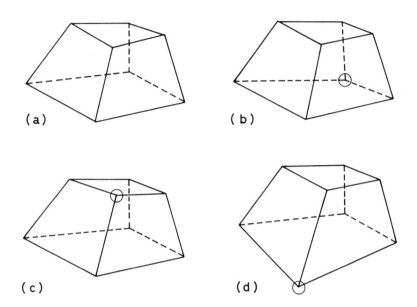

**Fig. 7.2.** Correction of a hidden-part-drawn picture of a hexahedron: (a) is an incorrect picture, and (b), (c), (d) are corrected pictures, where the circles denote the vertices moved for the correction.

Step 1. There is in general great freedom in the choice of $R^*$, and the result of the correction (i.e., the output of Method 7.1) depends on $R^*$. Probably the theoretically most complete way is to apply Method 7.1 to all possible $R^*$'s and to select among all the outputs the "best" one as the result of the correction. However, this is not practical; indeed the number of possible $R^*$'s is usually very large, and hence the check of all the possibilities would result in a combinatorial explosion.

One practical way is to employ some heuristic to choose a "good" subset as $R^*$. An example of such heuristics is the following.

**Heuristic 7.1.** Correct vertices with shorter edges first, where the lengths of edges are to be measured on the picture plane.

This heuristic is natural because shorter edges are more likely to contain errors in their positions if the picture is drawn by a human hand or is obtained by computer processing of a light intensity image. Now recall that the correction of the picture is carried out by displacing vertices in $V(R-R^*)$. Hence Heuristic 7.1 implies that vertices with shorter edges should be in $V(R-R^*)$; that is, the maximal subset $R^*$ should be searched for in such a way that incidence pairs containing vertices with longer edges are included in $R^*$ as much as possible. An efficient algorithm for finding $R^*$ with this property will be given in Chapter 8.

## 7.2. Set of All Scenes Represented by a Picture

The set of all scenes a labeled line drawing can represent is specified as the set of all solutions to the system consisting of (5.1) and (5.2). However, in Method 7.1 we use not (5.1) but (7.1) to reconstruct a spatial configuration of planar surfaces, from which the correct positions of vertices are determined. In other words, we regard (7.1) as an essential part of (5.1) and the other equations in (5.1) as a redundant part. Indeed what is done in Method 7.1 is to adjust the $x$ and $y$ coordinates of the vertices in $V(R-R^*)$ in such a way that the equations contained in (5.1) but not in (7.1) become linearly dependent on (7.1). Thus, for any corrected picture, (5.1) and (7.1) are equivalent. Using this fact, we can express the set of all scenes that the picture can represent more simply.

Let $D$ be a correct, or corrected, line drawing, let $I = (V,F,R)$ be its incidence structure, and let $I^* = (V,F,R^*)$ be the maximal generically reconstructible substructure of $I$ that has been used for the correction based on Method 7.1. Since the system of the equations (7.1), the equations associated with $I^*$, is linearly independent, the coefficient matrix $A(R^*)$ can be transformed by some permutation of the columns into $[A_1 \mid A_2]$, where $A_1$ is an $|R^*| \times |R^*|$ nonsingular matrix. Let $\eta$ and $\xi$ be the unknown vectors corresponding to the columns of $A_1$ and those of $A_2$, respectively, so that (7.1) can be expressed by

$$A_1\eta + A_2\xi = 0.$$

Since $A_1$ is nonsingular, we get

$$\eta = -(A_1)^{-1}A_2\xi. \tag{7.2}$$

This expression represents the solutions to (7.1) as a linear combination of the unknown variables in $\xi$. In other words, the set of vectors $w$ subject to (7.1) is identical with the set of vectors $(-(A_1)^{-1}A_2\xi,\ \xi)$ without any constraints. Moreover, it should be noted that in Method 7.1 the equations in (7.1) alone are used for the reconstruction of the polyhedral scene and the other equations in (5.1) are changed so that they become linearly dependent on (7.1). Therefore, (7.2) can be interpreted in the following way: the values of the unknowns in $\xi$ can be given arbitrarily, but once they are given, a solution to (7.1) is specified uniquely. Thus, the unknowns in $\xi$ form a base of the matroid $(H, \rho_H)$ defined by (5.4). This means that we can find the set of columns corresponding to $A_2$ by choosing a base of the matroid. If, for example, we want a base consisting of $z$ coordinates of vertices only, we can find one by Theorem 6.3 or Corollary 6.3.1; we need not check nonsingularity of submatrices of $A(R^*)$ numerically.

From (7.2), the vector $w$ subject to (7.1) can be represented by

$$w = h(\xi),  \tag{7.3}$$

where $h(\xi)$ is the vector obtained by a certain permutation of the entities of the vector $(-(A_1)^{-1}A_2\xi,\ \xi)$. Substituting (7.3) in (5.2) and (5.2'), we get, respectively,

$$Bh(\xi) > 0  \tag{7.4}$$

and

$$Bh(\xi) \geqq e.  \tag{7.4'}$$

The set of solutions to (5.1) and (5.2) is identical with the set of solutions to (7.4), and the set of solutions to (5.1) and (5.2') is identical with the set of solutions to (7.4'). Consequently, the set of all scenes that the picture can represent is identical with the set of all solutions to (7.4), and the picture is correct if and only if there exists a solution to (7.4').

The system (7.4) (or (7.4')) is much smaller than the original system; it has $n+3m-|R^*|$ unknowns and $|T|$ inequalities, whereas the system consisting of (5.1) and (5.2) (or (5.1) and (5.2')) has $n+3m$ unknowns, $|R|$ equations, and $|T|$ inequalities. In order to judge the correctness of a picture we only need to check whether the system (7.4') has a solution; we need not check directly the existence of a solution to the

larger system consisting of (5.1) and (5.2'). Hence, for example, Step 2 in
Method 7.1 can be replaced by this simpler step:

Step 2'.  Find a solution $\xi^*$ to (7.4'), and put $w^* = h(\xi^*)$ .

### 7.3.  Practical Judgment of the Correctness

Now we are ready to construct a practical method for judging the
correctness of labeled pictures. The outline of the method is shown by the
flow chart in Fig. 7.3.

Suppose that a labeled line drawing $D$ and its spatial structure $S$ =
$(V,F,R,T)$ are given. Our aim is to judge the correctness of the picture $D$
"flexibly" in the sense that the picture should be judged correct even if
the strict correctness is disturbed by a small deviation of the vertices.

Using Theorem 6.2, we judge whether the incidence structure $I$ =
$(V,F,R)$ is generically reconstructible. If so, we next check the existence
of a solution to the system defined by (5.1) and (5.2'). This can be done
by a method for finding a feasible solution to a linear programming problem
whose constraint set is given by (5.1) and (5.2'). Finally we judge the
correctness by Theorem 3.3 (or Theorem 4.1) directly; that is, if a
solution exists, $D$ is judged correct (Exit 1 in Fig. 7.3), and otherwise
incorrect (Exit 2).

If, on the other hand, $I$ is not generically reconstructible, we cannot
apply Theorem 3.3 directly, because Theorem 3.3 judges the correctness
"superstrictly." Therefore, using Theorem 6.2, we choose a subset $R^*$ of $R$
in such a way that the substructure $I^*$ = $(V,F,R^*)$ is generically
reconstructible and $R^*$ is maximal with this property, and construct the
associated system of the equations (7.1) and consequently the system of the
inequalities (7.4'). Since $I^*$ is generically reconstructible, we can search
for a solution to the system (7.4') without fearing numerical errors. If
the system does not have any solution, we conclude that $D$ is incorrect
(Exit 3). If it has a solution, we try to correct vertex position errors by
Method 7.1. If the correction is impossible, we conclude that $D$ is
incorrect (Exit 4). If it can be corrected, then we compare the corrected
line drawing with the original one, and judge whether the vertex position
errors are "permissible" or not by some criterion depending on
applications. (For example, we can judge that the errors are permissible if
the maximum distance between the original positions and the corrected
positions of vertices is smaller than a prespecified threshold, or,

line drawing $D$ and spatial structure $S=(V,F,R,T)$

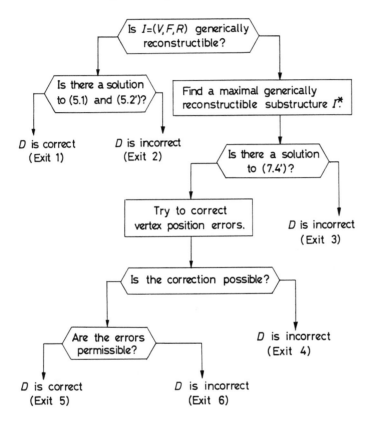

**Fig. 7.3.** Flow chart for a practical judgment of the correctness of pictures: if an input picture comes out through Exit 1 or 5, the picture is judged correct, and otherwise it is judged incorrect.

alternatively, if the sum of lengths of vertex displacements is smaller than a threshold, etc.). If the errors are permissible, we conclude that $D$ can be considered as being practically correct (Exit 5), and otherwise, we conclude that $D$ is incorrect (Exit 6).

   Thus, a machine can judge the correctness flexibly as human beings do. The point is that we do not judge directly whether the picture is correct but judge whether the incorrectness is permissible.

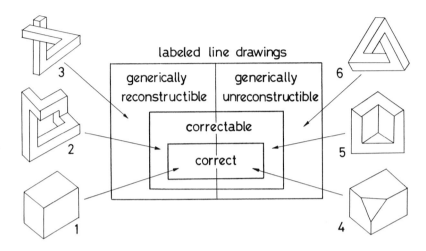

**Fig. 7.4.** Classification of labeled line drawings: picture 3 is adapted from Draper(1978), picture 5 from Huffman(1971), and picture 6 from Penrose and Penrose (1958).

## 7.4. A Classification of Line Drawings

We have considered labeled line drawings from several points of view, that is, whether they are, or are not, correct, correctable, and/or generically reconstructible. These points of view naturally form a framework for classifying labeled line drawings.

First, labeled line drawings have the associated incidence structures, and hence can be divided into *generically reconstructible* drawings and *generically unreconstructible* ones according to whether the incidence structures are generically reconstructible or not. The class of generically reconstructible line drawings is characterized by Theorem 6.2.

Second, labeled line drawings are divided into *correctable* drawings and *uncorrectable* ones according to whether they can be corrected by displacements of some vertices together with the lines incident to them. Here, we adopt the convention that correct pictures belong to the class of correctable pictures, because they can be "corrected" by displacing an empty set of vertices. Thus, correctable line drawings are subdivided into *correct* drawings and *incorrect* ones; the class of correct drawings is characterized by Theorem 3.3 or Theorem 4.1.

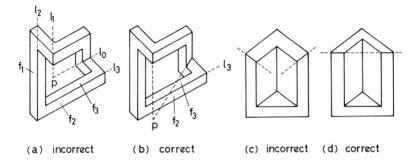

(a) incorrect    (b) correct    (c) incorrect    (d) correct

**Fig. 7.5.** Correction of the correctable pictures in Fig. 7.4.

Thus, labeled line drawings are divided into the six classes as shown in Fig. 7.4, where to each class is attached an example picture.

Pictures 1, 2, and 3 in the figure have generically reconstructible incidence structures, but pictures 2 and 3 are not correct.

We can understand the incorrectness of picture 2 in the following way (see Fig. 7.5(a)). Let $p$ be an intersection of the face $f_1$ and the line $l_0$ (the position of $p$ on the picture plane can be obtained as the intersection of the two lines $l_0$ and $l_1$). Let $L_p$ be the line that passes through $p$ and is perpendicular to the picture plane. Furthermore, let $z_1$, $z_2$, and $z_3$ be the $z$ coordinates of the points at which $L_p$ meets the faces $f_1$, $f_2$, and $f_3$, respectively, when the faces are extended. Recall that the picture is assumed to be in the $x$-$y$ plane and the positive direction of the $z$ axis faces toward the viewer. Therefore, a larger value of $z$ means that the point is nearer to the viewer. We get $z_1 > z_2$ because $f_1$ and $f_2$ share the convex edge $l_2$. Similarly, we get $z_2 > z_3$ because $f_2$ and $f_3$ share the convex edge $l_3$. On the other hand, $p$ is on both the faces $f_1$ and $f_3$ (note that $p$ is on $l_0$, which is on $f_3$), and hence we get $z_1 = z_3$, which is a contradiction. That is, picture 2 in Fig. 7.4 is incorrect. An example of the correction is shown in Fig. 7.5(b), where $p$ is on the lower side of $l_3$ in the picture plane and hence the convex edge $l_3$ gives the inequality $z_3 > z_2$ ; there is no contradiction.

Picture 3 is uncorrectable, because it cannot be corrected unless we change it drastically by interchanging the visible part and the invisible part.

Pictures 4, 5, and 6 in Fig. 7.4 have generically unreconstructible

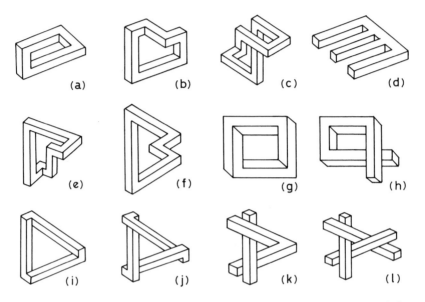

**Fig. 7.6.** Anomalous pictures: a, b, f, i, j, k, and l are adapted from Draper (1978), and g and h from Huffman (1971).

incidence structures. Picture 5 is not correct because the top face and the front face should meet at one line, but the two edges are not collinear, as shown in Fig. 7.5(c). It can be corrected, for example, as shown in Fig. 7.5(d). Picture 6 is not correct and cannot be corrected because its incorrectness is mainly due to contradictory inequalities caused by occluding edges, and the contradiction cannot be resolved even if the positions of the vertices are changed.

There is an intimate relationship between this classification framework and the procedures for discrimination between correct and incorrect pictures shown in Fig. 7.3. Suppose that a labeled line drawing is given to the procedure. Which exit it comes out of depends on which category it belongs to. For example, picture 1 in Fig. 7.4 comes out of Exit 1, and pictures 2 and 3 out of Exit 2. Picture 4 comes out of Exit 5 unless the threshold for the permissible errors is not very small, because the picture represents a polyhedron correctly only up to digitization errors. Picture 5 will come out of Exit 6 unless the threshold is not very large, and otherwise it comes out of Exit 5. Picture 6 comes out of Exit 3, because its incorrectness is due to inconsistency in the inequalities (3.4).

**Example 7.3.** In visual psychology, there is a class of pictures called 'anomalous pictures' or 'pictures of impossible objects' (Penrose and Penrose, 1958; Gregory, 1971; Robinson, 1972), and some of them have been discussed also from a mathematical point of view (Huffman, 1971; Cowan, 1974, 1977; Draper 1978; Térouanne, 1980; Kulpa, 1983; Thro, 1983). It seems interesting to classify these pictures from the viewpoint of our classification framework (Sugihara, 1982a). Fig. 7.6 shows some examples of anomalous pictures. From our point of view, various categories of pictures are included: (a), (b), (f), (g), and (i) are generically unreconstructible, uncorrectable pictures; (c), (j), (k), and (l) are generically reconstructible, correct pictures; (d) is an unlabelable picture; (e) is a generically reconstructible, incorrect, correctable picture; and (h) is a generically reconstructible, uncorrectable picture.

# 8. ALGORITHMIC ASPECTS OF GENERIC RECONSTRUCTIBILITY

The concept of generic reconstructibility has played the main role in the third module, the module for judging the correctness of pictures flexibly. Though we found a counting theorem for judging whether an incidence structure is generically reconstructible or not, it is not efficient from the time complexity point of view. In the present chapter we shall construct an efficient algorithm for checking the generic reconstructibility of an incidence structure and for finding a maximal generically reconstructible substructure; the time complexity of the algorithm is of the order of the square of the number of incidence pairs. Thus we complete the third module.

## 8.1. Network Flow Theory

A polynomially bounded algorithm for checking generic reconstructibility was first found by Sugihara (1979c); here the problem was reduced to the problem of finding complete matchings of a certain family of bipartite graphs and an $O(|R|^{3.5})$ algorithm was constructed, where $R$ denotes the set of incidence pairs. The algorithm was improved by Imai (1985), who found an algorithm for finding a maximal generically reconstructible substructure, which runs in $O(|R|^2)$ time. This algorithm includes the checking of generic reconstructibility, because an incidence structure is generically reconstructible if and only if its maximal generically reconstructible substructure coincides with the original structure itself.

This chapter presents Imai's algorithm for finding a maximal generically reconstructible substructure, which makes our third module more efficient. To this end we first review some basic results in network flow theory.

Let $R$ denote the set of real numbers, and let $R^+$ be the set of nonnegative real numbers. For a finite set $E$, a function from $E$ to $R$ is called a *vector* on $E$, and a vector on $E$ is called *nonnegative* if it is a function from $E$ to $R^+$. A vector is called *integral* if its value is an integer for any element of $E$. For a vector $g$ on $E$ and a subset $U$ of $E$, let $g|_U$ denote the restriction of $g$ to $U$; that is, $g|_U$ is a vector on $U$ and, for any $e \in U$, $g|_U(e) = g(e)$. For a vector $g$ on $E$ and a subset $U$ of $E$, we define $g(U) = \sum_{e \in U} g(e)$. For a subset $U$ of $E$, the characteristic vector $\chi_U$ is defined by $\chi_U(e) = 1$ if $e \in U$ and $\chi_U(e) = 0$ if $e \notin U$. A characteristic function of a singleton, say $\chi_{\{e\}}$ , is abbreviated as $\chi_e$ .

A *network* is a triple $Q = (N_Q, W_Q, c_Q)$ where $N_Q$ is a finite set, $W_Q$ is a subset of $N_Q \times N_Q$ , and $c_Q$ is a nonnegative vector on $W_Q$ . Elements of $N_Q$ are called *nodes*, those of $W_Q$ *arcs*, and $c_Q$ is the *capacity*. An alternating sequence of nodes and arcs $p = (u_0, e_1, u_1, e_2, u_2, \ldots, e_n, u_n)$ , where $u_i \in N_Q$ $(i = 0, 1, \ldots, n)$ and $e_i \in W_Q$ $(i = 1, 2, \ldots, n)$ , is called a *path from* the note $u_0$ to the node $u_n$ if for each $i = 1, 2, \ldots, n$ either $e_i = (u_{i-1}, u_i)$ or $e_i = (u_i, u_{i-1})$ . The arc $e_i$ is said to be *positive* in $p$ if $e_i = (u_{i-1}, u_i)$ and *negative* if $e_i = (u_i, u_{i-1})$ . A vector $g$ on $W_Q$ is called a *flow* on the network $Q$ if

$$0 \leq g(e) \leq c_Q(e) \text{ for any } e \in W_Q.$$

Intuitively, the network $Q = (N_Q, W_Q, c_Q)$ can be regarded as a directed graph having the node set $N_Q$ and the arc set $W_Q$ together with the capacity constraint such that for any arc $e$ the amount of commodity that flows through the arc $e$ in the positive direction in a unit time interval should be nonnegative and should not be greater than the capacity $c_Q(e)$ .

For any node $u$ in $N_Q$, let us denote by $W^+(u)$ and $W^-(u)$ the set of arcs going out of $u$ and the set of arcs coming into $u$, respectively. For a vector $g$ on $W_Q$ , we define a vector $\partial g$ on $N_Q$ by

$$\partial g(u) = \sum_{e \in W^+(u)} g(e) - \sum_{e \in W^-(u)} g(e).$$

For a flow $g$ on the network $Q$, a node $u$ $(\in N_Q)$ is called a *source* if $\partial g(u) > 0$ , a *sink* if $\partial g(u) < 0$ , and an *intermediate node* if $\partial g(u) = 0$ . Intuitively, $\partial g(u)$ denotes the difference in the amounts of flow going out of $u$ and coming into $u$. Consequently, $\partial g(u) = 0$ implies that the commodity passes through $u$ without stagnation, whereas $\partial g(u) \neq 0$ implies that the amount of commodity is not preserved at $u$; $\partial g(u) > 0$ implies that the commodity is supplied at $u$, and $\partial g(u) < 0$ implies that the commodity is consumed at $u$.

In what follows, we restrict our consideration to a network with a single sink, that is, a network in which a unique node, say $t$, is distinguished as the sink. A vector $g$ on $W_Q$ is called a *flow on the network* $Q = (N_Q, W_Q, c_Q)$ *with the sink* $t$ if $\partial g(t) \leq 0$ and $\partial g(u) \geq 0$ for $u \in N_Q - \{t\}$ .

Let $g$ be a flow on the network $Q = (N_Q, W_Q, c_Q)$ with the sink $t$. A path

$p = (u_0, e_1, u_1, \ldots, e_n, u_n)$ from a node $u_0$ to the sink $t$ $(u_n = t)$ is said to be *flow augmentable* if for each $i = 1, 2, \ldots, n$ either both $e_i$ is positive in $p$ and $g(e_i) < c_Q(e_i)$ or both $e_i$ is negative in $p$ and $0 < g(e_i)$. Suppose that the path $p$ is flow augmentable. Let us define $\Delta(e_i)$ by $\Delta(e_i) = c_Q(e_i) - g(e_i)$ if $e_i$ is positive in $p$ and $\Delta(e_i) = g(e_i)$ if $e_i$ is negative in $p$, and let $\Delta(p) = \min\Delta(e_i)$ where the minimum is taken over all arcs on the path $p$. Furthermore let us define the vector $\Delta g_p$ on $W_Q$ by $\Delta g_p(e) = \Delta(p)$ if $e$ is positive in the path $p$, $\Delta g_p(e) = -\Delta(p)$ if $e$ is negative in $p$, and $\Delta g_p(e) = 0$ if $e$ is not on $p$. Then the vector $g + \Delta g_p$ is a flow on $Q$; that is, the flow $g + \Delta g_p$ is obtained from the flow $g$ by augmenting the amount $\Delta(p)$ of additional flow of commodity through the path $p$. Thus, for a flow augmentable path $p$, we can increase the total amount of net flow coming into the sink $t$ by $\Delta(p)$. A node $u$ is said to be *flow augmentable* if there is a flow augmentable path from $u$ to the sink $t$.

For a given flow $g$ on the network $Q = (N_Q, W_Q, c_Q)$ with the sink $t$, an *auxiliary graph* $G(Q, g) = (N_G, W_G)$ having a node set $N_G$ and an arc set $W_G$ is defined by $N_G = N_Q$ and

$$W_G = \{e \mid e \in W_Q \text{ and } g(e) < c_Q(e)\} \cup \{e^r \mid e \in W_Q \text{ and } g(e) > 0\},$$

where $e^r$ denotes the reversal of $e$. That is, in the auxiliary graph $G(Q, g)$, an arc from $u$ to $u'$ exists if and only if there is an arc connecting $u$ and $u'$ in $W_Q$ (note that the direction of the arc in the original network is not necessarily from $u$ to $u'$; it may be from $u'$ to $u$) and the flow is augmentable along the arc in the direction from $u$ to $u'$. Let $G^r(Q, g)$ be the directed graph obtained by reversing the directions of all the arcs in $G(Q, g)$. Then, the problem of finding a flow augmentable path from a given node $u$ to the sink $t$ is reduced to the problem of searching for a directed path from $u$ to $t$ in the auxiliary graph $G(Q, g)$, and the problem of finding the set of all flow augmentable nodes is reduced to the problem of finding the set of all nodes reachable from $t$ in $G^r(Q, g)$. Both of them can be solved in $O(|W_Q|)$ time by a standard graph search technique such as the depth-first search or the breadth-first search (Aho et al., 1974).

Note that, for any network $Q$, the null vector $g$ (i.e., $g(e) = 0$ for any $e \in W_Q$) is a flow on $Q$. So, starting with a $g$ that is initially a null vector, we can augment the flow step by step by finding a flow augmentable path, say $p$, and replacing the flow $g$ with the new flow $g + \Delta g_p$ until we cannot find a flow augmentable path any more. Moreover, if the capacity $c_Q(e)$ is an integer at any arc $e \in W_Q$, the flow $g$ obtained at any stage of the above flow-augmenting process is an integral vector. This is first because the initial null vector is integral, and second because if $g$ is integral, $\Delta g_p$ is also integral for any flow augmentable path $p$. Thus, each time a flow augmentable path is found, the total amount of flow reaching the sink $t$ can be augmented by at least one unit.

## 8.2. Extraction of Generically Reconstructible Substructures

For an incidence structure $I = (V,F,R)$, we associate a network $Q(I) = (N_I,W_I,c_I)$ with the sink $t$ such that

$N_I = V \cup F \cup R \cup \{t\}$ ,
$W_I = \{(r,v), (r,f) \mid r=(v,f) \in R\} \cup \{(v,t) \mid v \in V\} \cup \{(f,t) \mid f \in F\}$ ,
$c_I(e) = \infty$ if $e = (r,v)$ or $e = (r,f)$ $(r = (v,f) \in R)$,
$c_I(e) = 1$ if $e = (v,t)$ $(v \in V)$,
$c_I(e) = 3$ if $e = (f,t)$ $(f \in F)$.

Then, for any subset $X$ of $R$, $V(X)$ and $F(X)$ coincide with the sets of nodes in $V$ and $F$, respectively, that are connected with some nodes in $X$. In what follows, we consider $R$ as the set of potential source nodes, whereas we consider $V \cup F$ as the set of intermediate nodes. Hence by a flow $g$ we refer to a vector $g$ on $W_I$ that satisfies $\partial g(r) \geq 0$ $(r \in R)$ , $\partial g(v) = \partial g(f) = 0$ $(v \in V, f \in F)$ , and $\partial g(t) \leq 0$. The next proposition is an immediate consequence of the so-called demand-supply theorem in network flow theory (Ford and Fulkerson, 1962; Iri, 1969a).

**Proposition 8.1.** For any nonnegative vector $h$ on $R$, there is a flow $g$ on the network $Q(I)$ such that $\partial g |_R = h$ if and only if, for any subset $X$ of $R$,

$h(X) \leq 3 |F(X)| + |V(X)|$ .

Now, we can state the next theorem.

**Theorem 8.1.** Let $I = (V,F,R)$ be an incidence structure and $X \subseteq R$. Suppose that the substructure $(V,F,X)$ is generically reconstructible. Then, for any $r \in R-X$, the following three statements are equivalent.
(1) $(V,F,X \cup \{r\})$ is generically reconstructible.
(2) For any $Y$ such that $r \in Y \subseteq X \cup \{r\}$ and $|F(Y)| \geq 2$, the inequality $|Y|+4 \leq |V(Y)|+3|F(Y)|$ holds.

(3) For any $x \in X$ such that $|F(\{x,r\})| = 2$, the network $Q(I) = (N_l, W_l, c_l)$ admits a flow $g$ such that $\partial g|_R = \chi_X + \chi_x + 4\chi_r$.

**Proof.** The equivalence of statements (1) and (2) follows immediately from Theorem 6.2.

Now assume that statement (2) is true. Let $x$ be an element of $X$ such that $|F(\{x,r\})| = 2$, and let $h$ be the vector on $R$ defined by $h = \chi_X + \chi_x + 4\chi_r$. Let $Z$ be any subset of $X \cup \{r\}$. Case 1: Suppose that $x \notin Z$. Then, $h(Z) \leq |Z| + 3$. If $|F(Z)| \geq 2$, it follows from the assumption and Theorem 6.2 that $|Z| + 3 \leq |Z| + 4 \leq 3|F(Z)| + |V(Z)|$. If $|F(Z)| = 1$, we get $|V(Z)| = |Z|$ and consequently $|Z| + 3 = |V(Z)| + 3 = |V(Z)| + 3|F(Z)|$. Thus, we get $h(Z) \leq |V(Z)| + 3|F(Z)|$. Case 2: Suppose that $x \in Z$. If $|F(Z)| \geq 2$, then $h(Z) = 2 + h(Z - \{x\}) \leq 2 + |Z| - 1 + 3 = |Z| + 4 \leq |V(Z)| + 3|F(Z)|$. If $|F(Z)| = 1$, then $|Z| = |V(Z)|$ and $r \notin Z$, and hence $h(Z) = |Z| + 1 \leq |V(Z)| + 3|F(Z)|$. Thus, for any subset $Z$ of $X \cup \{r\}$, $h(Z) \leq |V(Z)| + 3|F(Z)|$. Hence from Proposition 8.1, we get statement (3).

Conversely, assume that statement (3) is true. Let $Y$ be a subset of $X \cup \{r\}$ such that $r \in Y$ and $|F(Y)| \geq 2$. Then, there exists an element $x$ of $X$ such that $|F(\{x,r\})| = 2$. From our assumption it follows that there exists a flow $g$ on $Q(I) = (N_l, W_l, c_l)$ such that $\partial g|_R = \chi_X + \chi_x + 4\chi_r$, and hence from Proposition 8.1 $\chi_X(Y) + \chi_x(Y) + 4\chi_r(Y) \leq |V(Y)| + 3|F(Y)|$. Since $Y$ contains both $r$ and $x$, $\chi_X(Y) = |Y| - 1$, $\chi_x(Y) = 1$ and $4\chi_r(Y) = 4$; thus we get $|Y| + 4 \leq |V(Y)| + 3|F(Y)|$.

When a generically reconstructible substructure, say $(V,F,X)$, of an incidence structure $I = (V,F,R)$ is given, statement (3) in the theorem affords us an efficient way for augmenting the incidence pair set $X$ one by one while preserving generic reconstructibleness. Suppose that $(V,F,X)$ is generically reconstructible. Then, for any subset $Y \subsetneq X$, we have $|Y| \leq |V(Y)| + 3|F(Y)|$. Consequently, from Proposition 8.1, the network $Q(I)$ has a flow $g$ such that $\partial g|_R = \chi_X$. Moreover, since the capacities of arcs are all integers, we can find as $g$ a flow whose value is integral at every arc. Using the flow $g$, we can check, for an element $r$ of $R-X$, generic reconstructibility of $(V,F,X \cup \{r\})$ in the following way.

First, we search for flow augmentable paths from $r$ to the sink $t$. If they are found, we augment the flow until the total amount of supply of the commodity at $r$ reaches 4. Since the capacity at each arc is integral, at least one unit of flow can be augmented along each path; hence the flow augmentation is accomplished by finding at most four flow augmentable paths. If such paths do not exist, the substructure $(V,F,X\cup\{r\})$ is not generically reconstructible. Otherwise, we obtain the flow $g'$ such that $\partial g'|_R = \chi_X + 4\chi_r$. In order to check statement (3) in the theorem, we need not augment the flow any more; instead we only need to check whether every node $x$ in $X$ such that $|F(\{x,r\})| = 2$ is a flow augmentable node or not. If it is, statement (3) is true because at least one unit of flow can be added to $g'$ along any flow augmentable path (recall that the capacities are integral); we conclude that $(V,F,X\cup\{r\})$ is generically reconstructible. Otherwise, it is not.

From this observation, we can construct the following method, in which an initially empty set $X$ is augmented one by one while preserving generic reconstructibleness of $(V,F,X)$.

**Method 8.1 (Maximal generically reconstructible substructure).**

Input: Incidence structure $I = (V,F,R)$.

Output: A maximal generically reconstructible substructure of $I$.

Procedure:

Step 1. Let $X = \emptyset$, and let $Y = R$ and $g$ be a null flow on $Q(I)$.

Step 2. While $Y$ is not empty, choose and delete an element $r$ from $Y$ and do the following.

    2.1. Find a flow $h$ such that $h = g+g'$ and $\partial g'|_R = 4\chi_r$. If such an $h$ does not exist, go to Step 2.

    2.2. On the network $Q(I)$ with the flow $h$, find the set $Z$ of flow augmentable nodes.

    2.3. If $\{x \mid x \in X$ and $|F(\{x,r\})| = 2\} \subseteq Z$, then add $r$ to $X$ and augment the flow $g$ so that $\partial g|_R = \chi_{X\cup\{r\}}$.

Step 3. Return $(V,F,X)$.

The number of arcs in the network $Q(I)$ is of $O(|R|)$, because each element of $R$ is connected to exactly one element of $V$ and to exactly one element of $F$. Hence, the search for a flow augmentable path $p$ from a given node, the augmentation of the flow by $\Delta g_p$ along the path $p$, and the construction of the set of flow augmentable nodes all require $O(|R|)$ time. It is therefore obvious that Steps 2.2 and 2.3 require $O(|R|)$ time. Step 2.1 can also be done in $O(|R|)$ time, because it consists of at most four times for finding a flow augmentable path and augmenting the flow along this path. Since Steps 2.1, 2.2, and 2.3 are repeated $|R|$ times, the total amount of time required by Step 2 is of $O(|R|^2)$. Steps 1 and 3

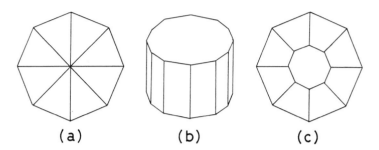

**(a)**          **(b)**          **(c)**

**Fig. 8.1.** Three different types of incidence structures used for checking the performance of Method 8.1: (a) is a top view of an $n$-gonal pyramid, (b) is a side view of a $2n$-gonal prism, and (c) is a top view of a truncated pyramid with an $n$-gonal base; the pictures are regarded as hidden-part-eliminated pictures.

can be done in, respectively, $O(|R|)$ and $O(1)$ time. Thus, Method 8.1 runs in $O(|R|^2)$ time.

**Example 8.1.** The efficiency of Method 8.1 was examined using various sizes of incidence structures. Fig. 8.1 shows the incidence structures used as input, and Fig. 8.2 plots the times required for finding maximal generically reconstructible substructures. Fig. 8.1(a) is a top view of a pyramid with an $n$-gonal base, whose incidence structure has $4n$ incidence pairs (recall that we also count the background face, which has $n$ incidence pairs; see Chapter 3), (b) is a picture of a prism with a $2n$-gonal base and $n$ visible side faces, whose incidence structure has $8n+2$ incidence pairs, and (c) is a top view of a truncated pyramid with an $n$-gonal base, whose incidence structure has $6n$ incidence pairs. The incidence structures associated with pictures (a) and (b) are generically reconstructible, whereas that associated with picture (c) is not. These three types of the incidence structures with various values of $n$ were used as the input to Method 8.1, and the times required were measured. The results are plotted in Fig. 8.2, where the horizontal axis represents the size of the incidence pair set, $|R|$, in a linear scale, and the vertical axis represents the time required in an algorithmic scale. The broken line shows the slope for $O(|R|^2)$. We can see that for large values of $|R|$ (i.e., for $|R|$ greater than 250), Method 8.1 runs in $O(|R|^2)$. The computer used in the

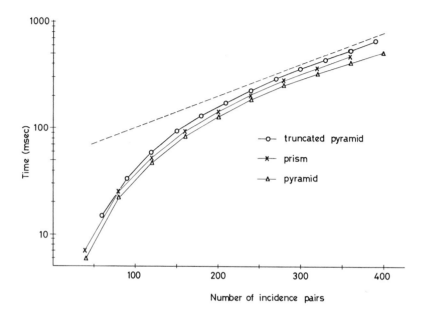

**Fig. 8.2.** Times required for finding maximal generically reconstructible substructures for various sizes of the incidence structures shown in Fig. 8.1.

experiment was M–382 of Fujitsu Ltd., and the computer program was written in Fortran77.

Method 8.1 has freedom in the order in which elements of $Y$ are chosen in Step 2. Indeed different orders create different substructures as the output. Even the size of the incidence pair set in the output substructure depends on this order. To check all such substructures is not practical because we come up against the problem of the combinatorial explosion. In practical implementation, therefore, we must define some appropriate order in which elements of $Y$ are chosen.

One natural order is the following. Recall that our purpose in finding a maximal generically reconstructible substructure $R^*$ is the correction of vertex position errors in the picture; the correction is made by displacing vertices in $V(R-R^*)$. As was shown in Section 7.1, the correction is possible only when each vertex to be corrected is on at most three faces in

$F_0$, where $F_0$ is the set of faces having four or more vertices in the
original incidence structure. Thus our first criterion is that incidence
pairs containing the vertices that are on more than three faces in $F_0$
should be chosen first. Next, as we pointed out in the discussion of
Heuristic 7.1, it seems that vertices incident to shorter edges are more
likely to have greater errors in their positions; they should be displaced
first in the correction. Thus, our second criterion is that incidence pairs
containing vertices that are on longer edges should be chosen as early as
possible. On the basis of these two criteria, we can define the order of
the incidence pairs in the following way.

First, $R$ is partitioned into $R_0$ and $R_1$ in such a way that $R_0$ consists
of incidence pairs containing the vertices that are on four or more faces
in $F_0$ (i.e., $R_0 = \{ (v,f) \mid (v,f) \in R, \ |F(\{v\}) \cap F_0| \geq 4 \}$) and $R_1 = R - R_0$.
In other words, vertices appearing in $R_1$ can be used for the correction
whereas those in $R_0$ cannot. Next, with each element $(v,f)$ of $R$ is
associated the maximum length of the line segments connected to the vertex
$v$ as its weight. Then, the order is defined by arranging elements of $R_0$ in
the decreasing order of the weights and next elements of $R_1$ also in the
decreasing order of the weights. When the incidence pairs are chosen in
this order in Step 2, the resultant maximal generically reconstructible
substructure, say $(V,F,R^*)$, is more likely to have the property that
vertices in $V(R - R^*)$ are on at most three faces in $F_0$ and that they are on
only shorter edges. This is what we want.

**Example 8.2.** The line drawing shown in Fig. 8.3 represents a planar-panel
object consisting of five panels, four of them forming a ring and the other
in the diagonal. The line drawing has the incidence structure $I = (V,F,R)$
where

$V = \{1,2, \ldots, 8\}$ ,
$F = \{1,2, \ldots, 5\}$ ,
$R = \{ (1,1),(1,2),(1,5),(2,2),(2,3),(3,1),(3,3),(3,4),(4,4),(4,5),$
$\quad (5,1),(5,2),(5,5),(6,2),(6,3),(7,1),(7,3),(7,4),(8,4),(8,5) \}$ ,

in which the vertex $v_\alpha$ ($\alpha = 1, \ldots, 8$) and the face $f_j$ ($j = 1, \ldots, 5$) are
abbreviated as $\alpha$ and $j$, respectively. It can be shown by primitive counting
that both $R_1^* = R - \{(1,1)\}$ and $R_2^* = \{(2,2),(4,4)\}$ give maximal
generically reconstructible substructures. Thus, the size of a maximal
generically reconstructible substructure is not necessarily unique. In Imai

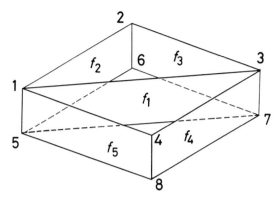

**Fig. 8.3.** Planar-panel object whose incidence structure has two different sizes of maximal generically reconstructible substructures.

(1985) is presented another example of an incidence structure that has maximal generically reconstructible substructures of different sizes.

# 9. SPECIFICATION OF UNIQUE SHAPE

The three modules established so far have enabled a machine to extract three-dimensional structures of objects from line drawings. However, what can be extracted are qualitative structures only; for example, the machine can tell which faces share an edge but cannot tell at what angle. From our mathematical point of view, a correct line drawing can represent infinitely many different objects. In the present and the next chapters, we consider methods for selecting from the set of all possible objects the one that is most consistent with additional information such as lengths of edges given by a designer or surface texture given in an image. Thus we shall construct the fourth module of our mechanism. This chapter considers the case where the additional data are accurate, whereas the next chapter treats the case where the additional data may contain noises.

## 9.1. Object Specification Using Precisely Drawn Pictures

First let us assume that a line drawing is a precise description of an object, that is, it is not a rough sketch, and hence the vertices are in correct position up to digitization errors. Then, the set of all objects the line drawing can represent is identical with the set of all solutions to the system consisting of (7.1) and (5.2). Therefore, to specify a unique shape is nothing but to remove the degrees of freedom in the choice of the solution to (7.1) and (5.2). As we have seen, the distribution of the degrees of freedom is characterized by the matroid $(H, \rho_H)$ defined by (5.4). In other words, an appropriate assignment of values to the unknowns in a certain subset of the unknown set $H = \{z_1, \ldots, z_n, a_1, b_1, c_1, \ldots, a_m, b_m, c_m\}$ determines the unique shape if and only if the subset forms a base, where "appropriate" means that the assignment of values does not violate the inequality (5.2).

Using the structure of the matroid $(H, \rho_H)$, a machine can check the insufficiency or the redundancy of additional information. Suppose that a designer gives some values to unknowns in a subset, say $X$, of $H$ in order to select one of the solution to (7.1). If $X$ is a dependent set of the matroid, the given values are in general inconsistent with (7.1); there is no solution to (7.1) that has the given values for the unknowns in $X$. If $X$ is an independent set, on the other hand, the given values are always consistent with (7.1), but the solution to (7.1) having the given values for the unknowns in $X$ is not necessarily unique. It is unique if and only if $X$ is a maximal independent set, that is, a base.

On the basis of this observation, we can construct the following two strategies for a machine to guide a designer in specifying the unique shape of the object.

In the first strategy, the machine shows to the user a set of unknowns that should be specified simultaneously for the unique reconstruction of the object. That is, after constructing (7.1) and (5.2) and correcting the input line drawing, the machine finds a base of the matroid $(H, \rho_H)$ and shows it to the user. Then, the user gives values to the unknowns in the base, by which he can specify the polyhedral object uniquely. In order to find a base, we can use Theorem 6.3. Let $I = (V, F, R)$ be the maximal generically reconstructible substructure of the original incidence structure that is used in the picture correction. Then, the size of a base must be equal to $|V| + 3|F| - |R|$. Since a base can be obtained by the greedy type of search, we can find one by scanning the elements of $V$ and adding them to an initially empty set $Y$ if the resultant set satisfies the condition in Theorem 6.3 until the size of $Y$ reaches $|V| + 3|F| - |R|$. Once a base is chosen and the user gives values to the unknowns in the base, the associated unique solution can be obtained by (7.2) where $\xi$ is the vector consisting of the given values of the unknowns in the base; thus the machine can construct the object shape quantitatively.

In the second strategy, on the other hand, a user selects the unknowns whose values should be given, and the machine guides the user not to select an inconsistent set of unknowns. At each step the machine shows to the user the set of unknowns any one of which can still be specified independently, and the user selects one of them. For simplicity, let us consider the case where the user specifies $z$ values of some vertices. As before, let $I = (V, F, R)$ be the maximal generically reconstructible substructure used for the picture correction. For any subset $Y$ of $V$, let us define $T(Y)$ by

$$T(Y) = \{v \mid v \in V-Y, \ \rho_V(Y) < \rho_V(Y \cup \{v\}) \} .$$

That is, $v$ is an element of $T(Y)$ if and only if $Y \cup \{v\}$ has greater degrees of freedom than $Y$ has. Hence, if the user has given $z$ coordinates to the vertices in $Y$, the $z$ coordinate of the vertex $v$ can still be given independently if and only if $v$ belongs to $T(Y)$. Note that the set $T(Y)$ can be constructed from Corollary 6.3.1. Therefore, the user and the machine can communicate in the following manner. After the machine corrects an input line drawing, the machine shows $T(\emptyset)$ to the user. The user first chooses from $T(\emptyset)$ any one vertex, say $v_1$, and gives a value to its $z$ coordinate. Then, the machine constructs $T(\{v_1\})$ and shows it to the user. The user next chooses one of its elements, say $v_2$, and gives its $z$ coordinate. Then, the machine shows $T(\{v_1, v_2\})$ to the user, and so on. They repeat the communication until the object shape is specified uniquely.

## 9.2. Object Specification Using Roughly Drawn Pictures

It has been assumed in Section 9.1 that the line drawings are drawn precisely within digitization errors; hence the $x$ and $y$ coordinates of vertices were regarded as given constants, and the problem was to determine only the $z$ coordinates. In human communication, on the other hand, pictures are often drawn only roughly; they represent only qualitative aspects of the objects. In that case vertex positions in the picture plane are not reliable, and consequently the exact shape of the object to be recovered does not necessarily belong to the set of solutions to (7.1) and (5.2). Hence, the mathematical structures as to the degrees of freedom in the choice of the objects will be quite different from that for the case of precisely drawn pictures.

Here we consider roughly drawn axonometric line drawings. This class includes usual line drawings in the sense that the usual line drawings can be regarded as axonometric line drawings in which no edges are parallel to the axonometric axes.

As is seen in Section 5.4, an axonometric line drawing is an orthographic projection of an object in which the axonometric axes are also drawn. The axonometric axes are three mutually orthogonal unit vectors, say $e_X$, $e_Y$, $e_Z$, which are usually chosen in such a way that many edges and faces of the object become parallel to them. Since the axonometric axes $e_X$, $e_Y$, $e_Z$ are of unit length, their projections, say $l_X$, $l_Y$, and $l_Z$, respectively, represent the ratios of compression of the lengths of edges that are parallel to the axonometric axes. In the axonometric projection the object posture is usually chosen so that no edge that is not parallel to an axonometric axis becomes accidentally parallel on the picture plane. Therefore, if a line segment in the picture is parallel to $l_X$, $l_Y$, or $l_Z$, the orientation and the exact length of the corresponding three-dimensional edge is determined uniquely (recall Heuristic 5.1).

In practical situations of engineering, we often use "axonometriclike" line drawings (instead of precise ones) to represent rough shapes of objects, where the line drawings are read with the following convention. Like axonometric line drawings, line segments that are nearly parallel to $l_X$, $l_Y$, or $l_Z$ are regarded as the projections of edges that are precisely parallel to the $X$, $Y$, or $Z$ axis. However, unlike axonometric line drawings, lengths of line segments drawn in the pictures are regarded as merely rough approximations to the true lengths of the projections of the edges. With this convention, the line drawing in Fig. 5.9 is thought of as a picture of a triangular prism whose side faces are perpendicular to the base triangle, but neither the precise shape of the base triangle nor the height is known. Thus, this convention allows us much greater degrees of freedom in the choice of the shape of the object than when the line drawings are drawn precisely. In the present section we consider line drawings with this convention.

Here, the algebraic approach taken in Section 5.4 seems useless. Indeed a position of a vertex $v_\alpha$ on the picture plane, $(x_\alpha, y_\alpha)$, may contain errors so that we must treat $x_\alpha$ and $y_\alpha$ as unknown variables instead of given constants. Consequently, (3.1) becomes nonlinear, and hence the resulting system of equations seems intractable.

However, if we restrict our objects to trihedral ones (i.e., the objects in which vertices lie on exactly three faces), we can reduce the problems to purely combinatorial problems.

One simple way to define the precise shape of an object represented by a line drawing $D$ and its spatial structure $S$ is to fix face planes one by one to the $(X, Y, Z)$ coordinate system. That is, we first choose an arbitrary face, say $f_1$, and specify the plane on which $f_1$ should lie, next choose another face, say $f_2$, and specify the associated plane, and so on. As we add new face planes, edges and vertices of the object are gradually generated as intersections of the planes.

This method is simple but does not always succeed in defining the shape. Recall that every face of a polyhedron must be planar. Hence, when we add a new face plane to the already constructed substructure, the plane must be chosen so that it passes through every vertex the face should have. However, if four or more vertices that a new face should have are already located in the substructure and are not coplanar, then it is impossible to add the new face plane; thus the method fails in defining the whole shape of the object.

The situation is quite different when we restrict our objects to trihedral ones. A trihedral vertex is shared by exactly three faces, and consequently the position of the vertex is determined only when all of the

three face planes are given. Therefore, at each step of adding a new face
to the already constructed substructure, any vertex that should be on the
new face has not yet been located; we can always add a new face plane and
augment the substructure. Thus, the method is always successful. This
observation leads us to the following solution to the problem.

Suppose that we are given an axonometriclike line drawing $D$. As in
Section 5.4, let $E_X$, $E_Y$, and $E_Z$ denote the sets of edges that are parallel
to $e_X$, $e_Y$, and $e_Z$, respectively. Furthermore, let $F_{XY}$, $F_{YZ}$, and $F_{ZX}$ denote
the sets of faces that are parallel to the $X$-$Y$ plane, the $Y$-$Z$ plane, and
the $Z$-$X$ plane, respectively, and let $F_X$, $F_Y$, and $F_Z$ denote the sets of
faces that are parallel only to the $X$ axis, the $Y$ axis, or the $Z$ axis,
respectively. These sets can be constructed from the labeled line drawing
$D$; for example, a face $f_i$ belongs to $F_X$ if and only if $f_i$ has an edge in $E_X$
but no edge in $E_Y \cup E_Z$, and $f_i$ belongs to $F_{XY}$ if and only if $f_i$ has both an
edge in $E_X$ and one in $E_Y$. Let $F_0$ be the set of faces that are parallel to
neither the $X$ axis, the $Y$ axis, nor the $Z$ axis. Thus,
$\{F_{XY}, F_{YZ}, F_{ZX}, F_X, F_Y, F_Z, F_0\}$ is a partition of $F$.

A face in $F_{XY}$ is parallel to the $X$-$Y$ plane, and hence it can be
represented by the equation $Z = a$, which contains only one parameter: $a$.
Similarly, faces in $F_{YZ}$ and in $F_{ZX}$ are represented by one-parameter
equations. A face in $F_X$, which is parallel to the $X$ axis, can be
represented by the equation $Z = aY + b$. Faces in $F_Y$ and in $F_Z$ are also
represented by two-parameter equations. A face in $F_0$, on the contrary, is
on a general plane, and is represented by a three-parameter equation $aX +$
$bY + cZ = 1$ (this equation cannot represent a plane that passes through the
origin of the $(x, y, z)$ coordinate system; however, note that the line
drawing does not specify the absolute position of the object in the space,
and consequently we can assume without loss of generality that no face is
on the plane passing through the origin). Thus, the total number of
parameters is

$$|F_{XY} \cup F_{YZ} \cup F_{ZX}| + 2|F_X \cup F_Y \cup F_Z| + 3|F_0|,$$

which is equal to the degrees of freedom in the choice of the object
represented by $D$. Note, however, that the degrees of freedom include the
freedom in the choice of the position and the posture of the object.
Therefore, the degrees of freedom in the choice of the shape itself, which
shall be denoted by $\tau(D)$, is obtained in the following equation:

$$\tau(D) = |F_{XY} \cup F_{YZ} \cup F_{ZX}| + 2|F_X \cup F_Y \cup F_Z| + 3|F_0| - p(D), \qquad (9.1)$$

where $p(D)$ is the degrees of freedom in the choice of the position and the posture of the object, that is,

$p(D) = 3$     if at least two of $E_X$, $E_Y$, $E_Z$ are nonempty,

$p(D) = 4$     if exactly one of $E_X$, $E_Y$, $E_Z$ is nonempty,

$p(D) = 6$     if $E_X$, $E_Y$, $E_Z$ are all empty.

The value of $p(D)$ can be interpreted in the following way. There are 6 degrees of freedom for us to fix a rigid object to the coordinate system: three for translation and three for rotation. Suppose first that $E_X$ and $E_Y$ are nonempty. Then, the edges in $E_X$ and $E_Y$ are constrained to be parallel to the associated axes; the object can admit translation, but not rotation. Thus, $p(D) = 3$. Next suppose that only $E_X$ is nonempty. Then, the edges in $E_X$ are constrained to be parallel to the $X$ axis, and hence the object admits translation in any direction and rotation about axes parallel to the $X$ axis. Thus, $p(D) = 4$. If $E_X$, $E_Y$, $E_Z$ are all empty, the object can admit any translation and any rotation, and hence $p(D) = 6$.

Note that in the case of an axonometriclike line drawing the degrees of freedom in the choice of the shape, $\tau(D)$, depend only on the face sets $F_{XY}$, $F_{YZ}$, $F_{ZX}$, $F_X$, $F_Y$, $F_Z$, $F_0$, and the edge sets $E_X$, $E_Y$, $E_Z$, whereas the degrees of freedom for an axonometric line drawing, $\sigma_H(H)-1$, defined in Section 5.4, depend also on the positions of the vertices in the picture $D$. This is because, unlike an axonometric line drawing, the positions of vertices on the picture plane are regarded as rough estimates about the precise positions, and consequently the degrees of freedom depend only on which faces contain which vertices and which edges are parallel to the coordinate axes.

Now we have seen that $\tau(D)$ additional data are required for us to define uniquely the shape of the object. The next question is which data are required. This can be answered easily in the following way. Assign a linear order to the faces such that the first three faces share a common vertex and, for $4 \leq i \leq |F|$, the $i$th face has two edges in common with the substructure consisting of the first $i - 1$ faces (this is always possible for a trihedral object). Give mutual angles between the first three faces, if they have not yet been given, and next for $i = 4, 5, \ldots,$ $|F|$, give appropriate data in order to fix the $i$th face with respect to the substructure consisting of the first $i - 1$ faces. Thus we can

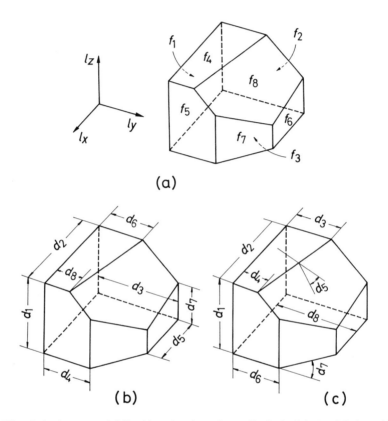

**Fig. 9.1.** Axonometriclike line drawing of a trihedral object: (a) is a line drawing, and (b) and (c) show two sets of additional data defining the unique shape of the object.

completely specify the shape of the object.

**Example 9.1.** Consider the line drawing $D$ shown in Fig. 9.1. The object has eight faces, and they are numbered as shown in the figure. The face $f_1$ is bounded by edges parallel to the $X$ axis and edges parallel to the $Z$ axis, and consequently belongs to $F_{ZX}$. The face $f_7$ has edges parallel to the $Z$ axis but no edges parallel to the $X$ axis or the $Y$ axis, and hence belongs to $F_Z$. The face $f_8$ belongs to $F_0$ because it has no edge that is parallel to the coordinate axes. Other faces are classified similarly, and we get

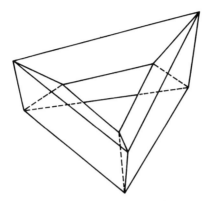

**Fig. 9.2.** Nontrihedral object whose faces cannot be specified in the step-by-step manner.

$F_{XY} = \{f_3, f_4\}$ , $F_{YZ} = \{f_2, f_5\}$ , $F_{ZX} = \{f_1, f_6\}$
$F_X = F_Y = \phi$ , $F_Z = \{f_7\}$ , $F_0 = \{f_8\}$ .

Moreover, since the line drawing has edges parallel to the $X$ axis and those parallel to the $Y$ axis, rotation of the object is not allowed; $p(D) = 3$. Hence we see

$$\tau(D) = 6 + 2 \times 1 + 3 \times 1 - 3 = 8;$$

that is, eight additional data are necessary to define the shape of the object.

In order to find a set of eight additional data, let us consider the linear order of the faces $(f_1, f_2, \ldots, f_8)$ . Since the mutual angles of the first three faces are given (i.e., they meet at right angles), we need not add any data for the specification of the relative position of these three faces. Since $f_4$ is parallel to $f_3$, $f_4$ is fixed to the substructure consisting of $f_1$, $f_2$, $f_3$ by giving the distance between $f_3$ and $f_4$ (the length $d_1$ in (b)). Similarly, since $f_5$ and $f_6$ are parallel to $f_2$ and $f_1$, respectively, they are fixed by the distances $d_2$ and $d_3$ in (b). The face $f_7$ is parallel to the $Z$ axis, and hence is fixed by giving two points through which the face should pass, which is done by lengths $d_4$ and $d_5$. Finally, since $f_8$ is not parallel to any coordinate axes, its definition requires three additional data; for example, $d_6$, $d_7$, $d_8$ in (b). Thus, the eight additional data $d_1$, ..., $d_8$ in (b) all together define the shape of the object uniquely.

Let us consider another linear order of the faces $(f_1, f_2, f_3, f_4, f_5, f_8, f_7, f_6)$. The first five faces are the same as in the previous order, so that the substructure consisting of these five faces is defined by $d_1$ and $d_2$. Next, in order to define $f_8$, three new data are necessary, and an example of the set of the three data is $\{d_3, d_4, d_5\}$ in (c), where $d_5$ is the angle between $f_4$ and $f_8$. The other faces, $f_7$ and $f_6$, are defined, for example, by $d_6$, $d_7$, $d_8$ in (c), where $d_7$ denotes the angle between $f_5$ and $f_7$. Thus, (c) represents another set of eight additional data.

**Example 9.2.** The method in this subsection is valid in the trihedral object world; it is not necessarily valid for objects outside this world. A counterexample is shown in Fig. 9.2. This line drawing represents an object bounded by nine quadrilateral faces forming a shape that is topologically equivalent to a torus. Note that every vertex of this object is shared by four faces. Therefore, when eight face planes are fixed in the space, the positions of all the vertices are determined, and in general the four vertices that should be on the ninth face are not coplanar. Thus, we cannot specify the face planes in the one-by-one manner.

## 10. RECOVERY OF SHAPE FROM SURFACE INFORMATION

Visual information on the surfaces of objects, such as shading and texture, affords us fruitful cues for recovering the three-dimensional structures of the objects. This chapter presents a method of using these cues as the additional information in order to determine the object structures quantitatively. While in the previous chapter the additional data are assumed to be accurate, surface cues extracted from real images are not always very accurate. Hence the shape recovery is considered as an optimization in the sense that among all the possible objects represented by a line drawing, the shape to be recovered is the one that is most consistent with the additional surface cues.

### 10.1. Shape Recovery as an Optimization

If line drawings are those extracted from photographic images of the outside world, surface information in the images is also available for the recovery of three-dimensional shape (Brady, 1982). There are exactly three degrees of freedom in the choice of a planar surface or a small portion of a curved surface that can be regarded as planar. These degrees of freedom can be lessened by various kinds of visual information, such as light intensity under a priori known illumination conditions (Horn, 1975; Woodham, 1977, 1981; Ikeuchi, 1981; Coleman and Jain, 1982), apparent distortion of known patterns (Kender, 1979; Kanade, 1981; Ikeuchi, 1984), surface contour (Stevens, 1981; Barrow and Tenenbaum, 1981; Marr, 1982), statistical properties of texture (Bajcsy and Lieberman, 1976; Witkin, 1981), vanishing points (Nakatani and Kitahashi, 1984), and the distribution of small pattern sizes (Ohta et al., 1981).

In general each of these cues alone is not enough to determine the surface completely; they can remove the degrees of freedom only partially. However, if we combine the surface information with the algebraic structure of line drawings, we can determine the object shape uniquely from single-view images; that is, from all the scenes that the line drawing can represent we can choose the one that is most consistent with the surface information. This is the basic idea of the shape recovery presented in this chapter (Sugihara, 1984a).

One general principle in computer vision is, "If surface information is not enough to determine each surface locally, use global constraints

that constrain relative configuration of the surfaces so that the total
degrees of freedom decrease" (Horn, 1975, 1977; Ikeuchi and Horn, 1981;
Kanade, 1981). The shape recovery method presented here is another example
of this principle, where the algebraic structure of line drawings is used
as the global constraint.

In the previous chapter the additional data were assumed to be
precise, and consequently the problem was to find a minimum set of
additional data that is sufficient to specify the object shape. In the case
of surface information obtained from real images, on the other hand, we
cannot expect that the data are always very accurate; they usually contain
noises. Therefore, instead of searching for a minimum set of additional
data, we must search for the shape that is most consistent with all of the
additional information. Keeping this in mind, we formulate the problem of
shape recovery as a kind of an optimization problem.

Let $D$ be a labeled line drawing extracted from a given image, and let
$I^* = (V, F, R^*)$ be a maximal generically reconstructible substructure of the
incidence structure of $D$. Then, there is a one-to-one correspondence
between the set of all solutions to the system consisting of (7.1) and
(5.2) and the set of all scenes that the picture $D$ can represent. Hence the
problem of shape recovery can be regarded as the problem of selecting a
solution to (7.1) and (5.2) that is most consistent with surface
information.

We consider any cue that can lessen the degrees of freedom of the
faces. Let $d_k$ denote an observed value of the $k$th cue, and for any $w$
satisfying (7.1) and (5.2), let $d_k^*(w)$ denote a theoretical value of the $k$th
cue that should be observed if the exact scene is $w$. For example, if a face
is covered with a grain texture of a known uniform density, we can adopt as
$d_k$ and $d_k^*(w)$, respectively, the observed value and the theoretical one of
the apparent a grain density on the surface; if the illumination condition
and the surface reflectance are known, we can adopt as $d_k$ and $d_k^*(w)$ the
observed value and the theoretical one of light intensity on the face.

Let $g_k(w)$ be the difference of the two values:

$$g_k(w) = d_k - d_k^*(w). \qquad (10.1)$$

If there is no error in observation, the true scene $w$ must satisfy $g_k(w)=0$;
this condition lessens the degrees of freedom of the face by 1. Since
noises are inevitable in real image data, we cannot expect $g_k(w)=0$ exactly.
However, if enough cues are available, we can seek a solution to the

following optimization problem:

**Problem 10.1.** Minimize $\sum_k s_k(g_k(w))^2$, subject to (7.1) and (5.2), where $s_k$ denotes a positive weight of the $k$th cue, and the summation is to be taken over all available cues.

A solution $\bar{w}$ to the optimization problem can be thought of as a scene that is most consistent with the surface cues under the quadric error criterion. Thus, the fundamental scheme of our shape recovery is to adopt the solution to the optimization problem as the shape to be recovered.

As we have seen in Section 7.2, the set of all solutions $w$ to (7.1) and (5.2) coincides with the set of all vectors of the form $w = h(\xi)$ satisfying (7.4). Hence, Problem 10.1 can be paraphrased by the next problem:

**Problem 10.2.** Minimize $\varphi(\xi) = \sum_k s_k(g_k(h(\xi)))^2$, subject to (7.4).

Note that the size of the vector $\xi$ equals $n+3m-|R^*|$ (where as before $n$ and $m$ denote the number of vertices and the number of faces, respectively), whereas the size of the vector $w$ equals $n+3m$. The size of $w$ increases as the scene becomes complicated, but the size of $\xi$ usually does not increase so rapidly as $w$; it often remains four or a little greater than four. Hence, Problem 10.2 is much more tractable than Problem 10.1 in the sense that the number of variables is very small.

Thus our problem of shape recovery has been reduced to the constrained optimization problem, where the constraints are expressed by the linear inequalities (7.4) and the objective function to be minimized is $\varphi(\xi)$. However, in order to solve the problem we have to consider one more point.

In Problem 10.2 the constraint set, the set of solutions $\xi$ to (7.4), is not a closed set, because some of the inequalities in (7.4) do not allow equalities (i.e., some inequalities are of the form $>$ but not $\geqq$). Generally a constrained optimization problem does not necessarily have a solution when its constraint set is not closed (Gill et al., 1981). In this sense Problem 10.2 seems unsound.

However, the unclosedness of the constraint set is a natural consequence of the properties of pictures of polyhedral scenes. For example, some of the inequalities represent the condition that faces bend along edges. An edge shared by two faces implies that the two faces meet at some angle other than $\pi$. This angle may be near to $\pi$, but is not equal to $\pi$

because, if so, the edge would disappear. Consequently, such inequalities do not include equalities.

The unclosedness of the constraint set seems unsound only when we consider Problem 10.2 as a "general" optimization problem. For our specific problem, the absence of equalities merely means that the shape to be recovered does not lie on the boundary of such constraints.

Let

$$B_1 h(\xi) \geqq 0 \qquad\qquad (10.2)$$

be the set of all improper inequalities (i.e., inequalities including equalities) in (7.4), and let

$$B_2 h(\xi) > 0 \qquad\qquad (10.3)$$

be the set of all proper inequalities (inequalities excluding equalities). Then, the shape to be recovered may lie on the boundary of the constraints (10.2), but never lies on the boundary of the constraints (10.3). That is, the inequalities in (10.3) are not "active" at the optimal point. In fact, this property is not a difficulty, but makes the problem easier in the following manner.

An optimization problem is usually solved by an iterated process; starting with a certain initial point in a solution space, we repeatedly seek for a better point until we reach the optimal point. One of the greatest difficulties in solving a constrained optimization problem is to control each step in such a way that the replaced point does not go out of the constraint set (Gill et al., 1981). This control is especially important when the optimal point lies on the boundary of the constraint set.

In our problem the optimal point does not lie on the boundary of the constraints (10.3). Hence, if an initial point is chosen near enough to the optimal point, we can ignore the inactive constraints (10.3). Thus we can lessen the number of constraints in the optimization.

Moreover, we can also ignore the other constraints (10.2) in the following sense. Note that our objective function to be minimized is the sum of quadric differences between the observed values and the theoretical values of the available cues. Hence the objective function is nonnegative, and if there is no error in observation, it becomes zero at the optimal point. This means that the optimal point remains optimal even if we remove active constraints. That is, the optimal point attains the local minimum of the objective function whether the constraints in (10.2) are considered or ignored. Hence if an initial point is chosen sufficiently near to the optimal point, we can reach the optimal point by any local optimization method (such as a steepest descent method) even if we skip the control for preventing the point from going out of the constraint set. Therefore, instead of solving Problem 10.2 directly, we search for the solution in the following manner. Starting with a certain initial point $\xi_0$ that satisfies (7.4), we search for the point $\bar{\xi}$ which yields the local minimum of the objective function of Problem 10.2. If $\bar{\xi}$ satisfies (7.4), we adopt $\bar{\xi}$ as a candidate of the shape to be recovered. Otherwise, we choose a new initial point and repeat the process. Thus, we can establish the next method for shape recovery.

**Method 10.1 (Shape recovery).**
Input:   Image of a polyhedral scene and the corresponding labeled line drawing with an incidence structure $I = (V,F,R)$.
Output: Three-dimensional shape represented in the image.
Procedure:
Step 1. Find a maximal generically reconstructible substructure $I^* = (V,F,R^*)$ of $I$, where $R^* \subseteq R$.
Step 2. Construct Problem 10.2.
Step 3. Choose a vector $\xi = \xi_0$ that satisfies (7.4).
Step 4. Find, starting with $\xi_0$, the locally minimum point $\xi = \bar{\xi}$ of the objective function $\varphi(\xi)$.
Step 5. If $\xi = \bar{\xi}$ satisfies (7.4) and $\varphi(\bar{\xi})$ is smaller than a certain prespecified threshold, go to Step 6. Otherwise, replace $\xi_0$ with a new initial point satisfying (7.4) and go to Step 4.
Step 6. Construct a three-dimensional scene using vector $\bar{w} = h(\bar{\xi})$ (whose components represent the $z$ coordinates of the vertices and the surface equations of the faces).
Step 7. If $R^* = R$, end the processing. If $R^* \neq R$ (note that, in this case, the scene constructed in Step 6 does not necessarily satisfy the incidence constraints in $R - R^*$ because these constraints have been removed), correct the positions of the vertices associated with elements in $R - R^*$ by finding intersections of the surfaces constructed in Step 6, and end the processing.

Step 1 can be done by Method 8.1. Step 2 consists of finding a set of vertices whose $z$ coordinates can be given independently (a method for this is given in Theorem 6.3), calculating (7.2), and constructing an objective function that depends on the cues available in the image. Since (7.4) is linear with respect to $\xi$, $\xi_0$ in Step 3 can be found, for example, by linear programming methods (Dantzig, 1963). Moreover, this step can be executed by Method 5.1 very quickly if there are exactly four degrees of freedom in the solutions to (7.4). Step 4 is an unconstrained local optimization; it can be done by any method (such as a steepest descent method). Steps 5 and 6 are obvious. Step 7 is the same as Step 3 in Method 7.1.

### 10.2. Some Examples

Here we shall show some examples in which Method 10.1 is applied to various kinds of objects and surface cues.

**Example 10.1 (Computer simulation for ideal images).** In the first example Method 10.1 is applied to ideal light intensity data of a scene generated by a computer. This example is intended to illustrate basic behavior of the method for a typical scene with typical surface information.

Fig. 10.1(a) shows a scene constructed in a computer, where a truncated pyramid lies on a desk surface. Seen from above, it is projected orthographically on the $x$-$y$ plane as shown in Fig. 10.1(b). Since this picture is also generated by a computer, the vertex positions are correct up to digitization errors. It has ten visible vertices and five visible faces, and they are numbered as in the figure.

Let $I = (V,F,R)$ be the incidence structure of the picture. Then, we get

$$V = \{1, 2, \ldots, 10\},$$
$$F = \{1, 2, \ldots, 5\},$$
$$R = \{(1,1), (2,1), (3,1), (3,2), (3,3), (4,2), (4,3), (4,4),$$
$$(5,2), (5,4), (5,5), (6,1), (6,2), (6,5), (7,3), (7,4),$$
$$(7,5), (8,1), (8,3), (8,5), (9,1), (10,1)\},$$

where $v_\alpha$ and $f_j$ are abbreviated to $\alpha$ and $j$ ($\alpha = 1, \ldots, 10$, $j = 1, \ldots, 5$) because it is obvious from the context whether a number denotes the vertex number or the face number. Since $|V|+3|F| = 25 < |R|+4 = 26$, $I$ is not generically reconstructible (see Theorem 6.2). If we delete from R any one incidence pair containing $f_2$, $f_3$, or $f_5$, then we get a generically

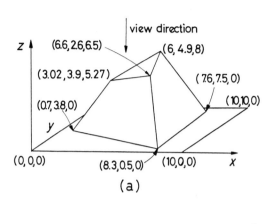

(a)

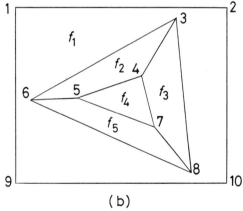

(b)

**Fig. 10.1.** Scene used in the computer simulation in Example 10.1: (a) shows an object on the floor that can be obtained by cutting off the upper part of a pyramid with a slant cutting plane, and (b) is a top view of the scene.

reconstructible substructure $I^* = (V,F,R^*)$. Let us put $R^* = R - \{(5,5)\}$. From $R^*$ we construct the system of equations (7.1), consisting of 21 equations, with respect to 25 unknowns $w = {}^t(z_1 \cdots z_{10}a_1b_1c_1 \cdots a_5b_5c_5)$. Corollary 6.2.1 assures us that the equations in (7.1) are linearly independent, and hence the solutions to (7.1) can be expressed as a linear combination of 4 free variables. According to the systematic way for finding a set of free variables (Theorem 6.3), we can, for example, put $\xi = {}^t(z_1,z_2,z_3,z_4)$. For the present example we easily see that when we specify $\xi$, the shape is determined uniquely. Thus we get the general form of solutions to (7.1) as

$$w = h(\xi), \quad \text{where} \quad \xi = {}^t(z_1,z_2,z_3,z_4).$$

Substituting this expression in (5.2), we get (7.4) and thus obtain the constraint set of Problem 10.2 explicitly.

A light intensity image of the scene is also generated by a computer. The scene is assumed to be illuminated by a parallel light. Let $-l$ be a direction vector along which the light is projected; that is, $l$ is a vector from a point on the surface toward the light source. Furthermore, it is assumed that the scene is covered with a Lambertian surface; light intensity at a point on the surface is $L\cos\theta$ where $L$ is a constant depending on the light source and surface reflectance, and $\theta$ is the incident angle, that is, the angle between a surface normal $n$ and the light source direction $l$. Then, when we have fixed the light source direction $l$, the light intensity on the surface depends only on its normal, and hence each planar face of the object has a constant intensity.

Let us define $n_k = (a_k,b_k,1)$; that is, $n_k$ is a vector normal to the $k$th surface $a_k x + b_k y + z + c_k = 0$ . Then, we obtain the light intensity $d_k$ on this surface:

$$d_k = L \cdot \cos\theta = \frac{L \cdot l \cdot n_k}{|l| \cdot |n_k|} = \frac{L \cdot l \cdot (a_k,b_k,1)}{|l| \sqrt{(a_k)^2 + (b_k)^2 + 1}} .$$

In the present experiment we put $L = 1$, $l = (-1,1,3)$, and thus get the observed value $d_k$ of the light intensity on the $k$th face ($k = 1, \ldots, 5$):

$$d_k = \frac{-a_k + b_k + 3}{\sqrt{11((a_k)^2 + (b_k)^2 + 1)}}, \quad k = 1,\ldots,5,$$

where $a_k$ and $b_k$ are fixed real numbers given in the scene in Fig. 10.1(a). Similarly, the theoretical value $d_k^*(w)$ of the light intensity on the $k$th face ($k = 1, \ldots, 5$) in a scene $w = {}^t(z_1 \cdots z_{10} a_1 b_1 c_1 \cdots a_5 b_5 c_5)$ is given by the right-hand side of the above equation in which $a_k$ and $b_k$ are regarded as variables. Thus we obtain the objective function in Problem 10.2 explicitly:

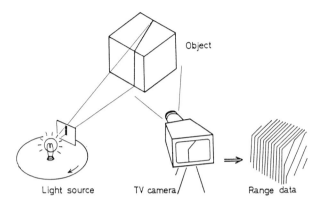

Light source          TV camera          Range data

**Fig.** 10.2. Light stripe image.

$$\varphi(\xi) = \sum_{k=1}^{5} s_k (d_k - d_k^*(w))^2$$

$$= \sum_{k=1}^{5} s_k (d_k - d_k^*(h(\xi)))^2, \quad \xi = {}^t(z_1, z_2, z_3, z_4),$$

where as the weight $s_k$ we adopt the area of the $k$th face on the picture plane.

Because of our assumption concerning the illumination condition, the light intensity data are invariant under the translation of the scene along the $z$ axis. Hence, without loss of generality we can fix one of the free parameters; we put $z_1 = 0$. Then, our problem has only three unknowns (i.e., $z_2$, $z_3$, and $z_4$), whereas the number of available cues is five, one for each face. We have thus enough cues to recover the shape uniquely.

Now, we start solving the optimization problem. In order to illustrate the behavior of the method, we have to display the recovered three-dimensional shape. For this purpose we use, in what follows, the light stripe representation. Suppose that a virtual light source is set to the left of the viewpoint and light is projected through a narrow vertical slit onto the scene, as is shown in Fig. 10.2. Then, an image of the slit on the surface of the scene forms a piecewise linear polygonal line. Changing the direction of the slit light and superimposing the resultant slit images upon each other, we get a light stripe image which reflects the shape of objects in the scene. While the light stripe image was originally

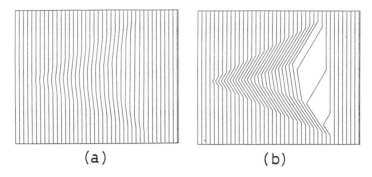

$$\text{(a)} \qquad\qquad\qquad\qquad \text{(b)}$$

**Fig. 10.3.** Result of the recovery: (a) shows an initial shape, and (b) shows the recovered shape that corresponds to the optimal point.

used for range finding (Shirai and Suwa, 1971; Oshima and Shirai, 1979), it is also suitable for shape display in that we can illustrate a three-dimensional shape without changing eye position.

Fig. 10.3(a) shows an initial shape satisfying (7.4), with which we start the optimization. The result of recovery is shown in Fig. 10.3(b). We can see that the initial shape (a) is not very near to the optimal shape (b). In our experience we find that the correct shape can be recovered from almost any initial shape provided that the initial shape satisfies (7.4). Hence, we need not repeat Steps 4 and 5 in Method 10.1 more than once.

On the other hand, if we start with the initial shape shown in Fig. 10.4(a), which does not satisfy (7.4), then we reach a local minimum that corresponds to the shape shown in Fig. 10.4(b), in which the edges forming ridges and those forming valleys are all interchanged with each other when compared with Fig. 10.3(b). Even if we come across this shape as a local minimum of the objective function, we can easily reject it in Step 5 because it does not satisfy the constraint (7.4). The interesting point is that Fig. 10.4(b) is very similar to what is called Necker's reversal (Gregory, 1971) or a "negative" object (Kanade, 1981), in which the relative depths are all reversed. It should be noted, however, that Fig. 10.4(b) is not the same as Necker's reversal in the following sense. A primal shape and its Necker's reversal are both correct interpretations of a picture, whereas Fig. 10.4(b) is incorrect because it does not make the objective function zero. Indeed, the value of the objective function at the local minimum point corresponding to Fig. 10.4(b) is equal to $\varphi(\xi) = 7.21$.

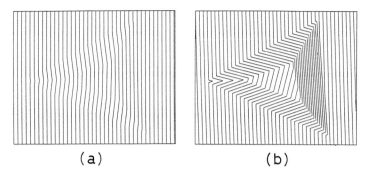

(a)                    (b)

**Fig. 10.4.** Reversed shape associated with a locally optimal point: (a) shows an initial shape, and (b) shows the shape that corresponds to a locally optimal point.

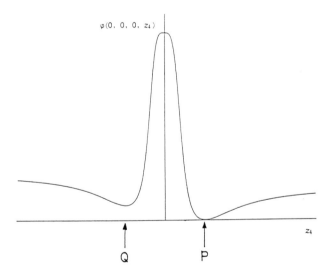

$\varphi(0, 0, 0, z_4)$

$z_4$

Q          P

**Fig. 10.5.** Profile of the objective function.

The situation is revealed more clearly when we plot the values of the objective function $\varphi(\xi)$ for various $\xi = {}^t(z_1, z_2, z_3, z_4)$. We put $z_1 = z_2 = z_3 = 0$ and move $z_4$ (that is, we fix the desk surface to the correct position and alter one of the top vertices of the truncated pyramid). Then,

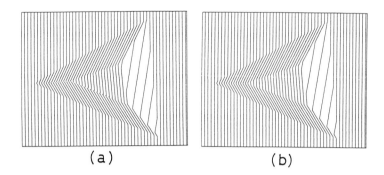

**Fig. 10.6.** Shape recovery from a picture containing vertex-position errors:
(a) shows the shape corresponding to the optimal point, where the surface
has discontinuity, and (b) shows the finally recovered shape, where the
discontinuity is repaired.

$\varphi(0,0,0,z_4)$ changes its value as shown in Fig. 10.5. When $z_4 > 0$, $\xi =$
$^t(0,0,0,z_4)$ satisfies (7.4), whereas all of the inequalities in (7.4) are
reversed if $z_4 < 0$ (note that this fact corresponds to the property stated
in Theorem 5.4). As is easily seen, $\varphi(0,0,0,z_4)$ has two locally minimum
points denoted by P and Q. P corresponds to the correct shape
(Fig. 10.3(b)), and Q corresponds to a reversed shape like Fig. 10.4(b)
(note that Q does not correspond to Fig. 10.4(b) exactly; in Fig. 10.4(b),
$z_2$ and $z_3$ also have nonzero values). Fig. 10.5 seems to suggest that the
correct optimal point can be attained by any local optimization method for
a very large range of initial points in the constraint set.

In the above observation it is not very easy for us to understand the
effect of the extraction of the generically reconstructible substructure $I^*$
from $I$. This is because our data do not contain vertex-position errors. Now
we perturb the vertex position; we change the position on the picture plane
of the vertex 7 from (6.6, 2.6) to (6.5, 2.5), and apply our method to the
new picture. The shape corresponding to the optimal point is shown in
Fig. 10.6(a). We can observe that the surface has gaps along the edges 5-6
and 5-7 (where the edge connecting $i$ and $j$ is denoted by $i$-$j$). This is
because we deleted the incidence pair (5, 5) when we constructed the
generically reconstructible substructure $I^*$. The incidence pair (5, 5)
represents the constraint that the vertex 5 should be on the face 5. Since
this constraint has been deleted, it is not satisfied by the recovered

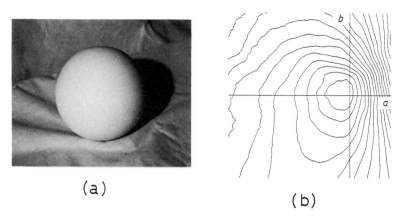

(a)

(b)

**Fig. 10.7.** Calibration of the illumination condition: (a) is a light intensity image of a sphere, and (b) shows the contours of the light intensity plotted in the gradient space.

shape in Fig. 10.6(a). It should be noted that, if we did not delete this constraint, we could not reconstruct any shape. Indeed, the picture is incorrect and hence Problem 10.1 has no solutions due to the superstrictness of the system of equations (5.1) associated with $I$.

All we have to do in order to repair the gaps in Fig. 10.6(a) is to find the exact point of intersection of the three recovered faces, the faces 2, 4, and 5. The result of the repair is shown in Fig. 10.6(b). This is the reason why Step 7 in Method 10.1 is necessary.

**Example 10.2** ( **Recovery of the shape from light intensity**). The second example is an application of Method 10.1 to real shading images of plaster objects.

The scenes were set on a desk surface in an ordinary room. The desk surface was covered with light gray cloth, and objects made of plaster were put on it. Photographs were taken by a camera with a 50-mm lens, which was about 1.3 m distant from the scenes. The scenes were illuminated by six 40-watt fluorescent lights on the ceiling together with a 300-watt bulb to the left of the camera.

In order to register the theoretical values, $d_k^*(w)$ in (10.1), of the light intensity cue, we first placed a sphere on the desk and took a photograph (Fig. 10.7(a)). In the real world, the light intensity of a

point on the surface is not determined only by the direct light from the
sources toward the point; it also depends on secondary light that reaches
the point after reflecting from other surfaces, and hence depends on the
shape around. As a rough approximation, however, we assumed in this example
that the light intensity depends only on the surface normal. Since a sphere
has a surface point for any normal direction, we can read from Fig. 10.7(a)
the light intensity value on a surface of any given normal.

The surface equation $ax+by+z+c = 0$ represents a family of mutually
parallel planes when we regard $a$ and $b$ as constants and $c$ as a variable.
This family is specified by the two parameters $a$ and $b$. Thus the pair $(a,b)$
can represent the orientation of the surface. Regarding $a$ and $b$ as the
horizontal and vertical coordinates, we can represent each orientation by a
point in a two-dimensional space. This space is called the *gradient space*.
Since we assume that the light intensity on the surface is determined only
by its orientation, the light intensity can be considered a two-variable
function defined on the gradient space. Fig. 10.7(b) shows contours (i.e.,
the curves on which the value does not change) of the light intensity
plotted on the gradient space. The smallest closed curve denotes a contour
of the highest light intensity, and the light intensity descends as we go
outward. The intensity descends rather slowly in the left lower direction
in Fig. 10.7(b). This is mainly because secondary light reflected on the
desk surface was stronger in the left lower part of the sphere.

Then, a scene to be recovered was set under the same illumination
condition. Fig. 10.8(a) is an image of a scene in which a dodecahedron lay
on the desk. Using an interactive system, we processed this image. The
system extracted edges as in (b), and an operator chose important lines as
in (c). Then, the system organized the lines and constructed a line drawing
as shown in (d), where the edge 7-8 was added according to an instruction
given by the operator.

The incidence structure of this line drawing is not generically
reconstructible. In order to get a generically reconstructible substructure
we deleted the constraint that vertex 8 lies on face 5 (see (e) for the
face numbers). We chose this constraint because the position of vertex 8
was determined as the intersection of only two lines, the lines 8-4 and
8-12, and hence it seems less reliable (recall that a vertex associated
with a deleted incidence pair may be displaced in Step 7 of Method 10.1).

Since the distance from the scene to the camera was not large enough,
we formulated the algebraic structure of the line drawing on the basis of
the perspective projection model in Section 3.7, and obtained the

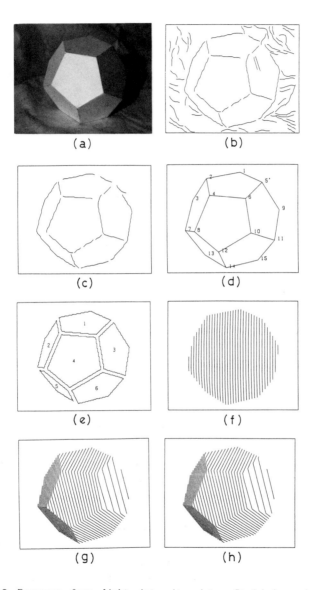

**Fig.** 10.8. Recovery from light intensity data, I: (a) is an image, (b) extracted edges, (c) selected edges, (d) a line drawing, (e) face regions, (f) an initial shape, (g) the shape corresponding to the optimal point, and (h) the finally recovered shape.

constraint set (7.4).

From the line drawing in (d) the system also found face regions as shown in (e). For a face $k$ ($k = 1, \ldots, 6$), the system computed the average intensity $d_k$ and the region area $s_k$; they are used in the objective function $\varphi(\xi)$ of Problem 10.2 as the observed value and the weight, respectively, of the $k$th cue.

The scene had four free parameters (we can, for example, choose $\xi = {}^t(z_1, z_2, z_3, z_4)$). However, in a way similar to that in Example 10.1, the present cues are invariant under scaling: $(x,y,z) \rightarrow (px,py,pz)$ (recall that the eye was at the origin). Hence, one of the free parameters can be fixed arbitrarily, and consequently the number of unknowns is three whereas the number of cues is six. Thus, we have enough cues to recover the shape uniquely.

Starting with an initial shape shown in (f), we got the optimal shape as shown in (g), where the surface has discontinuity along the edges 7-8 and 8-12. Discontinuity was repaired and the final result was obtained, as shown in (h).

Another example is shown in Fig. 10.9. The object is composed of a rectangular cone and a rectangular prism penetrating each other. Fig. 10.9(a) is a light intensity image, and (b) is a line drawing extracted from (a). If we ignore the background, the line drawing has six faces (they were numbered as shown in (b)), but the system was told that faces 3 and 4 and faces 5 and 6 are, respectively, coplanar. Therefore, its incidence structure has 16 vertices, 4 distinct planar surfaces, and 28 incidence pairs, and, consequently, four incidence pairs were deleted for the construction of a generically reconstructible substructure (note that $|R| + 4 - |V| - 3|F| = 4$). The optimal shape is shown in (c). We can see surface gaps along several edges, which are due to the deletion of some incidence pairs. Repairing the gaps, we obtained the final result, as shown in (d).

**Example 10.3 (Recovery of the shape from texture density).** In the present example, Method 10.1 was applied to orthographic images of scenes in which objects were covered with a grain texture of a known uniform density.

Scenes were composed of polyhedral objects covered with a grain texture. Sizes of the objects were about 180 mm $\sim$ 230 mm in their maximum diameters. Photographs were taken by a camera with a 200-mm telephoto lens that was about 5 m distant from the objects, which allows us to assume, as a rough approximation, that the photographs are orthographic projections of

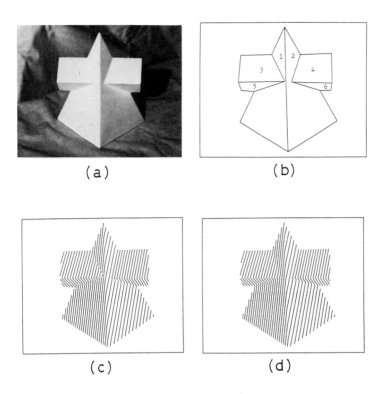

**Fig. 10.9.** Recovery from light intensity data, II: (a) is an image, (b) is a line drawing, (c) is the shape corresponding to the optimal point, and (d) is the recovered shape.

the scenes.

    Fig. 10.10(a) shows an image of a textured object. The object chosen here was what produces an "anomalous picture" (see Section 7.4). Fig. 10.10(b) is an image of the same object seen from another angle. This image is presented only to help readers to understand the shape of the object; it was not used for shape recovery. A rectangular plate covered with the same texture was also put in the scene. The normal to the plate faced toward the camera so that an apparent density might coincide with the real density. From the image of this plate we calculated the theoretical value of the grain density of a given planar surface.

    A line drawing of the object is shown in (c). The incidence structure

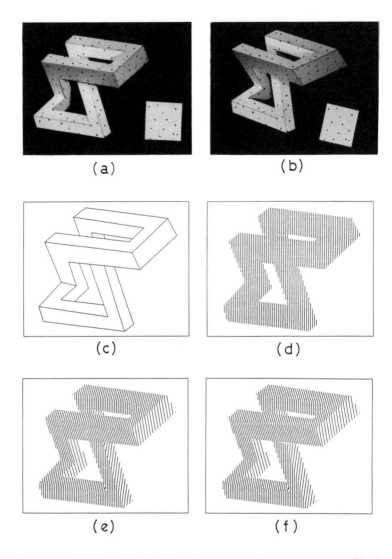

(a)                                    (b)

(c)                                    (d)

(e)                                    (f)

**Fig. 10.10.** Recovery from texture density: (a) is an input image, (b) shows the same scene viewed from another angle, (c) is a line drawing, (d) is an initial shape, (e) is the shape corresponding to the optimal point, and (f) is the recovered shape.

of this picture is not generically reconstructible. Starting with an initial shape in (d), we got the optimal shape, as shown in (e), in which the surface had discontinuity along some edges. Finding the correct intersections of the recovered faces, we got the final result of the recovery, as shown in (f).

## 11. POLYHEDRONS AND RIGIDITY

All the preceding chapters are devoted to one goal, machine extraction of
polyhedral structures from plane pictures; we have studied only those
aspects of line drawings that are necessary to attain this goal. However,
line drawings of polyhedrons have many other interesting characteristics.
In particular, it has been known for more than a century that there is a
beautiful and useful correspondence between line drawings of polyhedrons
and the rigidity of plane skeletal structures. This aspect has a close
relationship to the notions of "dual pictures" and the "gradient space,"
which are familiar in scene analysis. In this chapter we study this
correspondence from our combinatorial point of view, and establish generic
versions of the correspondence between two objects.

### 11.1. Gradient Space and Reciprocal Diagrams

In our computational mechanism we took an algebraic approach to checking
the correctness of labeled line drawings; the problem of judging the
correctness of a picture was reduced to the problem of judging the
satisfiability of certain linear constraints (recall Chapters 3 and 4). In
previous works on interpretation of line drawings, on the other hand, this
approach was not taken widely; instead, another approach, a gradient space
approach, has prevailed (Huffman, 1971, 1977a, 1977b; Mackworth, 1973;
Whiteley, 1979, 1982; Kanade, 1980, 1981; Draper, 1981). The algebraic
approach is more powerful than the gradient space approach in that the
former can give a necessary and sufficient condition for correctness,
whereas the latter gives in general only a necessary condition (Sugihara,
1984b). However, the gradient space approach seems useful for understanding
incorrectness of pictures "intuitively." Here, we review the basic idea of
the gradient space approach.

In addition to Assumptions 2.1 to 2.5, we put forth two more
assumptions for polyhedrons considered in this chapter. For a polyhedron $P$,
let $\text{Int}(P)$ denote the set of interior points of $P$; that is, $\text{Int}(P)$ consists
of those points of $P$ that are not on the surface of $P$. Next, for a point $p$
in $R^3$ and a positive real number $r$, let $\text{Ball}(p,r)$ denote the ball with the
radius $r$ and the center at $p$, that is, $\text{Ball}(p,r) =$
$\{q \mid q \in R^3, d(p,q) \leq r\}$ where $d(p,q)$ is the Euclidean distance between $p$
and $q$.

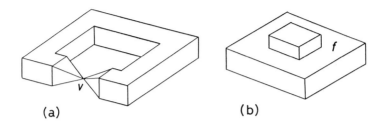

**Fig. 11.1.** A vertex and a face inhibited by the assumptions. The vertex $v$ in (a) does not satisfy Assumption 11.1, and the face $f$ in (b) does not satisfy Assumption 11.2.

**Assumption 11.1.** For any point $p$ on the surface of a polyhedron $P$, there exists a positive real number $r_0$ such that, for any $0 < r \leq r_0$, $\mathrm{Ball}(p,r) \cap \mathrm{Int}(P)$ is simply connected.

This assumption includes Assumption 2.2. Indeed, if a point $p$ is on the edge $e$ in Fig. 2.1, $\mathrm{Ball}(p,r) \cap \mathrm{Int}(P)$ consists of two mutually disconnected portions; thus, under Assumption 11.1 every edge is shared by exactly two faces. Moreover, this assumption enables us to exclude "pathological" vertices such as a vertex $v$ in Fig. 11.1(a), because, for this vertex $v$, $\mathrm{Ball}(v,r) \cap \mathrm{Int}(P)$ consists of two mutually disconnected portions. Thus, if Assumption 11.1 is valid, at every point on the surface of a polyhedron the neighboring space is partitioned into two connected portions, one occupied with material and the other vacant. Hence in particular, one can visit all edges and faces incident to a vertex in a certain cyclic order when one moves on the surface around the vertex.

**Assumption 11.2.** Every face of a polyhedron is simply connected.

This assumption implies that every face is a polygon and has no holes. Hence, the polyhedron shown in Fig. 11.1(b), for example, is excluded, because the face $f$ has a hole. This assumption assures us that the boundary of a face is connected in a graph theoretical sense, and hence one can visit all the edges and vertices on the boundary of a face in a certain cyclic order when one travels on the boundary.

Suppose that a viewer at an infinite distance in the positive direction of the $z$ axis sees a planar surface represented by an equation

$ax+by+z+c = 0$. We can consider that the surface equation defines $-z$ as a function of the two variables $x$ and $y$: $-z = ax+by+c$. Partially differentiating it by $x$ and $y$, respectively, we get

$$-\frac{\partial z}{\partial x} = a, \quad -\frac{\partial z}{\partial y} = b. \tag{11.1}$$

Hence, $a$ and $b$ represent the distances by which a point on the surface goes away from the viewer when it moves by unit length in the $x$ or the $y$ direction without departing from the surface. The ordered pair $(a,b)$ is called the *gradient* of the surface. The gradient represents how the surface tilts and slants. If $a = b = 0$, the surface faces precisely toward the viewer. A surface with $a \neq 0$ slants in the $x$ direction; if $a > 0$, the surface faces toward the right of the viewer, whereas if $a < 0$, it faces toward the left (note that this is true only for a right hand coordinate system; in the case of a left hand coordinate system, the surface faces toward the left of the viewer if $a > 0$, and toward the right if $a < 0$). Similarly, a surface with $b \neq 0$ slants in the $y$ direction; if $b > 0$, the surface slants upward, whereas if $b < 0$, it slants downward.

The gradient $(a,b)$ can be considered as a point on a plane whose first and second coordinates are represented by $a$ and $b$, respectively. The plane with the $(a,b)$ coordinate system defined as above is called the *gradient space*. Each point in the gradient space corresponds to some orientation of the surface, and hence it corresponds to a family of mutually parallel surfaces.

The use of the gradient space for line drawing interpretation is based on the following observation. Let $a_j x+b_j y+z+c_j = 0$ $(j = 1, 2)$ be equations of two surfaces. If they are not parallel, they intersect at a line and the orthographic projection of the line of intersection onto the $x$-$y$ plane is represented by

$$(a_1-a_2)x+ (b_1-b_2)y = -(c_1-c_2), \tag{11.2}$$

which is obtained if we eliminate the variable $z$ from the two surface equations. Eq (11.2) shows that the image of the line of intersection is perpendicular to the vector $(a_1-a_2,b_1-b_2)$. In other words, if the gradient space is superposed on the picture plane in such a way that the $a$ axis and the $b$ axis are parallel to the $x$ axis and the $y$ axis, respectively, then the image of the line of intersection is perpendicular to the line connecting the two associated gradients $(a_1,b_1)$ and $(a_2,b_2)$.

Let $(V,E)$ denote an undirected graph having the node set $V$ and the arc set $E$ without self-loops. A triple $(V,E,h)$ is called a *diagram* if $h$ is a mapping from the node set $V$ to the two-dimensional plane $R^2$. Intuitively, the diagram $(V,E,h)$ can be considered as a picture of the underlying graph $(V,E)$; the nodes are plotted at the positions specified by the mapping $h$, and the arcs are represented by straight line segments connecting the two terminal nodes. For the diagram $(V,E,h)$, elements of $V$ are called *points* and elements of $E$ *line segments*. Note that in the diagram two line segments may cross each other, and moreover two distinct nodes may occupy the same position.

Let $P$ be a polyhedron fixed to an $(x,y,z)$ Cartesian coordinate system, and let $V$, $E$, and $F$ be the sets of vertices, edges, and faces, respectively, of $P$. Furthermore, let $(x_\alpha,y_\alpha,z_\alpha)$ denote the coordinates of the $\alpha$th vertex $v_\alpha \in V$, and let $h_V$ be the mapping from $V$ to $R^2$ such that $h_V(v_\alpha) = (x_\alpha,y_\alpha)$. Then, $VD(P) = (V,E,h_V)$ is a diagram obtained by projecting $P$ orthographically onto the $x$-$y$ plane; that is, $VD(P)$ is a diagram composed of $|V|$ points and $|E|$ solid line segments where the points are the images of the vertices and the line segments are the images of the edges. $VD(P)$ is called the *vertex-edge diagram* of $P$. The vertex-edge diagram $VD(P)$ is slightly different from a hidden-part-drawn line drawing, considered in the previous chapters, in that in $VD(P)$ visible edges and hidden edges are not distinguished and accidental crossings of line segments are not counted in the node set. Intuitively, the introduction of the diagram $VD(P)$ corresponds to considering $P$ as an object made of transparent material.

For the polyhedron $P$ fixed in the space, let $a_jx+b_jy+z+c_j = 0$ denote the surface containing the $j$th face $f_j \in F$, and let $h_F$ be the mapping from $F$ to $R^2$ such that $h_F(f_j) = (a_j,b_j)$; that is, $h_F(f_j)$ denotes the gradient of the surface $f_j$. The ordered pair $(F,E)$ can be considered as an undirected graph if an element $e$ of $E$ is regarded as a pair of the side faces of the associated edge $e$ of the polyhedron $P$. Hence, we get another diagram $FD(P)$ $= (F,E,h_F)$; it is obtained from $P$ by first plotting the gradients of the faces on the gradient space and next connecting two gradients by a line segment if and only if the two associated faces share a common edge in $P$. $FD(P)$ is called the *face-edge diagram* of $P$. Note that $FD(P)$ can always be defined because the object $P$ is assumed to be in general position (Assumption 2.4). The diagram $FD(P)$ has $|F|$ points and $|E|$ line segments, and there is a natural one-to-one correspondence between the line segments in $VD(P)$ and those in $FD(P)$. Recall that the gradient represents the orientation of the surface; accordingly, if $P$ has mutually parallel faces, the corresponding points occupy the same position in the diagram.

Two diagrams are said to be *reciprocal* if there is a one-to-one correspondence between their line segments, so that one diagram can be superimposed on the other in such a way that corresponding line segments are perpendicular, and corresponding line segments that converge to a point in one diagram form a closed path in the other.

Now we get the next theorem, which has been known for a long time (Maxwell, 1864, 1870; see also Mackworth, 1973).

**Theorem 11.1.** For any polyhedron $P$, the vertex-edge diagram $VD(P) = (V,E,h_V)$ and the face-edge diagram $FD(P) = (F,E,h_F)$ are reciprocal.

**Proof.** The line segments in both of the diagrams come from the same edge set $E$, and hence there is a natural one-to-one correspondence between the two line segment sets. As has been observed in (11.2), the corresponding line segments become perpendicular if the two diagrams are superimposed in such a way that the $a$ and $b$ axes are parallel to the $x$ and $y$ axes, respectively.

For any vertex $v$ ($\in V$), let $(e_0,f_1,e_1,f_2,e_2,\ldots,f_k,e_k)$ (where $e_i \in E$, $f_j \in F$, $e_0 = e_k$) be an alternating sequence of edges and faces that are incident to the vertex $v$ and are found in this order when one moves on the surface counterclockwise around the vertex $v$. Note that because of Assumption 11.1 this alternating sequence is unique up to the choice of the starting edge $e_0$. Then, the edge set $\{e_1,e_2,\ldots,e_k\}$ forms the line segments converging to the point $h_V(v)$ in the diagram $VD(P)$, and simultaneously it forms a closed path connecting $k$ points $h_F(f_1)$, $h_F(f_2)$, $\ldots$, $h_F(f_k)$ in this order in the other diagram, $FD(P)$. Conversely, for any face $f(\in F)$, let $(e_0,v_1,e_1,v_2,e_2,\ldots,v_k,e_k)$ (where $e_i \in E$, $v_\alpha \in V$, $e_0 = e_k$) be an alternating sequence of edges and vertices surrounding the face $f$ counterclockwise in this order. This sequence is also unique up to the choice of the initial edge $e_0$ (recall Assumption 11.2). Then, the edge set $\{e_1,e_2,\ldots,e_k\}$ results in the line segments converging to the point $h_F(f)$ in $FD(P)$ on one hand, and it results in a closed path connecting the points $h_V(v_1)$, $h_V(v_2)$, $\ldots$, $h_V(v_k)$ in this order in $VD(P)$ on the other hand. Therefore, the two diagrams are reciprocal.

**Example 11.1.** Three pairs of mutually reciprocal diagrams are shown in Fig. 11.2. The diagrams (a), (b), and (c) are the projection of a tetrahedron, a tapered prism, and a hexahedron, respectively, and the diagrams (a'), (b'), and (c') are reciprocal to them. The same numbers are assigned to mutually corresponding line segments.

Since the incidence structure of a tetrahedron is generically reconstructible, diagram (a) continues to represent a tetrahedron correctly even if the four points are moved arbitrarily, provided that they are in generic position, and hence from Theorem 11.1 it always has a reciprocal figure. This observation leads to the following theorem: "Let $p_i$ ($i = 1,\ldots,4$) and $q_i$ ($i = 1,\ldots,4$) be two groups of points in generic position on a plane. If five out of six conditions $p_i p_j \perp q_i q_j$ ($1 \leq i < j \leq 4$; $\perp$ represents that the two lines are perpendicular to each other) are fulfilled, then the other one is also fulfilled." This theorem is called Reidemeister's theorem (Gurevich, 1960; see also Maxwell, 1864).

On the other hand, the incidence structure of a tapered prism and that of a hexahedron are not generically reconstructible; if the points of diagrams in (b) and (c) are displaced so that they are in generic position, they will not represent any polyhedrons. Indeed, in diagram (b) the three lines 1, 2, 3 are concurrent (this implies that the three side faces have a common point of intersection in the space), and in diagram (c) these four pairs of lines -- 1, 9; 2, 10; 3, 11; 4, 12 -- intersect at a common line (this implies that the top face and the bottom face intersect at a line). If these conditions are disturbed, they do not have reciprocal diagrams.

Theorem 11.1 implies that a diagram obtained as a projection of a polyhedron has a reciprocal diagram; in other words, a diagram having no reciprocal diagram cannot be a projection of any polyhedron. Moreover, as we have seen in Theorem 3.4, whether a diagram is a projection of a polyhedron does not depend on whether the projection is orthographic or perspective. Thus we get the following corollary.

**Corollary 11.1.1.** A diagram having no reciprocal diagram cannot be an orthographic or perspective projection of any polyhedron.

This corollary provides a graphical method for checking inconsistency in line drawings of polyhedrons. Given a hidden-part-drawn line drawing, we try to find its reciprocal diagram, and if it does not exist, we can conclude that the line drawing is not correct. This is the basic scheme

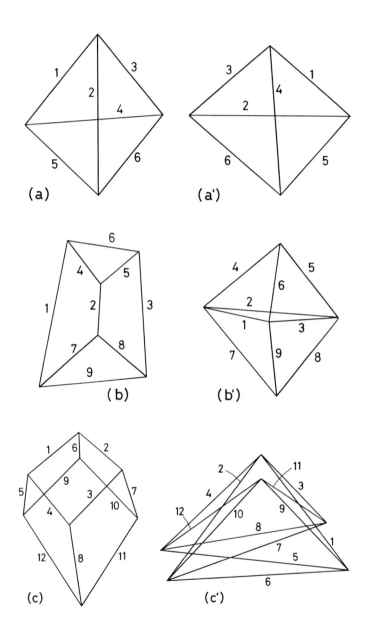

Fig. 11.2. Reciprocal pairs of diagrams.

adopted in the gradient space approach to checking inconsistency in interpretation of line drawings.

Note that the reciprocity stated in Theorem 11.1 holds only when all the edges of an object are drawn in the diagrams. If a line drawing represents only the visible part of a polyhedron $P$, it is in general a subdiagram of $VD(P)$ and consequently the last condition for the reciprocity (i.e., the condition that corresponding line segments that converge to a point in one diagram form a closed path in the other) cannot be expected. Thus, Corollary 11.1.1 cannot be applied directly to hidden-part-eliminated line drawings. However, a weaker condition, that is, the condition that corresponding lines are perpendicular, is still valid; it was widely used for checking inconsistency in line drawings (Huffman, 1971, 1977a, 1977b; Mackworth, 1973; Kanade, 1980, 1981).

It should be noted that even if the hidden part is drawn in the line drawing, Corollary 11.1.1 is not perfect for recognizing inconsistency. To have a reciprocal diagram is a necessary, but not sufficient, condition for a line drawing to represent a polyhedral scene. Indeed, diagram (c') in Fig. 11.2 has a reciprocal diagram, that is, (c), but obviously it does not represent any polyhedron. This is one of reasons why we have not taken the gradient space approach but have taken the algebraic approach, which gives us a necessary and sufficient condition for correctness, as shown in Theorems 3.3 and 4.1.

## 11.2. Rigidity of Plane Skeletal Structures

We have considered two-dimensional diagrams as projections of three-dimensional polyhedral objects. Here we introduce quite another way of interpreting the diagrams, namely, as two-dimensional frameworks composed of rigid rods and rotatable joints.

Let $D = (V,E,h)$ be a diagram whose underlying graph $(V,E)$ has $n$ nodes and $l$ arcs ($n = |V|$ and $l = |E|$). The diagram $D$ is called a *plane skeletal structure* (or a *skeletal structure* in short) when the line segments (the elements of $E$) are considered as rigid *rods* and the points (the elements of $V$) as rotatable *joints*. A joint connects end points of two or more rods in such a way that the mutual angles of the rods can change freely if the other ends are not constrained. This kind of a joint can be realized physically by a pin joint at which the rods are connected by a pin that is perpendicular to the plane on which the structure lies. The graph $(V,E)$ is called the *underlying graph* of the skeletal structure $D$.

Now let us consider how a skeletal structure can move and deform. Let $D = (V,E,h)$ be a plane skeletal structure, and let $h(v_\alpha) = (x_\alpha, y_\alpha)$ for a joint $v_\alpha \in V$. A rod connecting $v_\alpha$ and $v_\beta$ constrains the movement of $D$ in such a way that the distance between the joints is constant:

$$(x_\alpha - x_\beta)^2 + (y_\alpha - y_\beta)^2 = \text{const}.$$

Differentiating it by time parameter $t$, we get

$$(x_\alpha - x_\beta)(\dot{x}_\alpha - \dot{x}_\beta) + (y_\alpha - y_\beta)(\dot{y}_\alpha - \dot{y}_\beta) = 0, \tag{11.3}$$

where the dot denotes the differentiation by $t$. This equation implies that the relative velocity of the two terminal joints should be perpendicular to the rod; that is, the rod should not be stretched or compressed. Gathering all such equations, we get a system of linear equations

$$Hd = 0, \tag{11.4}$$

where $d$ is the unknown vector $d = {}^t(\dot{x}_1 \dot{y}_1 \cdots \dot{x}_n \dot{y}_n)$, and $H$ is an $(l \times 2n)$-dimensional matrix whose entities, say $h_{ij}$, are defined by $h_{i,2\alpha-1} = x_\alpha - x_\beta$ and $h_{i,2\alpha} = y_\alpha - y_\beta$ if one of the terminal joint of the $i$th rod is $v_\alpha$ where $v_\beta$ denotes the other joint, and $h_{i,2\alpha-1} = h_{i,2\alpha} = 0$ otherwise ($i = 1,2, \ldots, l$ and $\alpha = 1,2, \ldots, n$). A vector $d$ that satisfies (11.4) is called an *infinitesimal displacement* of the skeletal structure $D$. The infinitesimal displacements of $D$ form a linear subspace of $R^{2n}$, and its dimension is equal to $2n - \text{rank}(H)$. The rigid motions in a plane yield a three-dimensional subspace of this linear space. The skeletal structure $D$ is called *infinitesimally rigid* (or *rigid* in short) if $2n - \text{rank}(H) = 3$, that is, if the dimension of the linear space formed by the infinitesimal displacements equals the dimension of the linear space yielded by the rigid motions (this definition of rigidity is due to Laman, 1970; there are several other definitions of rigidity, such as "continuous rigidity" by Asimow and Roth, 1978, and "second order rigidity" by Connelly, 1980).

The rigidity of a structure depends on the positions of joints. The structure shown in Fig. 11.3(a) is rigid while the one in (b), which has the same underlying graph, is not rigid; the assignment of velocities indicated by the arrows (the vertices without arrows are assumed to have zero velocities) forms an infinitesimal displacement because the relative velocity of two terminal points of any rod is perpendicular to the rod.

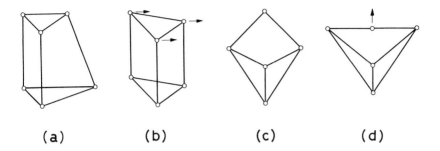

(a)                    (b)                    (c)                    (d)

**Fig. 11.3.** Rigid and nonrigid structures.

Similarly, though the structures in (c) and (d) have the same underlying graph, (c) is rigid and (d) is not. An infinitesimal displacement does not always correspond to an actual movement of a structure; the structure in (b) deforms mechanically, whereas the structure in (d) does not. The structure in (d) is categorized as nonrigid only because our definition of rigidity requires the absence of infinitesimal deformations.

For each rod $e_i$ ($\in E$), let us consider a real-valued quantity, say $u_i$, that satisfies the next two equations for any joint $v_\alpha$ ($\in V$) :

$$\sum_{e_i = \{v_\alpha, v_\beta\}} (x_\alpha - x_\beta) u_i = 0, \tag{11.5a}$$

$$\sum_{e_i = \{v_\alpha, v_\beta\}} (y_\alpha - y_\beta) u_i = 0, \tag{11.5b}$$

where the summations are taken over all rods that are incident to the joint $v_\alpha$. If the two-dimensional vector $((x_\alpha - x_\beta) u_i, (y_\alpha - y_\beta) u_i)$ (where $e_i = \{v_\alpha, v_\beta\} \in E$ ) is regarded as force which the joint $v_\alpha$ receives from the rod $e_i$, then the equations (11.5a) and (11.5b) together represent that the forces acting on $v_\alpha$ are in the state of equilibrium; (11.5a) represents the equilibrium in the $x$ components of the forces, and (11.5b) represents that in the $y$ components.

Gathering all the equations of the forms (11.5a) and (11.5b), we get $2n$ equations which can be written as

$uH = 0,$                                                                       (11.6)

where $H$ is the same coefficient matrix as in (11.4), and $u$ is the row vector $u = (u_1 u_2 \cdots u_l)$. A vector $u$ that satisfies (11.6) shall be called an *equilibrium vector*. For an equilibrium vector $u$, if $u_i > 0$, the force acts in such a way that the two terminal joints of the rod $e_i$ are pushed away from each other, and at its reaction the rod suffers compression. If $u_i < 0$, on the other hand, the force acts so that the two terminal joints are pulled together, and the rod suffers tension. The equilibrium vectors form a linear subspace of $R^l$, and its dimension is $l-\text{rank}(H)$.

From the definition of the matrix $H$, each row of $H$ corresponds to a rod. For any subset $X$ of $E$, let $H(X)$ be the submatrix of $H$ formed by the rows that correspond to the rods in $X$, and let us define a function $\tau_E$ by

$\tau_E(X) = \text{rank}(H(X)).$                                                (11.7)

Then, $(E,\tau_E)$ forms a matroid defined by the ground set $E$ and the rank function $\tau_E$ (Welsh, 1976). If $E$ is an independent set of this matroid, there is no redundancy in the rods and deletion of any rod from the structure results in an increase in the dimension of the linear space formed by the infinitesimal displacements. Moreover, $E$ being independent implies that the matrix $H$ is of row full rank and hence the only equilibrium vector is $u = 0$; the structure admits nonzero equilibrium vectors only when $E$ is dependent in the matroid $(E,\tau_E)$. The matroid $(E,\tau_E)$ was studied by Crapo (1979), Rosenberg (1980), Lovász (1980), Lovász and Yemini (1982), Sugihara (1983), Whiteley (1984b), Recski (1984a, 1984b, 1984c), and Tay and Whiteley (1984).

The joints of the skeletal structure $D = (V,E,h)$ are said to be *in generic position* if $x_1, y_1, \ldots, x_n, y_n$ are algebraically independent over the rational field (where $h(v_\alpha) = (x_\alpha, y_\alpha)$, $v_\alpha \in V$, $|V| = n$). In the case that the joints are in generic position, any polynomial of $x_1, y_1, \ldots, x_n, y_n$ with rational coefficients, and hence in particular the determinant of any submatrix of $H$, is 0 if and only if it is identically 0 when we consider $x_1, y_1, \ldots, x_n, y_n$ as indeterminate symbols. Therefore, if the joints are in generic position, the linear independence of the rows of $H$ depends only on the underlying graph $(V,E)$, and consequently the rigidity also depends only on the graph. For any subset $X$ of the edge set $E$ of the graph $(V,E)$, $X$ is called *generically independent* if $\tau_E(X) = |X|$ for a skeletal structure $D = (V,E,h)$ whose joints are in generic position, and *generically dependent* otherwise. The graph $(V,E)$ is called *generically independent* if $E$ is generically independent. Furthermore, the graph $(V,E)$ is called *generically rigid* if a skeletal structure $D = (V,E,h)$ with the joints in generic position is rigid.

The generic independence is characterized by the next theorem, which was first proved by Laman (1970) (other proofs are also given by Asimow and Roth, 1979, and Lovász and Yemini, 1982).

**Theorem 11.2 (Laman's theorem).** A graph $(V,E)$ is generically independent if and only if

$$2|V(X)| - 3 \geq |X| \tag{11.8}$$

holds for any nonempty subset $X$ of $E$, where $V(X)$ $(\subseteq V)$ denotes the set of nodes that are terminals of arcs in $X$.

Since the motions on a plane have three degrees of freedom, the dimension of the linear space formed by the infinitesimal displacements is at least three. Consequently, the size of a generically independent subset of $E$ cannot be greater than $2n-3$, where $n = |V|$. Thus, the condition stated in Theorem 11.2 is obviously necessary for $E$ to be generically independent. The theorem says that the condition is also sufficient.

**Remark 11.1.** Characterization of the rigidity as stated in Theorem 11.2 was considered by Laman (1970), Asimow and Roth (1979), and Lovász and Yemini (1982). There are, however, differences not only in their approaches but also in their results. What Laman proved is that there exists at least one skeletal structure $(V,E,h)$ such that $\text{rank}(H) = |E|$ if and only if the underlying graph $(V,E)$ satisfies the condition in Theorem 11.2. Asimow and Roth said that the joints of the skeletal structure $(V,E,h)$ are *in general position* if every submatrix of $H$ has the possible maximum rank over all skeletal structures with the same underlying graph, and proved that, for any skeletal structure $(V,E,h)$ with the joints in general position, $\text{rank}(H)$ $= |E|$ is equivalent to the condition stated in Theorem 11.2. Thus, they stated more clearly the case when the condition implies independence of the rows of $H$. Lovász and Yemini proved what is just stated in Theorem 11.2 as a corollary of a certain more general result. If the joints are in generic position, no polynomial of $x_1$, $y_1$, ..., $x_n$, $y_n$ vanishes unless it is identically equal to 0, and hence in particular the determinant of any submatrix of $H$ is not 0 unless it is identically 0. Thus, being in generic position implies being in general position; Asimow and Roth proved the strongest case.

From an engineering point of view, however, their results are almost equivalent, because they all imply that, for a point $(x_1,y_1,\ldots,x_n,y_n)$ almost anywhere in $R^{2n}$, the condition stated in Theorem 11.2 is equivalent to rank$(H) = |E|$.

Here we follow the Lovász-Yemini generic version simply because we have considered realizability of polyhedrons also in the generic sense.

A generically rigid graph with $n$ nodes should have $2n$-3 generically independent arcs, and hence the next corollary results directly from Theorem 11.2.

**Corollary 11.2.1.** A graph $(V,E)$ having $n$ nodes and $2n$-3 arcs ($|V| = n$, $|E| = 2n$-3) is generically rigid if and only if (11.8) holds for any nonempty subset $X$ of $E$.

For a skeletal structure $D = (V,E,h)$, if $E$ is independent in the matroid $(E,\tau_E)$, that is, if $\tau_E(E) = |E|$, then the only solution to (11.6) is a zero vector. Thus, the structure admits nonzero equilibrium vectors only when the rod set $E$ is dependent. In particular, if the arc set $E$ is generically dependent in the underlying graph $(V,E)$, the associated skeletal structure with the joints in generic position admits nonzero equilibrium vectors. However, whether components of an equilibrium vector are positive or negative (i.e., whether the forces are compression or tension) cannot be determined by the underlying graph only; it depends on the positions of the joints.

**Example 11.2.** For the diagram in Fig. 11.4(a), the condition in Theorem 11.2 is not fulfilled, and hence the arc set is generically dependent. One of the sign patterns of the equilibrium vectors is shown by the labels + and –, where + implies that the force along the edge is compression and – implies tension. If $u$ is an equilibrium vector, $-u$ is also an equilibrium vector; thus the pattern obtained by exchanging all the + and – labels in (a) is also a sign pattern of an equilibrium vector. The structure satisfies rank$(H) = 5$, because the deletion of any one rod from the structure results in a structure that satisfies the condition in Theorem 11.2. Hence the dimension of the linear space formed by the equilibrium

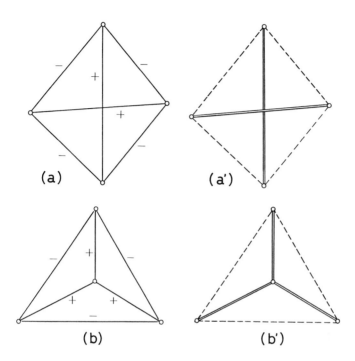

**Fig. 11.4.** Sign patterns of equilibrium vectors and tensegrity structures. In (a) and (b) the label + represents force of compression and the label − represents force of tension, and the structures in (a) and (b') are the tensegrity structures obtained from the sign patterns in (a) and (b).

vectors equals *l*-rank(*H*) = 6-5 = 1, and therefore the sign pattern of an equilibrium vector is unique up to the exchange of all the signs simultaneously.

The structure in Fig. 11.4(b) has the same underlying graph as that in (a) but joint positions are different. As a result, it has a different sign pattern of an equilibrium vector, as shown in (b). Since the equilibrium vectors of this structure form a one-dimensional linear space, the sign pattern is unique up to the simultaneous exchange of all the signs. Thus, even if structures have the same underlying graph, in general they give different sign patterns of equilibrium vectors.

A structure with a nonzero equilibrium vector has the remarkable property that the structure remains rigid when the tensed rods are replaced with cables and the compressed rods are replaced with struts, where a *cable* is a structure element that provides an upper bound for the distance between the two terminal points and a *strut* gives a lower bound for the distance between the two terminal points. A structure composed of rigid rods, cables, and struts is called a *tensegrity structure*. From the sign patterns shown in (a) and (b) in Fig. 11.4 we get the rigid tensegrity structures shown in (a') and (b'), where the broken lines represent cables and the double lines represent struts. The tensegrity structures are studied by Connelly (1980) and Roth and Whiteley (1981).

### 11.3. Graphical Correspondence

We have considered the two ways of interpreting plane diagrams: the interpretation as line drawings of polyhedrons and the interpretation as plane skeletal structures. Here we establish a correspondence between the two ways of interpretation, which has been known for more than a century (Maxwell, 1864, 1870; Cremona, 1890; Whiteley, 1982).

For a polyhedron $P$, we define two graphs. First let $VG(P) = (V,E)$ be the graph having the vertex set $V$ as the node set and the edge set $E$ as the arc set; an arc in $E$ connects the two terminal vertices of the corresponding edge. The graph $VG(P)$ is called the *vertex-edge graph* of $P$. Next, let $FG(P) = (F,E)$ be the graph having the face set $F$ as the node set and the edge set $E$ as the arc set; an arc connects the two side faces of the corresponding edge of $P$. The graph $FG(P)$ is called the *face-edge graph* of $P$. Obviously, the underlying graph of the vertex-edge diagram $VD(P)$ and that of the face-edge diagram $FD(P)$ of a polyhedron $P$ are identical to the vertex-edge graph $VG(P)$ and the face-edge graph $FG(P)$, respectively, of the polyhedron $P$.

The vertex-edge graph $VG(P)$ comes from vertices and edges of the polyhedron $P$. Hence, the original vertices and edges can be regarded as the graph embedded on the surface of the object $P$, that is, as the graph drawn on the surface of $P$ in such a way that the arcs do not cross except at nodes.

The face-edge graph $FG(P)$ can also be drawn on the same surface. Indeed, we can choose an arbitrary point on each face and connect it with the midpoint of each edge on the boundary of the face by a (if necessary curved) line, where the lines do not cross each other, as shown in Fig. 11.5. All together, these lines give an embedding of the face-edge graph $FG(P)$. Note that the above embedding in general is not equivalent to

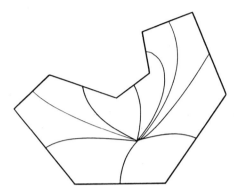

**Fig. 11.5.** Part of arcs of the face-edge graph $FG(P)$ drawn on a face of the polyhedron $P$.


the embedding on a plane, because the polyhedron $P$ is not necessarily topologically equivalent to a sphere. If $P$ is topologically equivalent to, for example, a torus, then the vertex-edge graph or the face-edge graph cannot necessarily be drawn on a plane unless arcs cross each other.

For a vertex $v$ ($\in V$), let $C(v) = (e_0, f_1, e_1, \ldots, f_k, e_k)$ be the alternating sequence of arcs (= edges) and nodes (= faces) in the embedding of $FG(P)$ that surrounds the vertex $v$ counterclockwise in this order when seen from the outside of the polyhedron $P$, where $e_0 = e_k$. From Assumption 11.1, $C(v)$ is unique up to the choice of the starting arc $e_0$.

In the embedding of $FG(P)$ each arc $e_i$ ($\in E$) forms the common boundary of the two side regions that contain the terminal vertices of the corresponding edge $e_i$ of $VG(P)$. Therefore, every edge $e$ ($\in E$) appears exactly twice in some $C(v)$, and the two appearances are in the opposite direction. This observation can be summarized in the next lemma.

**Lemma 11.1.** Let $e$ be an edge of a polyhedron $P$, $v_\alpha$ and $v_\beta$ be the two terminal vertices of $e$, and $f_j$ and $f_k$ be the two side faces of $e$. Then, the edge $e$ appears in $C(v_\alpha)$ and $C(v_\beta)$, and in them only, once in the order $\ldots$, $f_j$, $e$, $f_k$, $\ldots$ and the other time in the opposite order, $\ldots$, $f_k$, $e$, $f_j$, $\ldots$ .


Now we are ready to prove the next theorem, which is a slightly generalized version of what was proved by Maxwell (1864, 1870).

**Theorem 11.3.** If a diagram $D$ is obtained as an orthographic or perspective projection of a polyhedron, the corresponding skeletal structure $D$ admits an equilibrium vector whose components are all nonzero.

**Proof.** It follows from Theorem 3.4 that if $D$ is a perspective projection of a polyhedron, then $D$ is an orthographic projection of some other polyhedron. Therefore, without loss of generality we assume that $D$ is given as an orthographic projection of a polyhedron $P$; that is, $D$ is the vertex-edge diagram $VD(P) = (V,E,h_V)$. Then, from Theorem 11.1, the face-edge diagram $FD(P) = (F,E,h_F)$ of the same polyhedron $P$ is a reciprocal diagram of $D$. Turning the reciprocal diagram $FD(P)$ round by the amount of $\pi/2$ in the picture plane, we get the diagram, say $FD^*(P)$, whose line segments are parallel to the corresponding line segments in $VD(P)$.

Now, we can interpret line segments in $FD^*(P)$ as force in equilibrium in the following way. First, from the definition of reciprocity, line segments converging to a vertex $v$ in $VD(P)$ form a closed path in $FD^*(P)$. Indeed, the closed path is given by $C(v)$. Next, since the corresponding line segments in $VD(P)$ and $FD^*(P)$ are parallel to each other, the line segments in $FD^*(P)$ can be regarded as forces that the vertex $v$ receives from the corresponding rods in $D$; the force acts in the direction in which the line segment is traversed when one travels along the closed path $C(v)$. Since the path is closed, all the forces that the vertex $v$ receives are in a state of equilibrium. Finally, from Lemma 11.1 an edge $e$ appears in exactly two closed paths, and moreover it is contained in mutually opposite directions; consequently the force along the rod $e$ is either the "pushing" at both the terminal joints or the "pulling" at both the terminal joints. Thus, the collection of all the forces represented by $FD^*(P)$ is in a state of equilibrium.

Let us consider signed lengths of line segments in $FD^*(P)$ where the sign is defined as $+$ if the corresponding force pushes the two terminal vertices away and as $-$ if the force pulls them together. Dividing the signed lengths of line segments in $FD^*(P)$ by the lengths of the corresponding line segments in $D$, we get an equilibrium vector. Adjacent faces on $P$ have different orientations, and hence they are plotted in different positions on the gradient space. Consequently, every line segment in $FD(P)$ has a nonzero length, so that every component of the equilibrium vector is nonzero.

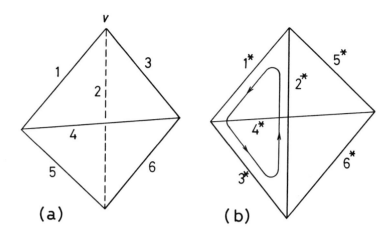

**Fig. 11.6.** Interpretation of a reciprocal diagram as force in equilibrium in the original diagram.

**Example 11.3.**    Fig 11.6(a) shows one interpretation of the diagram in Fig. 11.2(a) as a line drawing of a polyhedron $P$. Indeed the polyhedron $P$ is a tetrahedron, and the broken line represents a hidden edge. Fig. 11.6(b) is the corresponding $FD^*(P)$, which is obtained if we rotate the diagram in Fig. 11.2(a') by $\pi/2$ counterclockwise. For the line segments 1 to 6 in (a), the corresponding line segments in $FD^*(P)$ are assigned the numbers $1^*$ to $6^*$, respectively. Let $v$ be one vertex on $P$ as shown in (a). If one moves on the surface of $P$ around the vertex $v$ counterclockwise, one crosses the three edges 1, 3, 2 cyclically in this order. The corresponding three line segments in $FD^*(P)$ form a closed path on which they appear in the order $1^*$, $3^*$, $2^*$, as shown in (b). Copying the direction of the closed path to the corresponding line segments in (a), we see that on the line segment 1 or 3 it goes away from $v$ whereas on the line segment 2 it comes toward $v$. Therefore, the designated force is tension on the rods 1 and 3 and is compression on the rod 2. In this way, the rotated reciprocal diagram in (b) gives the sign pattern of force shown in Fig. 11.4(a).

The converse of Theorem 11.3 does not hold. A counterexample is given in Fig. 11.2(c'). Diagram (c') has a reciprocal diagram, (c), and indeed the reciprocal diagram gives an equilibrium vector whose components are all nonzero; obviously, however, the diagram in (c') cannot be a projection of any polyhedron. (Whiteley, 1982, introduced a new concept, named "oriented polyhedrons," so that the converse of the theorem may hold. However, the oriented polyhedrons include physically unrealizable objects, because the surface is allowed to penetrate itself and consequently we cannot pack material inside the surface while preserving its orientation.)

A quite different type of a correspondence between line drawings of polyhedrons and rigidity of structures is also studied by Whiteley (1984c) (see also Crapo and Whiteley, 1982).

## 11.4. Generic Correspondence

The correspondence established in the previous section is metrical, or in other words graphical, in the sense that the correspondence was established through diagrams whose nodes are definitely given on the picture plane. In this section, on the other hand, we see that a similar but nonmetrical correspondence also holds. We establish a correspondence between a class of line drawings whose vertices are in generic position and a class of skeletal structures whose joints are in generic position.

Let $I = (V,F,R)$ be an incidence structure, that is, $V$ and $F$ are mutually disjoint finite sets and $R$ is a subset of $V \times F$; elements of $V$ and $F$ are called vertices and faces, respectively. If $(v,f) \in R$ for $v \in V$ and $f \in F$, then we say that $v$ is on $f$ and $f$ has $v$. As in the previous chapters, we assume that any element of $V$ is on at least one element of $F$, and any element of $F$ has at least three elements of $V$. Here, we concentrate our attention upon the class of incidence structures that satisfy the next condition.

**Condition 11.1.**    (a)    $|V|+3|F| = |R|+4$    and    (b)    $|V(X)|+3|X| \geq |R(X)|+4$  for any $X \subseteq F$  such that $|X| \geq 2$.

The condition implies the following. From Theorems 6.1 and 6.2, an incidence structure that satisfies Condition 11.1(b) is generically reconstructible and the associated coefficient matrix $A$ in (5.1) is of row full rank. Therefore, Condition 11.1(a) together with (b) implies that there are $\rho_V(V) = |V|+3|F|-\text{rank}(A) = 4$ degrees of freedom in the choice of a solution to (5.1) when the projected vertices are in generic position. That is, Condition 11.1 is fulfilled if and only if the incidence structure $I$ is generically reconstructible and admits exactly four generic degrees of freedom. As we have seen in Corollary 5.3.1, a picture with an incidence structure having exactly 4 degrees of freedom has the remarkable property that the images of intersections of faces do not depend on the choice of a solution to (5.1).

Next consider a graph $G = (V,E)$ satisfying the following condition, where, for any $X \subseteq V$, $E(X)$ denotes the set of arcs connecting nodes in $X$.

**Condition 11.2.** (a) $2|V| = |E|+2$ and (b) $2|X| \geq |E(X)|+3$ for any proper subset $X$ of $V$ such that $|X| \geq 2$.

From Condition 11.2(a), the graph $G$ is generically dependent (recall Theorem 11.2). For any arc $e$ $(\in E)$, however, the graph $(V,E-\{e\})$ satisfies the condition in Theorem 11.2, and hence is generically independent. Thus, among all the subsets of $E$, $E$ only is generically dependent. Moreover, it follows from Corollary 11.2.1 that $(V,E-\{e\})$ is generically rigid and consequently $G$ is also generically rigid.

Let $D = (V,E,h)$ be a plane skeletal structure whose underlying graph is $G$ and whose joints are in generic position. Then, Condition 11.2 implies the following.

First, the structure $D$ has one more rod than is necessary to make the structure rigid (recall Corollary 11.2.1, which states that $n$ points in generic position can be connected rigidly by $2n-3$ rods), and the redundancy is used most effectively in the sense that the structure $D$ remains rigid even if any one rod is broken. Second, since $D$ is rigid, rank$(H) = 2|V|-3 = |E|-1$ (where $H$ is the coefficient matrix in (11.6)) and hence the equilibrium vectors form a one-dimensional linear space. Moreover, all components of the vectors are nonzero, because $E$ is the only dependent set (note that the equilibrium vector represents the coefficients of a linear combination of row vectors in $H$ that results in a zero vector). Thus, the structure $D$ admits an internal force in equilibrium that is unique up to scalar multiplication and that is nonzero on every rod.

For a polyhedron $P$, let $VG(P) = (V,E)$ be the vertex-edge graph of $P$, and let $I(P) = (V,F,R)$ be the incidence structure associated with $P$. Our purpose here is to show that, under some condition, $I(P)$ satisfies Condition 11.1 if and only if $VG(P)$ satisfies Condition 11.2. For this purpose we need some preparation.

For convenience let $\mu_I$ be the integer-valued function on $2^F$ defined, for any $X \subseteq F$, by

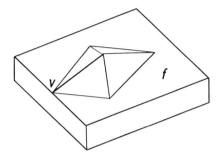

**Fig. 11.7.** Polyhedron whose vertex-edge graph is not 2-connected.

$$\mu_I(X) = |V(X)| + 3|X| - |R(X)| - 4. \tag{11.9}$$

Similarly let $\mu_G$ be the integer-valued function on $2^E$ such that, for any $X \subseteq V$,

$$\mu_G(X) = 2|X| - |E(X)| - 3. \tag{11.10}$$

A graph $G$ is said to be *2-connected* if it remains connected when any one node and the incident arcs are deleted from $G$.

**Lemma 11.2.** Let $P$ be a polyhedron. If Condition 11.1 is fulfilled by the incidence structure $I(P) = (V,F,R)$, the vertex-edge graph $VG(P)$ is 2-connected.

**Proof.** From Assumption 11.2 it follows that $VG(P)$ is connected. Let us assume, contrary to the lemma, that $VG(P)$ is not 2-connected. Then there exists a vertex, say $v$, such that deletion of $v$ makes the graph disconnected. Moreover, from Assumption 11.1 it follows that there is a face, say $f$, whose boundary touches the vertex $v$ twice or more, as shown in Fig. 11.7. Hence, the face $f$ divides the other part of the surface of $P$ into at least two connected regions. Let $F_1$ be the set of faces that belong to any one connected region, and let $F_2 = F - F_1 \cup \{f\}$. Then, $F_1$, $F_2$, and $\{f\}$ form a partition of $F$; hence in particular we get

$$|F| = |F_1| + |F_2| + 1. \tag{11.11a}$$

Let $V_1$ [resp. $V_2$] be the set of vertices that are on some faces in $F_1$ [resp. $F_2$]. Since $v$ is the only vertex that is common to $V_1$ and $V_2$, we get

$$|V| = |V_1| + |V_2| - 1. \tag{11.11b}$$

Let $R_1$ [resp. $R_2$] be the set of incidence pairs whose second entities are in $F_1$ [resp. $F_2$]. Let, furthermore, $k_1$ [resp. $k_2$] be the number of vertices in $V_1 - \{v\}$ [resp. $V_2 - \{v\}$] that are on the face $f$. Then, we get

$$|R| = |R_1| + |R_2| + k_1 + k_2 + 1. \tag{11.11c}$$

Now we get

$$
\begin{aligned}
&|V| + 3|F| - |R| - 4 \\
={}& |V_1| + k_1 + 3(|F_1| + 1) - (|R_1| + k_1 + k_2 + 1) - 4 \\
&+ |V_2| + k_2 + 3(|F_2| + 1) - (|R_2| + k_1 + k_2 + 1) - 4 - 1 - 3 \times 1 + 1 + 4 \\
={}& \mu_I(F_1 \cup \{f\}) + \mu_I(F_2 \cup \{f\}) + 1 \geqq 1,
\end{aligned}
$$

where the first equality comes from (11.11a), (11.11b), and (11.11c), and the inequality comes from Condition 11.1(b). The above inequality contradicts Condition 11.1(a), and consequently $VG(P)$ is 2-connected.

Now we can state the next theorem.

**Theorem 11.4.** Let $P$ be a polyhedron that is topologically equivalent to a sphere. Then, the incidence structure $I(P)$ satisfies Condition 11.1 if and only if the vertex-edge graph $VG(P)$ satisfies Condition 11.2.

**Proof.** First, Condition 11.1(a) is equivalent to Condition 11.2(a), because $\mu_I(F) = -\mu_G(V) - 1$ follows directly from $|R| = 2|E|$ and Euler's formula $|V| + |F| - |E| = 2$.

Suppose that $I(P)$ satisfies Condition 11.1. Let $X$ be any proper subset of $V$ such that $|X| \geqq 2$.

Case 1: Suppose that the graph $(X, E(X))$ is connected. Let $F_1$ ($\subseteq F$) be the set of faces whose vertices are all in $X$, and let $F_2 = F - F_1$. Let $V_0$ be the set of vertices in $X$ that belong to the boundaries of the faces in $F_2$, and let $V_1 = X - V_0$ and $V_2 = V - X$. Furthermore, let $E_0$ be the set of edges in

$E(X)$ that belong to the boundaries of the faces in $F_2$, and let $E_1 = E(X)-E_0$ and $E_2 = E-E(X)$. Then, $\{F_1,F_2\}$, $\{V_0,V_1,V_2\}$, and $\{E_0,E_1,E_2\}$ are partitions of $F$, $V$, and $E$, respectively.

Suppose that the polyhedral surface $P$ is topologically deformed to a sphere, say $K$, and that the vertex-edge graph $VG(P)$ is drawn on $K$ as the vestiges of vertices, edges, and faces of $P$. Regions on $K$ bounded by the edges correspond to the faces in $F$. If we delete the vertices in $V_2$ and the edges incident to them, the faces in $F_2$ are merged into connected regions, say $A_i$ $(i = 1,\ldots,k)$, on $K$. Note that $k \geqq 1$ because $X \neq V$.

Let $F_2^i$ $(\subseteqq F_2)$ be the set of the faces constituting $A_i$, and let us define $E_2^i = E(F_2^i)\cap E_2$, $E_0^i = E(F_2^i)\cap E_0$ $(i = 1,\ldots,k)$, where, for any face set $Y$, $E(Y)$ denotes the set of edges belonging to the boundaries of the faces in $Y$. Similarly, let us define $V_2^i = V(F_2^i)\cap V_2$, $V_0^i = V(F_2^i)\cap V_0$ $(i = 1,\ldots,k)$. Note that $|F_2^i| \geqq 2$ for any $i$ $(1 \leqq i \leqq k)$, and $F_2^i\cap F_2^j = \phi$, $E_2^i\cap E_2^j = \phi$, $V_2^i\cap V_2^j = \phi$ for any $i$ and $j$ $(1 \leqq i < j \leqq k)$.

A connected region $A_i$ $(1 \leqq i \leqq k)$ is bounded by edges in $E_0^i$; the edges in $E_0^i$ form a closed path surrounding $A_i$. If one travels along the closed path around $A_i$, one passes through each vertex in $V_0^i$ at least once. Hence we get $|V_0^i| \leqq |E_0^i|$, where the equality holds when every vertex in $V_0^i$ appears exactly once in the closed path.

Let $R_i$ be the set of incidence pairs concerned with faces in $F_2^i$. Each face $f_j \in F_2^i$ had $|V(\{f_j\})|$ vertices, and $|R_i|$ equals the sum of such numbers of vertices over all faces in $F_2^i$: $|R_i| = \sum|V(\{f_j\})|$ where the summation is taken over all faces $f_j$ in $F_2^i$. From Lemma 11.2, no vertex appears twice or more on the boundary of any face in $F_2^i$. Consequently, $|V(\{f_j\})|$ equals also the number of edges on the boundary of $f_j$. Thus, we get $|R_i| = 2|E_2^i|+|E_0^i|$, because in the summation elements of $E_2^i$ are counted twice and those in $E_0^i$ are counted once.

Then, we get

$$
\begin{aligned}
\mu_G(X) &= 2(|V_0|+|V_1|)-(|E_0|+|E_1|)-3 \\
&= 3(|V_0\cup V_1|-|E_0\cup E_1|+|F_1|+k)-|V_0\cup V_1|+2|E_0\cup E_1|-3|F_1|-3k-3 \\
&= -(|V|+3|F|-|R|-4)+|V_2|+3|F_2|-3k-2|E_2|-1 \\
&= \sum_{i=1}^{k}(|V_2^i|+3|F_2^i|-2|E_2^i|-3)-1 \\
&\geqq \sum_{i=1}^{k}(|V_2^i\cup V_0^i|+3|F_2^i|-2|E_2^i|-|E_0^i|-3)-1 \\
&\geqq \sum_{i=1}^{k}(|V_2^i\cup V_0^i|+3|F_2^i|-2|E_2^i|-|E_0^i|-4)
\end{aligned}
$$

$$= \sum_{i=1}^{k} \mu_I(F_2^i) \geq 0,$$

where the first equality is the definition of $\mu_G$, the second one comes from simple counting, the third one follows from Euler's formula $|V_0 \cup V_1| - |E_0 \cup E_1| + |F_1| + k = 2$ for the subgraph $(V_0 \cup V_1, E_0 \cup E_1)$ and $|R| = 2|E| = 2(|E_0| + |E_1| + |E_2|)$, the fourth one comes from Condition 11.1(a), the next inequality follows from $|V_0^i| \leq |E_0^i|$ for $1 \leq i \leq k$, and the last equality comes from $|R_i| = 2|E_2^i| + |E_0^i|$.

Case 2: Suppose that the graph $(X, E(X))$ is not connected. Then, Condition 11.2(b) can be derived easily from the fact that every connected component of $(X, E(X))$ satisfies $\mu_G(X_j) \geq 0$, where $X_j$ represents the set of vertices belonging to the $j$th connected component of $(X, E(X))$.

Therefore, Condition 11.2(b) is satisfied in both the cases.

Conversely, suppose that $VG(P)$ satisfies Condition 11.2. Let $X$ be any subset of $F$ such that $|X| \geq 2$. Let us define $F_1 = X$, $F_2 = F - F_1$, $V_0 = V(F_1) \cap V(F_2)$, $V_1 = V(F_1) - V_0$, $V_2 = V(F_2) - V_0$, $E_0 = E(F_1) \cap E(F_2)$, $E_1 = E(F_1) - E_0$, $E_2 = E(F_2) - E_0$. Let $G_X = (V_0 \cup V_1, E_0 \cup E_1)$ denote the subgraph of $VG(P)$ having the vertex set $V_0 \cup V_1$ and the edge set $E_0 \cup E_1$.

Case 1: Suppose that $G_X$ is connected. Suppose that the graph $VG(P)$ is drawn on the sphere $K$. If we delete the edges in $E_2$ from the graph, the faces in $F_2$ are merged into connected regions, say $A_1$, ..., $A_k$, on $K$. Let $F_2^i \ (\subseteq F_2)$ be the set of the faces belonging to $A_i$, and let us define $V_0^i = V(F_2^i) \cap V_0$, $V_2^i = V(F_2^i) \cap V_2$, $E_0^i = E(F_2^i) \cap E_0$, $E_2^i = E(F_2^i) \cap E_2$ $(i = 1, \ldots, k)$. Note that $V_2^i \cap V_2^j = \phi$ and $E_2^i \cap E_2^j = \phi$ for $1 \leq i < j \leq k$. Moreover, note that for every edge in $E_0$, one side face belongs to $F_1$ and the other belongs to $F_0$, so that first we have $E_0^i \cap E_0^j = \phi$ for $1 \leq i < j \leq k$, and second we have $|V_0^i| = |E_0^i|$ for $1 \leq i \leq k$. If $k = 0$, then $X = F$ and hence $\mu_I(X) = 0$. If $k \geq 1$, then $|V(F_2^i)| \geq 3$ for any $i$ $(1 \leq i \leq k)$ and hence we get

$$\mu_I(X) = |V_0| + |V_1| + 3|F_1| - (2|E_1| + |E_0|) - 4$$
$$= 3(|V_0 \cup V_1| + |F_1| + k - |E_0 \cup E_1|) + |E_1| + 2|E_0| - 2|V_0 \cup V_1| - 3k - 4$$
$$= |E| - 2|V| + 2 - |E_2| + |E_0| + 2|V_2| - 3k$$
$$= \sum_{i=1}^{k} (2|V_2^i \cup V_0^i| - |E_2^i \cup E_0^i| - 3)$$
$$= \sum_{i=1}^{k} \mu_G(V(F_2^i)) \geq 0.$$

In the above equations, the third equality follows from Euler's formula for the graph $(V_0 \cup V_1, E_0 \cup E_1)$, and the fourth equality from Condition 11.2(a) and $|V_0'| = |E_0'|$.

Case 2: Suppose that the graph $G_X$ is not connected. Then Condition 11.1(b) can be derived from the fact that each connected component of $G_X$ satisfies $\mu_l(X_j) \geqq 0$, where $X_j$ denotes the subset of $X$ bounded by edges belonging to the $j$th connected component of $G_X$.

Therefore, Condition 11.1(b) is fulfilled in both the cases.

The next corollary follows directly from Theorem 11.4 and the physical meanings of Conditions 11.1 and 11.2.

**Corollary 11.4.1.** Let $P$ be a polyhedron that is topologically equivalent to a sphere. Then, the following three statements are equivalent.
(1) The incidence structure $I(P)$ is generically reconstructible and admits exactly four degrees of freedom.
(2) The vertex-edge graph $VG(P)$ is generically rigid, and remains generically rigid if any one arc is deleted, but deletion of any two arcs yields a graph that is not generically rigid.
(3) For any plane skeletal structure whose underlying graph is $VG(P)$ and whose joints are in generic position, the equilibrium vector is unique up to scalar multiplication and its component is nonzero at every rod.

A graph $G$ is called *planar* if $G$ can be drawn on a plane in such a way that the nodes correspond to distinct points and the arcs correspond to (curved, if necessary) line segments and no line segments intersect except at nodes. A graph $G$ is called *3-connected* if it remains connected when any two nodes and the incident arcs are deleted from $G$.

If a polyhedron $P$ is topologically equivalent to a sphere, the vertex-edge graph $VG(P)$ is planar. Conversely, Steinitz's theorem says that if a graph $G$ having at least four nodes is planar and 3-connected, then there exists a convex polyhedron whose vertex-edge graph is isomorphic to $G$ (Grünbaum 1967; Barnette and Grünbaum, 1969). Hence, from Theorem 11.4, we get the following corollary.

**Corollary 11.4.2.** Let $G$ be a planar 3-connected graph with four or more nodes. Then, the following three statements are equivalent.
(1) There is a line drawing with the underlying graph $G$ such that
    (1a) it represents a convex polyhedron, and there are exactly 4 degrees

of freedom in the choice of the heights of the vertices,

(1b) the property (1a) remains true even if the vertex positions are changed slightly in any direction.

(2) There is a plane skeletal structure with the underlying graph $G$ such that

(2a) it is rigid, and remains rigid if any one rod is removed, but becomes flexible if any two rods are removed,

(2b) the property (2a) remains true even if the joint positions are changed slightly in any direction.

(3) There is a plane skeletal structure with the underlying graph $G$ such that

(3a) it admits a nonzero equilibrium vector, and the vector is unique up to scalar multiplication and nonzero at every rod,

(3b) the property (3a) remains true even if the joint positions are changed slightly in any direction.

It is also known that, for any planar 3-connected graph $G$, there are exactly two "different" ways of embedding $G$ in the surface of a sphere, where "different" means that one embedding cannot be deformed to the other while the arcs are kept uncrossed (Whitney, 1933). Moreover, the two ways of embedding are mirror images of each other. Therefore, any convex polyhedron that can be represented by any line drawing specified by statement (1) in Corollary 11.4.2 yields one and the same incidence structure.

It may be interesting to note that, if a polyhedron $P$ is topologically equivalent to a sphere and its incidence structure $I(P)$ satisfies Condition 11.1(a), then the number of the faces is equivalent to the number of the vertices. Indeed $|V| = |F|$ follows immediately from $|V|+3|F| = |R|+4$, $|V|-|E|+|F| = 2$, and $|R| = 2|E|$.

**Example 11.4.** In Fig. 11.8, the line drawing in (a) represents a polyhedron (a cone with a quadrilateral base) and there are exactly 4 degrees of freedom in the choice of the polyhedron. Moreover, the property is preserved if one changes the positions of vertices slightly on the picture plane. Thus, statement (1) in Corollary 11.4.2 is fulfilled. The corresponding skeletal structure shown in (a') is rigid, and remains rigid if any one rod is removed, but becomes flexible if two or more rods are removed. The property is preserved if the joint positions are perturbed. Thus, statement (2) in Corollary 11.4.2 is fulfilled.

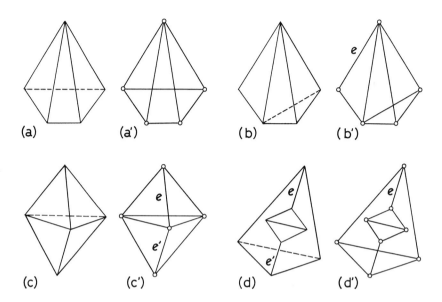

(a)          (a')          (b)          (b')

(c)          (c')          (d)          (d')

**Fig. 11.8.** Generic correspondence between interpretation as polyhedrons and interpretation as skeletal structures.

In contrast, the line drawing in (b) does not represent any polyhedron, and the corresponding skeletal structure shown in (b') becomes flexible when only one rod, the rod $e$ for instance, is deleted. Next, the line drawing in (c) represents a polyhedron, but there are 5 degrees of freedom in the choice of the object; indeed all the faces are triangular so that we have to specify the $z$ coordinates of all the vertices in order to fix the object in the space. The corresponding skeletal structure shown in (c') remains rigid even if we delete two edges, the edges $e$ and $e'$ for example. Finally, the line drawing in (d) represents a polyhedron and there are exactly 4 degrees of freedom in the choice of the object, but the property is not preserved when some vertices are displaced on the picture plane; it represents a polyhedron correctly only when the two edges $e$ and $e'$ are collinear. The corresponding skeletal structure shown in (d') becomes flexible if only one rod, the rod $e$ for instance, is removed.

## 11.5. Principal Partitions and Submodular Decompositions

In addition to the correspondences stated in the previous sections, line drawings of polyhedrons and plane skeletal structures admit several other common mathematical properties. These common properties enable us to treat the two objects in a unifying manner; in particular, some internal structures of the objects can be recognized in terms of principal partitions of matroids and decompositions of submodular systems, which we summarize in this section.

Let us reconsider the system of equations (5.1). Each row of the coefficient matrix $A$ represents the constraint that a vertex should be on a face. Hence, there is a natural one-to-one correspondence between the set of rows of $A$ and the incidence pair set $R$. For any subset $X$ of $R$, let $A(X)$ be the submatrix formed by the rows corresponding to elements in $X$, and let us define a function $\tau_R$ by

$$\tau_R(X) = \text{rank}(A(X)). \tag{11.12}$$

Then, $(R, \tau_R)$ forms a matroid (Welsh, 1976).

This matroid and the matroid $(E, \tau_E)$ associated with a plane skeletal structure defined by (11.7) are analogous in the following sense. First, they both come from linear dependence of row vectors in matrices, $A$ in (5.1) and $H$ in (11.4). Second, the ground sets, $R$ and $E$, both correspond to constraints about geometrical configurations: an element of $R$ represents the constraint that a vertex should be on a face, and an element of $E$ represents the constraint that the distance between two points should be kept unchanged. Hence, for either matroid, if the ground set is dependent, the constraints are redundant and consequently deletion of some constraints does not change the linear space formed by the solutions to the system of (5.1) or (11.4).

The redundancy is in general distributed nonuniformly in the structure; the redundancy is dense in one part but sparse in another part. Let $(M, \tau)$ be a matroid. For any $X \subseteq M$, the density of redundant constraints can be defined by $(|X| - \tau(X))/|X|$. We shall concentrate our attention on the numerator and consider a parametric form defined by

$$f(X) = \tau(X) - \alpha |X|, \tag{11.13}$$

where $\alpha \in [0, 1]$. If the redundancy is dense in the substructure associated with $X$, $\tau(X)$ is relatively small and $|X|$ is relatively large. Therefore, the subset $X$ that minimizes $f(X)$ can be expected to give some information about the distribution of the redundancy.

The family of subsets that minimize (11.13) generates a partially ordered structure of $M$, which is called the principal partition of the matroid. The theory of principal partitions of matroids was developed by Iri (1979a) as a unifying generalization of apparently different results found in several fields of mathematics and engineering, such as Dulmage-Mendelsohn decompositions of bipartite graphs (Dulmage and Mendelsohn, 1958, 1959), maximally distant tree-pairs of a graph (Kishi and Kajitani, 1967; Baron and Imrich, 1968), the minimum-rank maximum-term-rank theorem on matrices (Iri, 1969b), and strong irreducibility of matroids (Tomizawa, 1976). This theory provides a decomposition of a matroid based on nonuniform distribution of dependence, and has been applied to system analysis in various fields of engineering (Iri, 1979b; Iri and Fujishige, 1981). It is also applicable to our systems, as the following outline indicates.

Let $(M,\tau)$ be a matroid and let $\mathfrak{D}(\alpha)$ be the family of subsets $X$ of $M$ such that $X$ minimizes $f(X)$ in (11.13) for $\alpha \in [0,1]$. Furthermore, let $\mathfrak{D} = \cup \mathfrak{D}(\alpha)$, where the union is taken over all $\alpha$ such that $0 \leq \alpha \leq 1$. Then $\mathfrak{D}$ is closed under union and intersection and $\mathfrak{D}$ contains $\emptyset$ and $M$. Therefore, any longest chain $X_0 = \emptyset \subsetneqq X_1 \subsetneqq \cdots \subsetneqq X_n = M$ $(X_i \in \mathfrak{D})$ defines the same family of difference sets $\mathfrak{F}(\mathfrak{D}) = \{X_1 - X_0, X_2 - X_1, \ldots, X_n - X_{n-1}\}$, which is a partition of $M$ (Iri and Han, 1977). Partial order $\ll$ is defined on $\mathfrak{F}(\mathfrak{D})$ in such a way that $M_i \ll M_j$ $(M_i, M_j \in \mathfrak{F}(\mathfrak{D}))$ if and only if $M_j \subsetneqq X$ implies $M_i \subsetneqq X$ for any $X \in \mathfrak{D}$. Matroid $(M,\tau)$ itself is partitioned into "principal minors" $(M_i, \tau_i)$, where $M_i \in \mathfrak{F}(\mathfrak{D})$ and

$$\tau_i(X) = \tau(X \cup \{Y \mid Y \in \mathfrak{F}(\mathfrak{D}), Y \ll X, X \neq Y\}) - \tau(\{Y \mid Y \in \mathfrak{F}(\mathfrak{D}), Y \ll X, X \neq Y\}) \quad (11.14)$$

for any $X \subseteq M_i$.

Applying the above principal partition to the matroids $(R, \tau_R)$ and $(E, \tau_E)$, we can partition the structures according to nonuniform distribution of redundant constraints and obtain partial orders among the partitioned substructures.

**Example 11.5.** Let $(R, \tau_R)$ be the matroid defined by (11.12) associated with the line drawing of a polyhedron shown in Fig. 11.9(a). The incidence structure of this picture is not generically reconstructible, and $R$ is

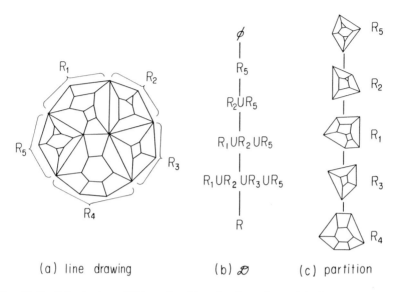

(a) line drawing          (b) $\mathcal{D}$          (c) partition

**Fig. 11.9.** Principal partition of a line drawing of a polyhedron.

dependent in the matroid. We get

$\mathcal{D}(\alpha) = \{\phi\}$       if $\alpha \in [0, 29/32)$,

$\mathcal{D}(\alpha) = \{R_5\}$       if $\alpha \in (29/32, 12/13)$,

$\mathcal{D}(\alpha) = \{R_2 \cup R_5\}$       if $\alpha \in (12/13, 29/31)$,

$\mathcal{D}(\alpha) = \{R_1 \cup R_2 \cup R_5\}$       if $\in (29/31, 19/20)$,

$\mathcal{D}(\alpha) = \{R_1 \cup R_2 \cup R_3 \cup R_5\}$       if $\in (19/20, 29/30)$,

$\mathcal{D}(\alpha) = \{R\}$       if $\alpha \in (29/30, 1]$,

and $\mathcal{D}(\alpha)$ for a "critical" value of $\alpha$ is a simple union of $\mathcal{D}(\alpha)$'s in both sides of the critical value (for example, $\mathcal{D}(29/32) = \{\phi, R_5\}$), where $R_1, \ldots, R_5$ are sets of incidence pairs, shown in Fig. 11.9(a). Family $\mathcal{D}$ and the principal partition are shown in (b) and (c), respectively. In this accidental case, the result of the principal partition coincides with the partition of the matroid into "nonseparable" components (see Welsh, 1976, for "nonseparable" components). Hence, the order among components represents nothing but the difference of ratios of the ranks to the sizes of the support sets; redundant incidence pairs are denser in upper components in (c) than in lower components.

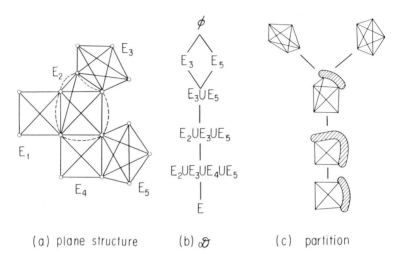

(a) plane structure          (b) $\mathcal{D}$          (c) partition

**Fig. 11.10.** Principal partition of a plane skeletal structure.

**Example 11.6.**    Fig. 11.10 shows an example of the principal partition for the plane skeletal structure.   Let $(E, \tau_E)$ be the matroid defined by (11.7) associated  with a plane skeletal structure shown in (a).   For this matroid we get

$$\mathcal{D}(\alpha) = \{\emptyset\} \qquad\qquad \text{if } \alpha \in [0,\ 3/5),$$
$$\mathcal{D}(\alpha) = \{\emptyset, E_3, E_5, E_3\cup E_5\} \qquad \text{if } \alpha = 3/5,$$
$$\mathcal{D}(\alpha) = \{E_3\cup E_5\} \qquad\qquad \text{if } \alpha \in (3/5,\ 3/4),$$
$$\mathcal{D}(\alpha) = \{E_3\cup E_5, E_2\cup E_3\cup E_5, E_2\cup E_3\cup E_4\cup E_5\} \qquad \text{if } \alpha = 3/4$$
$$\mathcal{D}(\alpha) = \{E_2\cup E_3\cup E_4\cup E_5\} \qquad \text{if } \alpha \in (3/4,\ 4/5),$$
$$\mathcal{D}(\alpha) = \{E_2\cup E_3\cup E_4\cup E_5, E\} \qquad \text{if } \alpha = 4/5,$$
$$\mathcal{D}(\alpha) = \{E\} \qquad\qquad \text{if } \alpha \in (4/5,\ 1],$$

where $E_1$, $\ldots$, $E_5$ are the sets of rods shown in  (a).   Family $\mathcal{D}$  and  the principal  partition  are  shown  in  (b) and (c), where hatches represent additional rigid objects to which skeletal structures are  fixed  (this  is the physical meaning of the principal minors defined in (11.14)). Redundant rods are more crowded in upper elements in (c) than in lower elements,  and hence  upper substructures are stronger than lower ones.   For instance, the lowest component in (c) remains rigid when any  one  rod  is  deleted,  and becomes  flexible  when  any  two rods are deleted.   On the other hand, the second lowest component remains rigid even if some two rods are deleted (for example, the two slant rods), and so on.

Now let us turn our attention to another analogy between line drawings and skeletal structures. The analogy we concentrate on here is the combinatorial characterization of generic properties stated in Theorems 6.2 and 11.2. The conditions stated in those theorems are very similar to each other. The similarity can be represented clearly in terms of the functions $\mu_I$ and $\mu_G$ defined by (11.9) and (11.10), respectively.

For a finite set $M$ and a function $\mu$ on $2^M$, consider a condition of the next form.

**Condition 11.3.** For any subset $X$ of $M$ such that $|X| \geq p$, the inequality $\mu(X) \geq 0$ holds.

The equivalence of statements (1) and (2) in Theorem 6.2 can be paraphrased as follows: "An incidence structure $I = (V,F,R)$ is generically reconstructible if and only if Condition 11.3 is fulfilled, where $M = R$, $\mu = \mu_I$, and $p = 2$." Theorem 11.2 can be paraphrased in this way: "A graph $G = (V,E)$ is generically independent if and only if Condition 11.3 is fulfilled, where $M = E$, $\mu = \mu_G$, and $p = 1$." Thus, both the generic reconstructibility of an incidence structure and the generic independence of a graph are characterized by a combinatorial condition of the same "form."

Moreover, the two functions $\mu_I$ and $\mu_G$ are analogous in the following way. A function $\mu$ on $2^M$ is said to be *submodular* if, for any subsets $X$ and $Y$ of $M$, the inequality

$$\mu(X \cup Y) + \mu(X \cap Y) \leq \mu(X) + \mu(Y) \tag{11.15}$$

holds. The functions $\mu_I$ and $\mu_G$ are not exactly submodular, but are *almost submodular* in the sense that (11.15) is satisfied for any subset $X$ and $Y$ such that $|X \cap Y| \geq p$, where $p = 2$ for $\mu = \mu_I$, and $p = 1$ for $\mu = \mu_G$.

The inequality (11.15) is of the same form as (5.7c), the third condition that should be satisfied by a rank function of a matroid. A submodular function generates a certain decomposition of the ground set (Fujishige, 1980). Although rank functions of matroids should be submodular, a certain subclass of almost submodular functions also defines matroids (Imai, 1983; see also Edmonds, 1970; Sugihara, 1985). Moreover,

Fujishige's decomposition based on submodular functions can be modified  so
that  almost  submodular  functions  also  define decompositions.  The modified
decomposition is useful for the analysis of our present systems.

Let $M$ be a finite set, and let $\mu$ be a function on $2^M$  that  is  almost
submodular  in  the  sense  that  (11.15) is fulfilled by any $X$, $Y \subseteq M$ such
that  $|X \cap Y| \geqq p$, where $p$ is  a  positive  constant.  Let  $q$  be  another
constant such that $q \geqq p$, and let us define $\beta^*$ by

$$\beta^* = \min \{ \mu(Y) \mid Y \subseteq M, \ |Y| \geqq q \} .$$

We define, for each $x \in M$,

$$K(x) = \cap \{ X \mid x \in X \subseteq M, \ |X| \geqq q, \ \mu(X) = \beta^* \} \qquad (11.16)$$

with  the  convention that $K(x) = \{x\}$  if there is no $X$ that satisfies the
conditions stated on the right of (11.16).

Let $G = (M,A)$ be a directed graph having $M$ as the node  set  and  $A =$
$\{(x,y) \mid y \in K(x), \ x,y \in M\}$  as the arc set.  Decomposing $G$ into strongly
connected components, we get the partition of $M$ and the  partial  order  in
it.  Fujishige's decomposition corresponds to the case where $p = q = 0$.  If
we choose $q$ appropriately, the above partition and partial order help us to
understand  internal  structures  of  generically reconstructible incidence
structures and generically  independent  skeletal  structures,  as  in  the
following examples.

**Example 11.7.**  Let  us  consider  the  incidence  structure  $I = (V,F,R)$
associated with the line drawing of a polyhedron shown in Fig. 11.11(a).  $I$
is  generically  reconstructible,  and hence the constraints represented by
incidence pairs are not redundant.  Let us consider the  almost  submodular
function $\mu_I$  defined  by  (11.9).  Putting $M = R$, $\mu = \mu_I$, and $q = 3$, we get
$\beta^* = 0$ and

$K(1) = K(3) = \{1,3\}$ ,  $K(2) = \{1,2,3\}$ ,  $K(4) = \{1,3,4\}$ ,
$K(5) = \{5\}$ ,  $K(6) = \{6,7,10\}$ ,  $K(7) = \{7,10\}$ ,  $K(8) = \{8,10\}$ ,
$K(9) = \{9\}$ ,  $K(10) = \{10\}$ ,  $K(11) = \{6,7,8,10,11,12\}$ ,
$K(12) = \{8,10,12\}$ ,

and consequently obtain the partition and the partial  order  as  shown  in
(b).  This partition represents the distribution of subsets $X$ of $F$ such that

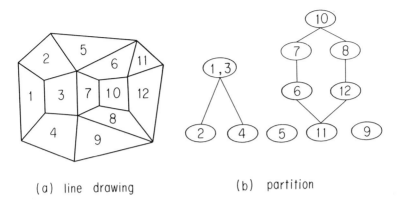

(a) line drawing                        (b) partition

**Fig. 11.11.** Partition based on the almost submodular function $\mu_l$ associated with a line drawing of a polyhedron.

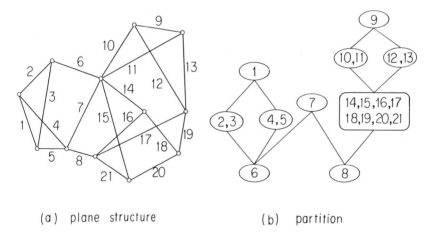

(a) plane structure                     (b) partition

**Fig. 11.12.** Partition based on the almost submodular function $\mu_G$ associated with a plane skeletal structure.

$\mu_l(X) = 0$. Therefore, for any component of this partition, the union of all upper components together with this component constitutes a minimal substructure with exactly 4 degrees of freedom that includes this component.

**Example 11.8.** Another example is shown in Fig. 11.12. Let $(V,E)$ be the underlying graph of the plane skeletal structure illustrated in (a), which is generically independent and generically rigid. Putting $M = E$ and $\mu = \mu_G$ and $q = 3$, we get $\beta^* = 0$ and

$K(1) = \{1\}$ , $K(2) = K(3) = \{1,2,3\}$ , $K(4) = K(5) = \{1,4,5\}$ ,
$K(6) = \{1,2,3,4,5,6,7\}$ , $K(7) = \{7\}$ , $K(8) = \{7,8,\ldots,21\}$ ,
$K(9) = \{9\}$ , $K(10) = K(11) = \{9,10,11\}$ , $K(12) = K(13) = \{9,12,13\}$ ,
$K(14) = K(15) = \ldots = K(21) = \{9,10,\ldots,21\}$ ,

and hence obtain the partition and the partial order as shown in (b). The partition and the partial order represent the distribution of rigid and generically independent substructures, and also represent which part of the structure supports the rigidity of which part. If a rod in a certain component is removed from the structure, all the rods belonging to the same component or the lower components become flexible, while the substructure composed of rods in the upper components remains rigid. The chosen value of $q$ (i.e., 3) is equal to the minimum number of rods that form a nontrivial rigid structure.

REFERENCES


Aho, A. V., Hopcroft, J. E., and Ullman, J. D., 1974. *The Design and Analysis of Computer Algorithms*, Addison-Wesley, Reading, Massachusetts.

Aldefeld, B., 1983. Automatic 3D reconstruction from 2D geometric part descriptions, *Proceedings of IEEE Conference on Computer Vision and Pattern Recognition '83*, pp. 66-72.

Asada, M., Yachida, M., and Tsuji, S., 1984. Analysis of three-dimensional motions in blocks world, *Pattern Recognition*, vol. 17, pp. 57-71.

Asimow, L., and Roth, B., 1978. The rigidity of graphs, *Transactions of the American Mathematical Society*, vol. 245, pp. 279-289.

Asimow, L., and Roth, B., 1979. The rigidity of graphs II, *Journal of Mathematical Analysis and Applications*, vol. 68, pp. 171-190.

Bajcsy, R., and Lieberman, L., 1976. Texture gradient as a depth cue, *Computer Graphics and Image Processing*, vol. 5 pp. 52-67.

Ballard, D. H., and Brown, C. M., 1982. *Computer Vision*, Prentice-Hall, Englewood Criffs, New Jersey.

Barnette, D., and Grünbaum, B., 1969. On Steinitz's theorem concerning convex 3-polytopes and on some properties of planar graphs, *The Many Facets of Graph Theory*, Lecture Notes on Mathematics, no. 110, Springer, Berlin, pp. 27-40.

Baron, G., and Imrich, W., 1968. On the maximal distance of spanning trees, *Journal of Combinatorial Theory*, vol. 5, pp. 378-385.

Barrow, H. G., and Tenenbaum, J. M., 1981. Interpreting line drawings as three-dimensional surfaces, *Artificial Intelligence*, vol. 17, pp. 75-116.

Brady, M., 1982. Computational approaches to image understanding, *Computing Surveys*, vol. 14, pp. 3-71.

Chien, R. T., and Chang, Y. H., 1974. Recognition of curved objects and object assemblies, *Proceedings of the 2nd International Conference on Pattern Recognition*, pp. 496-510.

Clowes, M. B., 1971. On seeing things, *Artificial Intelligence*, vol. 2, pp. 79-116.

Cohen, P. R., and Feigenbaum, E. A., 1982. *The Handbook of Artificial Intelligence*, Volume III, Pitman, London.

Coleman, Jr., E. N., and Jain, R., 1982. Obtaining 3-dimensional shape of textured and specular surfaces using four-source photometry, *Computer Graphics and Image Processing*, vol. 18, pp. 309-328.

**Connelly, R., 1980.** The rigidity of certain cabled frameworks and the second-order rigidity of arbitrarily triangulated convex surfaces, *Advances in Mathematics*, vol. 37, pp. 272-299.

**Cowan, T. M., 1974.** The theory of braids and the analysis of impossible figures, *Journal of Mathematical Psychology*, vol. 11, pp. 190-212.

**Cowan, T. M., 1977.** Organizing the properties of impossible figures, *Perception*, vol. 6, pp. 41-56.

**Crapo, H., 1979.** Structural rigidity, *Structural Topology*, vol. 1, pp. 26-45.

**Crapo, H., 1981.** The combinatorial theory of structures, Lecture Note at the Colloquium on Matroid Theory, Szeged, Hungary, 30 August - 3 September.

**Crapo, H., and Whiteley, W., 1982.** Statics of frameworks and motions of panel structures --- A projective geometric introduction, *Structural Topology*, vol. 6, pp. 43-82.

**Cremona, L., 1890.** *Graphical Statics* (Beare, T. H., trans.), Clarendon Press, London.

**Dantzig, G. B., 1963.** *Linear Programming and Extensions*, Princeton Univ. Press, Princeton.

**Draper, S. W., 1978.** The Penrose triangle and a family of related figures, *Perception*, vol. 7, pp. 283-296.

**Draper, S. W., 1981.** The use of gradient and dual space in line-drawing interpretation, *Artificial Intelligence*, vol. 17, pp. 461-508.

**Duda, R. O., and Hart, P. E., 1973.** *Pattern Classification and Scene Analysis*, Wiley, New York.

**Dulmage, A. L., and Mendelsohn, N. S., 1958.** Coverings of bipartite graphs, *Canadian Journal of Mathematics*, vol. 10, pp. 517-534.

**Dulmage, A. L., and Mendelsohn, N. S., 1959.** A structure theory of bipartite graphs of finite exterior dimension, *Transactions of the Royal Society of Canada*, Ser. 3, Sect. III, vol. 53, pp. 1-13.

**Edmonds, J., 1967.** Systems of distinct representatives and linear algebra, *Journal of Research of National Bureau of Standards*, vol. 71-B, pp. 241-245.

**Edmonds, J., 1970.** Submodular functions, matroids, and certain polyhedra, in Guy, R., et al. (eds.), *Combinatorial Structures and Their Applications*, Gordon and Breach, New York, pp. 69-87.

**Edmonds, J., 1971.** Matroids and the greedy algorithm, *Mathematical Programming*, vol. 1, pp. 127-136.

**Falk, G., 1972.** Interpretation of imperfect line data as a three-dimensional scene, *Artificial Intelligence*, vol. 3, pp. 101-144.

**Ford, L. R., Jr., and Fulkerson, D. R., 1962.** *Flows in Networks*, Princeton University Press, Princeton, New Jersey.

**Fujishige, S., 1980.** Principal structures of submodular systems, *Discrete Applied Mathematics*, vol. 2, pp. 77-79.

**Fukui, Y, Hirotani, T, Ohira, T., and kishi, Y, 1983.** An input method for solid models by drawing, preprint, Industrial Products Research Institute, Ministry of International Trade and Industry of Japan.

**Gill, P. E., Murray, W., and Wright, M. H., 1981.** *Practical Optimization*, Academic Press, London.

**Grape, G. R., 1973.** Model based (intermediate-level) computer vision, Stanford Artificial intelligence Memo, AIM-201 (STAN-CS-73-366).

**Gregory, R. L., 1971.** *The Intelligent Eye* (3rd edition), Weidenfeld and Nicolson, London.

**Grünbaum, B., 1967.** *Convex Polytopes*, Interscience Publishers, London.

**Gurevich, G. B., 1960.** *Proektivnaya Geometriya*, Gosudarstvennoe Izdatel'stvo, Fiziko-Matematicheskoi Literatury, Moskva.

**Guzman, A., 1968a.** Computer recognition of three-dimensional objects in a visual scene, Technical Report MAC-TR-59, Artificial Intelligence Laboratory, MIT.

**Guzman, A., 1968b.** Decomposition of a visual scene into three-dimensional bodies, *Proceedings of AFIPS Fall Joint Conference*, pp. 291-304.

**Hall, P., 1935.** On representatives of subsets, *Journal of London Mathematical Society*, vol. 10, pp. 26-30.

**Haralick, R. M., and Queeney, D., 1982.** Understanding engineering drawings, *Computer Graphics and Image Processing*, vol. 20, pp. 244-258.

**Haralick, R. M., and Shapiro, L. G., 1979.** The consistent labeling problem, Part I, *IEEE Transactions on Pattern Analysis and Machine Intelligence*, vol. PAMI-1, pp. 173-184.

**Haralick, R. M., and Shapiro, L. G., 1980.** The consistent labeling problem, Part II, *IEEE Transactions on Pattern Analysis and Machine Intelligence*, vol. PAMI-2, pp. 193-203.

**Hohenberg, F., 1966.** *Konstruktive Geometrie in der Technik*, Springer, Berlin.

**Horn, B. K. P., 1975.** Obtaining shape from shading information, in Winston, P. H. (ed.), *The Psychology of Computer Vision*, McGraw-Hill, New York, pp. 115-155.

**Horn, B. K. P., 1977.** Understanding image intensities, *Artificial Intelligence*, vol. 8, pp. 201-231.

Huffman, D. A., 1971. Impossible objects as nonsense sentences, in Meltzer, B., and Michie, D. (eds.), *Machine Intelligence* 6, Edinburgh Univ. Press., pp. 295-323.

Huffman, D. A., 1976. Curvature and creases: A primer on paper, *IEEE Transactions on Computer*, vol. C-25, pp. 1010-1019.

Huffman, D. A., 1977a. A duality concept for the analysis of polyhedral scenes, in Elcock, E. W., and Michie, D. (eds.), *Machine Intelligence 8*, Ellis Horwood, England, pp. 475-492.

Huffman, D. A., 1977b. Realizable configurations of lines in pictures of polyhedra, in Elcock, E. W., and Michie, D. (eds.), *Machine Intelligence 8*, Ellis Horwood, England, pp. 493-509.

Huffman, D. A., 1978. Surface curvature and applications of the dual representation, in Hanson, A. R., and Riseman, E. M. (eds.), *Computer Vision Systems*, Academic Press, New York, pp. 213-222.

Idesawa, M., Soma, T., Goto, E., and Shibata, S., 1975. Automatic input of line drawing and generation of solid figure from three-view data, *Proceedings of International Computer Symposium 1975*, vol. II, pp. 304-311.

Ikeuchi, K., 1981. Determining surface orientation of specular surfaces by using the photometric stereo method, *IEEE Transactions on Pattern Analysis and Machine Intelligence*, vol. PAMI-3. pp. 661-669.

Ikeuchi, K., 1984. Shape from regular patterns, *Artificial Intelligence*, vol. 22, pp. 49-75.

Ikeuchi, K., and Horn, B. K. P., 1981. Numerical shape from shading and occluding boundaries, *Artificial Intelligence*, vol. 17, pp. 141-184.

Imai, H., 1983. Network-flow algorithms for lower-truncated transversal polymatroids, *Journal of the Operations Research Society of Japan*, vol. 26, pp. 186-211.

Imai, H., 1985. On combinatorial structures of line drawings of polyhedra, *Discrete Applied Mathematics*, vol. 10, pp. 79-92.

Iri, M., 1969a. *Network Flow, Transportation and Scheduling: Theory and Algorithms*, Academic Press, New York.

Iri, M., 1969b. The maximum-rank minimum-term-rank theorem for the pivotal transforms of a matrix, *Linear Algebra and Its Applications*, vol. 2, pp. 427-446.

Iri, M., 1979a. A review of recent work in Japan on principal partitions of matroids and their applications, *Annals of the New York Academy of Sciences*, vol. 319, pp. 306-319.

Iri, M., 1979b. Applications of matroid theory to engineering system problems, *Proceedings of the 6th Conference on Probability Theory*, Brasov, Romania, pp. 107-127.

Iri, M., and Fujishige, S., 1981. Use of matroid theory in operations research, circuits and system theory, *International Journal of Systems Science*, vol. 12, pp. 27-54.

Iri, M., and Han, T.-S., 1977. *Linear Algebra --- Standard Forms of Matrices* (in Japanese), Kyoiku-Shuppan, Tokyo.

Ishii, M., and Nagata, T., 1976. Feature extraction of three-dimensional objects and visual processing in a hand-eye system using laser tracker, *Pattern Recognition*, vol. 8, pp. 229-237.

Kanade, T., 1980. A theory of Origami world, *Artificial Intelligence*, vol. 13, pp. 279-311.

Kanade, T., 1981. Recovery of the three-dimensional shape of an object from a single view, *Artificial Intelligence*, vol. 17, pp. 409-460.

Kanatani, K., 1986. The constraints on images of rectangular polyhedra, *IEEE Transactions on Pattern Analysis and Machine Intelligence* (to appear).

Kender, J. R., 1979. Shape from texture: A computational paradigm, *Proceedings of ARPA Image Understanding Workshop*, Science Application, Inc., pp. 134-138.

Kishi, G., and Kajitani, Y., 1967. On maximally distant trees, *Proceedings of the 5th Annual Allerton Conference on Circuit and System Theory*, pp. 635-643.

Kupla, Z., 1983. Are impossible figures possible?, *Signal Processing*, vol. 5, pp. 201-220.

Lafue, G., 1978. A theorem prover for recognizing 2-D representations of 3-D objects, in Latombe, J.-C. (ed.), *Artificial Intelligence and Pattern Recognition in Computer Aided Design*, North-Holland, Amsterdam, pp. 391-401.

Laman, G., 1970. On graphs and rigidity of plane skeletal structures, *Journal of Engineering Mathematics*, vol. 4, pp. 331-340.

Lee, S. J., Haralick, R. M., and Zhang, M. C., 1985. Understanding objects with curved surfaces from a single perspective view of boundaries, *Artificial Intelligence*, vol. 26, pp. 145-169.

Liardet, M., Holmes, C., and Rosenthal, D., 1978. Input to CAD systems --- Two practical examples, in Latombe, J.-C. (ed.), *Artificial Intelligence and Pattern Recognition in Computer Aided Design*, North-Holland, Amsterdam, pp. 403-427.

Lovász, L., 1980. Matroid matching and some applications, *Journal of*

*Combinatorial Theory*, vol. B-28, pp. 208-236.

Lovász, L., and Yemini, Y., 1982. On generic rigidity in the plane, *SIAM Journal on Algebraic and Discrete Methods*, vol. 3, pp. 91-98.

Mackworth, A. K., 1973. Interpreting pictures of polyhedral scenes, *Artificial Intelligence*, vol. 4, pp. 121-137.

Mackworth, A. K., 1977a. Consistency in networks of relations, *Artificial Intelligence*, vol. 8, pp. 99-118.

Mackworth, A. K., 1977b. How to see a simple world --- An exegesis of some computer programs for scene analysis, in Elcock, E. W., and Michie, D. (eds.), *Machine Intelligence 8*, Ellis Horwood, England, pp. 510-537.

Markowsky, G., and Wesley, M. A., 1980. Fleshing out wire frames, *IBM Journal of Research and Development*, vol. 24, pp. 582-597.

Marr, D., 1982. *Vision*, Freeman and Company, San Francisco.

Maxwell, J. C., 1864. On reciprocal figures and diagrams of forces, *Philosophical Magazine*, ser. 4, vol. 27, pp. 250-261.

Maxwell, J. C., 1870. On reciprocal figures, frames, and diagrams of forces, *Transactions Royal Society of Edinburgh*, vol. 26, pp. 1-40.

McGregor, J. J., 1979. Relational consistency algorithms and their applications in finding subgraph and graph isomorphisms, *Information Sciences*, vol. 19, pp. 229-250.

Mirsky, L., 1971. *Transversal Theory*, Academic Press, London.

Mirsky, L., and Perfect, H., 1967. Applications of the notion of independence to problems of combinatorial analysis, *Journal of Combinatorial Theory B*, vol. 2, pp. 327-335.

Montanari, U., 1974. Networks of constraints --- Fundamental properties and applications to picture processing, *Information Sciences*, vol. 7, pp. 95-132.

Nakatani, H., and Kitahashi, T., 1984. Inferring 3-d shape from line drawings using vanishing points, *Proceedings of the 1st International Conference on Computers and Applications*, Peking, pp. 683-688.

Nevatia, R., 1982. *Machine Perception*, Prentice-Hall, Englewood Criffs, New Jersey.

Nitzan, D., Brain, A. E., and Duda, R. O., 1977. The measurement and use of registered reflectance and range data in scene analysis, *Proceedings of IEEE*, vol. 65, pp. 206-220.

Nudel, B., 1983. Consistent-labeling problems and their algorithms --- Expected-complexities and theory-based heuristics, *Artificial Intelligence*, vol. 21, pp. 135-178.

Ohta, Y., Maenobu, K., and Sakai, T., 1981. Obtaining surface orientation from texels under perspective projection, *Proceedings of the 7th International Joint Conference on Artificial Intelligence*, pp. 748–751.

Oshima, M., and Shirai, Y., 1979. A scene description method using three-dimensional information, *Pattern Recognition*, vol. 11, pp. 9–17.

Penrose, L. S., and Penrose, R., 1958. Impossible objects: a special type of visual illusion, *British Journal of Psychology*, vol. 49, pp. 31–33.

Preiss, K., 1981. Algorithms for automatic conversion of a 3-view drawing of a plane-faced part to the 3-D representation, *Computers in Industry*, vol. 2, pp. 133–139.

Recski, A., 1984a. A network theory approach to the rigidity of skeletal structures, Part I --- Modelling and interconnection, *Discrete Applied Mathematics*, vol. 7, pp. 313–324.

Recski, A., 1984b. A network theory approach to the rigidity of skeletal structures, Part II --- Laman's theorem and topological formulae, *Discrete Applied Mathematics*, vol. 8, pp. 63–68.

Recski, A., 1984c. A network theory approach to the rigidity of skeletal structures, Part III --- An electric model of planar frameworks, *Structural Topology*, vol. 9, pp. 59–71.

Roberts, L., 1965. Machine perception of three-dimensional solids, in Tippett, J. et al. (eds.), *Optical and Electro-Optical Information Processing*, MIT Press, Cambridge, Mass., pp. 159–197.

Robinson, J. O., 1972. *The Psychology of Visual Illusion*, Hutchinson, London.

Rosenberg, I. G., 1980. Structural rigidity I --- Foundations and rigidity criteria, *Annals of Discrete Mathematics*, vol. 8, North-Holland, pp. 143–161.

Rosenfeld, A., Hummel, R. A., and Zucker, S. W., 1976. Scene labeling by relaxation operations, *IEEE Transactions on Systems, Man and Cybernetics*, vol. SMC-6, pp. 420–433.

Roth, B., and Whiteley, W., 1981. Tensegrity frameworks, *Transactions of the American Mathematical Society*, vol. 265, pp. 419–446.

Sanker, P. V., 1977. A vertex coding scheme for interpreting ambiguous trihedral solids, *Computer Graphics and Image Processing*, vol. 6, pp. 61–89.

Shafer, S. A., 1985. *Shadows and Silhouettes in Computer Vision*, Kluwer Academic Publishers, Boston.

Shafer, S. A., and Kanade, T., 1983. Using shadows in finding surface orientations, *Computer Vision, Graphics, and Image Processing*, vol. 22, pp. 145–176.

Shapira, R., 1974. A technique for the reconstruction of a straight-edge, wire-frame object from two or more central projections, *Computer Graphics and Image Processing*, vol. 3, pp. 318-326.

Shapira, R., 1984. The use of objects' faces in interpreting line drawings, *IEEE Transactions on Pattern Analysis and Machine Intelligence*, vol. PAMI-6, pp. 789-794.

Shapira, R., 1985. More about polyhedra --- Interpretation through constructions in the image plane, *IEEE Transactions on Pattern Analysis and Machine Intelligence*, vol. PAMI-7, pp. 1-16.

Shapira, R., and Freeman, H., 1979. The cyclic order property of vertices as an aid in scene analysis, *Communications of ACM*, vol. 22, pp. 368-375.

Shirai, Y., and Suwa, M., 1971. Recognition of polyhedrons with a range finder, *Proceedings of the 2nd International Joint Conference on Artificial Intelligence*, pp. 80-87.

Stevens, K. A., 1981. The visual interpretation of surface contours, *Artificial Intelligence*, vol. 17, pp. 47-73.

Sugihara, K., 1978. Picture language for skeletal polyhedra, *Computer Graphics and Image Processing*, vol. 8, pp. 382-405.

Sugihara, K., 1979a. Range-data analysis guided by a junction dictionary, *Artificial Intelligence*, vol. 12, pp. 41-69.

Sugihara, K., 1979b. Automatic construction of junction dictionaries and their exploitation for the analysis of range data, *Proceedings of the 6th International Joint Conference on Artificial Intelligence*, pp. 859-564.

Sugihara, K., 1979c. Studies on Mathematical Structures of Line Drawings of Polyhedra and Their Applications to Scene Analysis (in Japanese), Dissertation for Dr. of Engineering submitted to University of Tokyo (also published as Researches Electrotechnical Laboratory, no. 800).

Sugihara, K., 1982a. Classification of impossible objects, *Perception*, vol. 11, pp. 65-74.

Sugihara, K., 1982b. Mathematical structures of line drawings of polyhedrons --- Toward man-machine communication by means of line drawings, *IEEE Transactions Pattern Analysis and Machine Intelligence*, vol. PAMI-4. pp. 458-469.

Sugihara, K., 1983. On some problems in the design of plane skeletal structures, *SIAM Journal on Algebraic and Discrete Methods*, vol. 4, pp. 355-362.

Sugihara, K., 1984a. An algebraic approach to shape-from-image problems,

*Artificial Intelligence*, vol. 23, pp. 59-95.

Sugihara, K., 1984b. A necessary and sufficient condition for a picture to represent a polyhedral scene, *IEEE Transactions on Pattern Analysis and Machine Intelligence*, vol. PAMI-6, pp. 578-586.

Sugihara K., 1984c. An algebraic and combinatorial approach to the analysis of line drawings of polyhedrons, *Discrete Applied Mathematics*, vol. 9, pp. 77-104.

Sugihara, K., 1985. Detection of structural inconsistency in systems of equations with degrees of freedom and its applications, *Discrete Applied Mathematics*, vol. 10, pp. 297-312.

Tay, T.-S., and Whiteley, W., 1984. Recent advances in the generic rigidity of structures, *Structural Topology*, vol. 9, pp. 31-38.

Térouanne, E., 1980. On a class of 'impossible' figures: a new language for a new analysis, *Journal of Mathematical Psychology*, vol. 22, pp. 24-47.

Thro, E. B., 1983. Distinguishing two classes of impossible objects, *Perception*, vol. 12, pp. 733-751.

Tomizawa, N., 1976. Strongly irreducible matroids and principal partitions of a matroid into strongly irreducible minors (in Japanese), *Transactions of the Institute of Electronics and Communication Engineers of Japan*, vol. 59-A, pp. 83-91.

Turner, K. J., 1974. Computer perception of curved objects using a television camera, Doctoral dissertation, School of Artificial Intelligence, Edinburgh University.

Waltz, D., 1972. Generating semantic descriptions from drawings of scenes with shadows, Technical Report AI-TR-271, MIT.

Waltz, D., 1975. Understanding line drawings of scenes with shadows, in Winston, P. H. (ed.), *The Psychology of Computer Vision*, McGraw-Hill, New York, pp. 19-91.

Welsh, D. J. A., 1976. *Matroid Theory*, Academic Press, London.

Wesley, M. A., and Markowsky, G., 1981. Fleshing out projections, *IBM Journal of Research and Development*, vol. 25, pp. 934-954.

Whiteley, W., 1979. Realizability of polyhedra, *Structural Topology*, vol. 1, pp. 46-58.

Whiteley, W., 1982. Motions and stresses of projected polyhedra, *Structural Topology*, vol. 7, pp. 13-38.

Whiteley, W., 1984a. Some matroids on hypergraphs with applications in scene analysis and geometry, Preprint, Champlain Regional College (900 Riverside Drive, St. Lambert, Quebec, J4P 3B8, Canada).

Whiteley, W., 1984b. Infinitesimal motions of a bipartite framework,

*Pacific Journal of Mathematics*, vol. 110, pp. 233–255.

**Whiteley, W.**, 1984c. A correspondence between scene analysis and motions of frameworks, *Discrete Applied Mathematics*, vol. 9, pp. 269–295.

**Whitney, H.**, 1933. A set of topological invariants for graphs, *American Journal of Mathematics*, vol. 55, pp. 231–235.

**Winston, P. H.**, 1977. *Artificial Intelligence*, McGraw-Hill, New York.

**Witkin, A. P.**, 1981. Recovering surface shape and orientation from texture, *Artificial Intelligence*, vol. 17, pp. 17–45.

**Woodham, R. J.**, 1977. A cooperative algorithm for determining surface orientation from a single view, *Proceedings of the 5th International Joint Conference on Artificial Intelligence*, pp. 635–641.

**Woodham, R. J.**, 1981. Analysing images of curved surfaces, *Artificial Intelligence*, vol. 17, pp. 117–140.

The MIT Press, with Peter Denning as consulting editor, publishes computer science books in the following series:

**Artificial Intelligence,** Patrick Winston and Michael Brady, editors

**Computer Systems** Herb Schwetman, editor

**Foundations of Computing,** Michael Garey, editor

**Information Systems,** Michael Lesk, editor

**Logic Programming,** Ehud Shapiro, editor

**Scientific Computation,** Dennis Gannon, editor